A Psychotheraɪ

How to be Gay and Happy

The Book for Gay, Lesbian, Bisexual, Trans, and Queer People or Those Who Think They Might Be

Peter Field

How to Be Gay AND Happy
Peter Field, MA, MBACP, FRSH

Cover Design: Kir Lysenka
Interior Design: Adina Cucicov, Flamingo Designs

A Rainbow Champions Publication

info@rainbowchampions.com

In memory of my brother,
Bob Field.

Contents

Introduction

If you were to go online and type 'gay' into a search engine, what would you find? I can tell you because I've done it. Enter 'gay' and you will see entry after entry for homosexual websites: gay porn, gay dating, gay clubs, gay saunas, gay magazines, gay news. But you will find nothing that tells you the original meaning of gay — joyful, carefree and bright.

Why is this? Have we forgotten that gay once meant happy? Is gay now solely a matter of sex and sexual orientation, something divorced from joy and happiness?

As a psychotherapist I have met and worked with quite a few gay people — men and women — whose lives were far from happy. Many came carrying the burden of a past that still seemed to weigh heavily on their shoulders and on their minds. And in that past they had learned to expect so little, simply because they were gay. So often, their lives were anything but 'gay.'

Yet in the many countries I have visited, worked and lived in, I have known countless gay people whose lives could be described as bright, relatively carefree and joyful; men and women who claimed their share of happiness and lived life to the full — gay in the original, truest sense of the word.

In this book you will learn about those things that can act as blocks to happiness for gay people — things such as homophobia, shame and low self-esteem, and how they influence our thinking and affect the way we feel. And you will learn how you can deal with such negative forces and actually *choose* to be happy.

The strategies you will be introduced to and the techniques you will learn can help you to claim or reclaim your birthright and live assertively, with your head held high.

We may not choose our sexuality or our sexual orientation, but we *can* choose our behavior and the way we respond to life. If you are gay, if you belong to that great minority of lesbian, gay, bisexual, trans, or intersex people, then you can be what you were born to be; you can be gay AND happy. That is the purpose of this book.

Chapter One

On Being Gay AND Happy

"Is life not a hundred times too short for us to stifle ourselves..."
~ Friedrich Nietzsche

"But you don't *look* gay," said the man seated next to me at the convention. "If you hadn't told me, I'd never have known."

He meant it as a compliment. To him, as to so many others, I simply didn't fit the stereotypical homosexual image, and in his own way, he was praising me because of it. My response must have taken him aback.

"Oh?" I said. "What if I were to tell you that you don't look straight, and that if you hadn't told me, I'd never have known?"

Why should one be a compliment and the other not?

I am gay. And I am happy to be gay. In fact, I've been that way for a very long time.

The response of the man at the convention was in many ways understandable. A society and a media that have painted a narrow and distorted picture of gay people have influenced him, like so many others.

In this vision, which is largely out of sync with reality, gay men are flamboyant, in-your-face personalities abandoned to a life of hedonistic pursuit. We are either creatures of the night, spending our time cruising gay bars and clubs, drinking and drugging as we run from one anonymous sexual encounter to another; or else we are tortured souls furtively living out our days, our true identity cloaked in secrecy and subterfuge.

We either lack masculinity or we flaunt it. We either wiggle and lisp, spending endless hours in front of the mirror fixing our hair and plucking our eyebrows; or live our lives in the gym perfecting our 'Muscle Mary' physiques. We have an intense dislike of women, or else are 'one of the girls.'

Women who are gay face stereotypes, as well. They are dark and brooding, homely and overweight. They lumber around in shapeless flannel shirts, wear their hair cropped, and never don makeup. They care little for family, and they hate men.

Bisexuals face biases from every side. Those who are gay can see bisexuals as avoiding their 'true' gay identity, and straights may assume that bisexuals are oversexed and indiscriminate.

Likewise, transgender people are often categorized as gay, as drag queens or kings, or as simply confused. And those who are intersex may be ignored completely, dismissed as being altogether too bewildering to bother about.

We will discuss these separate orientations and identities in more detail later in this chapter.

According to these myths, we can do and be all of these things, but we cannot really sit comfortably in our own skin. We cannot be gay *and* happy.

Yet, the fact is that it is entirely possible for anyone to be gay AND happy.

(While recognizing and respecting the inherent differences, for ease of reading, throughout this book I will use the word 'gay' as a collective noun for LGBTIQ people. I ask for forbearance from those who do not identify as such.)

I have met people who have tried to fit neatly into all of these stereotypes — and who have experienced real difficulty because of it. A stereotype, after all, is not a person, and only people can ever really be happy.

But I have also met far more gay people who could not be further removed from these descriptions. In fact, the countless gay people that I have met away from therapy — all over the world and in practically every walk of life — usually lead perfectly ordinary, three-dimensional, balanced lives. Of course, we all sometimes have difficulties, problems that come with this experience we call life. But like me, and I hope most of you, they are in almost every sense of the word quite happy.

Being gay is simply an aspect of human diversity. It is a fact of life, part of the broad spectrum of experience that contributes to the richness of humanity, adding to its color and its vibrancy.

The importance of diversity in sexual orientation and gender identity cannot be overestimated. No law or edict will ever banish it, no vaccine or extermination program will ever eliminate it. It cannot be prayed or punished away. With each new generation, gay people will be born; we will be found in every race, class, and religion, and in every part of the world. We are brothers and sisters, mothers and fathers, children, relatives, friends, acquaintances, colleagues, co-workers, and neighbors.

As long as the human race survives, gay people will never disappear, never go away.

What Is Happiness?

We know something about what it is to be gay, and we will look further into this a little later. Since this book is about being gay *and* happy, however, perhaps it would be good to have a clearer understanding of what we mean by happiness.

There is a multitude of definitions of happiness. A good working definition might be that it is an inner sense of wellbeing and joy; a feeling that tells us our life is good and has some kind of meaning.

As we move through this book, you'll find that there really is no single secret to happiness. Just as there are many definitions, there are many components. There is, however, one thing that is essential in order for us to be authentically happy:

We need to accept ourselves.

Experience and research have shown that genuine happiness comes from the inside. Only when we accept ourselves can we begin to be at peace with ourselves. And being at peace with ourselves is the key that unlocks the door to enduring happiness.

> *"For me happiness occurs arbitrarily: a moment of eye contact on a bus, where all at once you fall in love; or a frozen second in a park where it's enough that there are trees in the world."*
>
> **~ Russell Brand**

We know that life can be difficult. Even the happiest amongst us will sometimes experience difficulty in living. Being gay does not mean that we live our lives free of difficulty; just as being straight does not guarantee this, either. But there are special challenges that come with being gay that people who are straight simply do not have to face.

In this book, we will look at some of those challenges and how we might best overcome them. It is how we handle life's difficulties — the choices we make, and the attitude we adopt — that really determines the degree of happiness that we, or anyone else, can experience.

Happiness Is a Choice

If there is one thing that my life and my work have taught me about happiness, it's that happiness is not something that can be found: it is something that we *choose*. If we spend our lives looking for happiness, then we will spend our lives doing just that — *looking*.

As we move forward we will discuss how gay people can *choose* happiness. I'll show you useful, practical strategies that have been proven to work; as well as approaches, attitudes, and techniques that you can learn and put into action in order to live your life assertively and to experience your share of happiness.

The simple fact is that being gay and happy is not only something that every gay person deserves to be, it is something that any gay person can *learn* to be.

Despite the difficulties we must all encounter in life, being gay and happy is immensely achievable. In fact, being happy is the birthright of every person who is attracted to the same sex, just as it is the birthright of every person who is attracted to the opposite sex. Being gay is the reality for untold millions of people all over the world, and has been since the beginning of our time here on Earth.

Gay or straight, man, woman, or simply human, if we expect to live every single moment of our lives in a state of constant contentment and happiness, then we will be sadly disappointed. Such a scenario may work in fairy tales and children's stories, but it can never work in real life. As human beings, each of us has the ability to experience the full range of human emotion: joy, surprise, and trust, as well as the more difficult ones such as fear, anger, and sadness.

Happiness was never intended to be a constant state. It is not something that we can always feel or always be, but it is something that we *can* experience on a regular basis — just as we experience other emotions — as we progress with our journey in life.

Perhaps happiness is best thought of as *part* of the human experience, something that co-exists with other moods, other states, and other ways of being. Consider the case of Ben, for instance.

Ben is an excellent example of someone who understands the nature of happiness. As a successful record producer living in London and Los Angeles, he enjoys life to the fullest and would be the first to admit that he has more than his share of happiness. But for Ben, life wasn't always like this.

He grew up in a place where anyone who was not overtly heterosexual was ridiculed. For years he struggled with and hid his sexuality. Moving to Los Angeles and its offer of big city anonymity, Ben finally allowed himself the freedom to express his sexuality.

Soon Ben found himself drinking and drugging, spending night after night clubbing and cruising, jumping into and out of bed with men he barely remembered the next morning — all in the endless *pursuit* of happiness. Though he did sometimes experience pleasure, he just couldn't be happy, and this really troubled him.

Like so many before, he had bought into the idea that he was entitled to live his life, if not actually in a perpetual state of happiness, then at least in pursuit of it. The trouble was that the more he pursued happiness, the more it seemed to elude him. The harder he tried, the less happy he became.

Ben was gay, and the old conditioning ran deep. Maybe, he thought, the fact that he was gay was the reason for his unhappiness. He certainly was desperately unhappy. Perhaps if he were straight things would be different. It was only when he began to accept himself and his sexuality and to realize that life was not meant to be spent in a constant state of euphoria or in its pursuit that he could relax into and better understand himself. As he did this, he came to experience more moments of true happiness.

As we have seen, this is the real key to being gay and happy, or indeed, to being anything and happy: *Before we can be really happy, we first need to accept themselves.*

Ben discovered that being gay and happy is far from a myth, just as being straight and happy is not a myth. It might take work, and it will take the realization that no one can remain perpetually happy, but *anyone can learn to be happy*, provided he or she is willing to put the effort in and let go of unreasonable demands and expectations. Above all, happiness depends on dropping the pretense, losing the act, and allowing ourselves to be who and what we are. It means reclaiming ourselves and our rights as human beings and as valuable members of society.

We will be returning to these themes time and again as we move through *How to Be Gay AND Happy.*

> *"All happiness depends on courage and work."*
>
> **~ Honoré de Balzac**

Real happiness, like real unhappiness, comes from who we most consistently allow ourselves to be. And it is in this that we have a choice. We can allow ourselves to be what the media and a big chunk of society tell us that we must be — stereotypes and distorted images of what we truly are — or we can have the courage to be what we were meant to be: good, decent individuals whose lives have meaning and purpose.

Happiness happens when we stop believing in the myths and false stories. It happens when we let go of our fears and embrace all that we are, while working toward being all that we can be.

It takes courage to claim or to reclaim your life, courage to *live* your life, courage to be yourself. This courage has to start from where you are, not from where you would like to be. It has to start from a profound understanding, a profound truth: if you are attracted to the same sex, there is nothing wrong with you. There really never was.

You are gay, and that is absolutely okay.

Where Did We Get the Idea That Being Gay Isn't Okay?

So many of society's proscriptions against being gay exist for reasons other than rationality or practical necessity. They are the product of the two essential ingredients of prejudice — ignorance and fear.

As human beings evolved from their primitive origins, rules and laws were needed in order to protect children and the very young — to guard against rape, and to ensure that genetic flaws were not endlessly perpetuated through the inbreeding of incest, for example.

Attitudes, laws, and injunctions against homosexuality stemmed from these early origins, becoming enshrined in religious dogma and philosophical beliefs. At the very root of these beliefs and positions lies a very simple yet fundamental idea — sex is shameful. That which brings shame must be a sin, and with sin comes damnation; consequently, sex is to be feared.

This was the position adopted by the Abrahamic religions — Judaism, Christianity, and Islam (taken in chronological order of founding). It is these religions, more than any others, that have influenced our society's attitude toward sex and toward homosexuality.

Recognizing that without sex, groups, tribes, and the whole human race would rapidly become extinct, those who influenced or wielded power — the shamans, priests, and interpreters of nature or of 'God's Law' — had little option but to condone it. This was done, often begrudgingly, and sex was sanctioned, but with restrictions.

Most often it was decided that sexual congress should be restricted to acts done behind closed doors, in secret, hidden from others the way shame should always be hidden. Usually, sex was limited to a single partner or to a very small number of committed partners. Though it was inherently dirty and embarrassing, it was seen as a necessary evil, sanctioned because of its ability to strengthen the group, helping it to multiply and grow stronger and more secure. The offspring of sex – children – would be born through sin and into sin, but at least the group, the society, would expand and grow stronger.

In this way, sex served a function other than the mere gratification of 'carnal desire.' It was not simply the giver of guilty pleasure, because pleasure was frowned upon by many religions (female circumcision and genital mutilation, unfortunately still practiced in many cultures, is a remnant of this). Sex served a purpose beyond the self, something that benefitted the group as a whole. It was 'productive.'

> *"To discriminate against our sisters and brothers who are lesbian or gay, on grounds of their sexual orientation, for me is as totally unacceptable and unjust as apartheid ever was."*
>
> **~ Archbishop Desmond Tutu**

Sex between members of the same sex, though, could not be productive. It added nothing to the group, the tribe, or the country. All it could be was the bringer of pleasure to those who engaged in it. Life was not supposed to be about pleasure, but about work and devotion. Sex between men and men or women and women was a shame, and so it was a sin. And sin needed to be hated, rebuked, and outlawed. Above all, it needed to be punished.

And so laws were passed and as societies grew, judicial systems incorporated the old attitudes and injunctions into their penal codes. In 1120 AD, the Church Council of Nablus described homosexuality as a "sin against nature," enshrining it as the devil's work and further strengthening social disapproval. Being gay was listed as "a crime against nature" — as if there were any place other than nature from which it could possibly spring.

Philosophical and religious beliefs and dogma do not confine themselves to the walls of the church, synagogue, mosque, or temple, of course. They sweep out, directly or indirectly influencing the whole of a society. Eventually they become part of the customs, attitudes, and ethos, affecting even those who claim no religious affiliations or beliefs.

Despite this, homosexuality continued to exist. It always has and it always will. History shows that there are ample instances of same-sex love in almost all ancient civilizations, as well as in all modern ones.

In some countries, Britain included, having sex with someone of the same gender became punishable by death. In eleven countries today — Afghanistan, Iran, Iraq, Nigeria, Mauritania, Saudi Arabia, Somalia, Sudan, Qatar, United Arab Emirates, and Yemen, the death penalty still applies and may be meted out to anyone found to have committed "the sin that dare not speak its name" (to use the term Lord Alfred Douglas, Oscar Wilde's lover, gave it). Even in the 21st century, being gay remains a crime in more than seventy countries.

In the UK, homosexuality remained a criminal offence until as recently as 1967, when it was repealed under the Sexual Offences Act. In the US, it was still a crime in thirteen of the fifty states until the Supreme Court forced those states to repeal the law in 2003.

With a history of social intolerance and condemnation, blind prejudice against same-sex relations and gender variance was elevated into something more than mere difference. Not only was being gay seen as a sin and a crime, it also became viewed as a form of mental illness. Because it departed from the norm, psychiatry saw it as an aberration. As we shall see later in this chapter, difference became disease and being gay was classified as a mental illness or disorder.

'Disease', though, can have its lighter side. As comic Robin Tyler quipped, "If homosexuality is a disease, let's all call in queer to work: 'Hello. Can't work today; still queer.' "

Because of negative religious, legal, and medical underpinnings, being gay continues to incite irrational condemnation from people who might otherwise lead relatively ordinary, unprejudiced, and quite tolerant lives.

Though the situation for gay people has improved greatly in Western countries such as the US and the UK, there are a good many people who see it as something inherently wrong and sinful. There are those who are unsettled by sex and disturbed by difference; people who view those who are gay as a threat, and so homophobia continues to exist in many quarters.

(We will look more deeply into this thing called 'homophobia' a little later in *How to Be Gay And Happy,* because it is one of the biggest blocks in our ability to be genuinely happy.)

For these reasons it is not surprising that so many gay people, and those who are in some degree attracted to the same sex, choose to stay hidden, keeping their heads down and remaining in the closet.

It is this, too, that forces so many of us to live lives of subterfuge and secrecy, an existence full of quiet desperation and inner torment. This is what drives the unhappy among us into conflicted, unhappy marriages, where *both* partners end up paying an awful price. Into the arms of unsound therapists and twisted forms of certain religions that further corrupt and disturb, bringing untold pain and suffering to our fellow human beings in the name of 'goodness' and the false promise of release from endless, unrelenting misery.

> *"There is a tendency to consider anything in human behavior that is unusual, not well known, or not well understood, as neurotic, psychopathic, immature, perverse, or the expression of some other sort of psychological disturbance."*
>
> **~ Alfred Kinsey**

And all of this contributes to the illusion that being gay is something sad, abnormal, and relatively rare, another stereotype that plays such a large part in the popular perception of gay people.

How Many Gay People Are There?

Because so many gay people choose to remain below the radar, it is immensely difficult to correctly estimate the actual number of human beings who are attracted to the same sex.

Do we count those who have simply had a few same-sex encounters, but who now restrict themselves solely to a heterosexual relationship? How about those who sometimes have same-sex encounters, and occasionally have sex with the opposite sex — are they as 'gay' as those who exclusively have same-sex relationships? And what about those who remain celibate, for whatever reason, and don't engage in any kind of same-sex activity with another, but who fantasize and dream about it on a regular basis? Are all of these people to be counted as gay?

Estimating the number or assigning a figure very much depends on how we define this word 'gay.' Is it something that one does, or something that one is?

Sexual relations with the same sex are not confined to the Western world, of course. They have always existed and have been found in all cultures, though more prevalent or apparent in some than in others.

In some parts of the world, especially in the non-Western countries, many men who have sex with other men do not think of themselves as being either gay or homosexual. Accordingly, the acronym 'MSM' or 'MESMEN' has been coined to signify the *behavior* — men who have sex with men — and WSW — women who have sex with women — while 'gay' is usually used in order to describe what is considered to be an obvious sexual identity or accepted orientation.

We know that while the sexual orientation of men and women may vary over time, it tends to remain constant for most adults.

Research has focused on gay as something that people do sexually and not necessarily on who they are. It has been very much concerned with homo*sexuality,* and not necessarily with being *gay* — as an identity that encompasses more than sexual activity.

The terms 'homosexual' and 'homosexuality' refer to sexual activity between members of the same sex. You will find no mention of these words in any ancient text. They are not in the *Torah,* the *Bible,* or the *Qur'an.* This is because they are neologisms — new words. The history of these words provides an interesting keyhole through which we can understand aspects of our society's attitude toward gay people.

It was not until the late 19th century that the word 'homosexuality' was used. Austrian-born Hungarian doctor Karoly Maria Benkert (Karoly Maria Kertbeny in some sources) coined the terms *homosexual* (*homosexualität*), and also *heterosexual* (having a sexual attraction to the opposite sex), in an attempt to classify sexual orientation. The prefix *homo* he took from the Greek word meaning 'same' and the suffix *sexual* also came from the Greek. (The first vowel 'o' of the Greek suffix 'homo' meaning 'same' is pronounced as the 'o' sound in 'honest' is pronounced. The Latin suffix 'homo' means 'man' and is pronounced with the 'o' sounding as it does in the word 'only.' Because of confusion between the Greek and the Latin, most people pronounce the word *homosexual* incorrectly).

> *"No, I've never thought that I was gay. And that's not something you think. It's something you know."*
>
> ~ **Robert Plant**

Benkert himself seems to have been an enlightened psychologist and human rights campaigner. Amongst his acquaintances were luminaries such as Hans Christian Anderson (himself gay),

Heinrich Heine, and the Brothers Grimm. Little did Benkert realize that through his creation of the word 'homosexuality,' gay people would more easily become discriminated against and persecuted.

Once the classification had been created and the label applied, being 'homosexual' could be seen as something amenable to scientific investigation. It was now viewed as a distinct medical condition, an abnormality that could be dissected and pathologized. Their difference and variance from the average meant that homosexuals could now be treated as if sick or having a clinical disorder, something to be cured through surgical lobotomy, castration, electric shock, or drugs.

Homosexuals could now simply be locked away together with other "mental defectives."

As Hitler's Third Reich swept to power, gay people across Europe were arrested and interred in camps such as Auschwitz, Belsen, Buchenwald, and their prototype, Dachau. Here they were issued striped pajama uniforms, an inverted pink triangle attached to the arm.

In these camps, just as there were no happy Jews or happy Gypsies, there was little possibility of being gay and happy. And in these camps they became the lowest of the low in the pecking order of despair, shunned by other internees who themselves shared the distorted societal belief that homosexuals were immoral, willfully wicked, and irredeemably wrong. They were beaten, bullied, and castrated. And like the other internees, they could be experimented upon, tortured, starved, and murdered.

Such barbaric and inhumane treatment may seem remote and belonging to a long gone era, until we realize that castration of gay people was still legal in seven states in the US until as late as the 1970s.

The word "homosexual" was first used in an English language broadcast medium in 1953 by Dr. Jacob Bronowski on a BBC radio program, *Behind the News*. In 1961, the first American documentary film about homosexuality — *The Rejected* — produced by John W. Reavis for Public Broadcasting Service station KQED in San Francisco, was broadcast. In the same year, British actor Dirk Bogarde starred in the film *Victim,* in which he courageously played a homosexual barrister fighting blackmail.

We will look again at some of our gay history later in this book — at how gay people have fought for the right to exist and at the wonderful accomplishments and advances that have been made because of this.

Though much of this history may be unknown to many gay people, it is undeniably connected with social attitudes toward homosexuality that exist today. Homophobia is sadly present in our society, and it may be found at many levels. It is a fact of life that those of us who are gay have to be aware of and deal with, sometimes on a regular basis. This is a subject that we will discuss in the next chapter.

Given all this history, and the fact that homophobia still exists, sometimes in its most virulent and violent forms, it is little wonder that so many gay people choose to remain 'in the closet,' where they cannot be identified, discriminated against, or counted.

The Kinsey Research

Difficult though it may be to determine just how many gay people there are, we do have some idea of the number of people who are attracted to the same sex because of research conducted more than half a century ago in the US. So thorough and well conducted was this research that it was foundational to the field of sexology. Even today, it retains much of its validity. This groundbreaking work has profoundly influenced and deepened our understanding of human sexuality and of homosexuality in particular.

In the most extensive study ever conducted into human sexuality, researchers, under the direction of Dr. Alfred Kinsey from the University of Indiana, conducted interviews with more than 17,000 people over a ten-year period. The findings, published in two volumes: *Sexual Behavior in the Human Male* (1948) and *Sexual Behavior in the Human Female* (1953), caused astonishment and outrage, challenging conventional beliefs and shedding new light on an area that had for so long remained off-limits and taboo.

The statistic that most shocked people was the finding that one man in ten is exclusively homosexual, as are approximately six percent of women.

Kinsey himself was at pains to point out, however, that "males do not represent two discrete populations, heterosexual and homosexual." For him, "the world is not divided into sheep and goats;" so he devised a scale from 0 to 6. (Later an additional category was added by Kinsey's associates, in order to signify asexuality). The figure 6 represented those who were exclusively homosexual, while 0 meant someone was completely heterosexual. What Kinsey found was that most people fell somewhere in between these numbers. Human sexuality was far too complex to be designated simply as gay and straight.

> *"Males do not represent two discrete populations, heterosexual and homosexual. The world is not to be divided into sheep and goats. Not all things are black nor all things white."*
>
> **~ Alfred Kinsey**

Importantly — and of course, controversially — Kinsey's research pointed to the fact that fully thirty-seven percent of all men had had a homosexual experience and that almost half of all adult men (forty-six percent) had 'reacted' sexually to someone of the same sex. For women, seven percent of single females and four percent of previously married females were given a rating of 3 (about equal heterosexual and homosexual experience/response).

So astonishing and provocative were these findings that they met with enormous incredulity and massive opposition, not only from religious leaders and organizations, but also from powerful politicians and the media. People didn't want to believe anything that so contradicted their traditional beliefs and disturbed their cherished moral precepts. It simply didn't jibe with the way they believed human sexuality *should* be.

Even today, there are those who spend enormous amounts of energy attempting to deny the validity of Kinsey's research, often disparaging its irreproachable methodology and distorting its inconvenient findings. Though Kinsey's position was that of the scientist, opponents of the research are not above attempting some form of character assassination on Kinsey himself (for example, wrongly accusing him of encouraging child abuse — in direct contradiction to the facts). Such, unfortunately, is the irrational hysteria and deep-seated prejudice that homosexuality still can elicit.

> *"There are people that very strongly identify themselves as gay and then lesbian, and then I think there are a lot of people who are kind of some percentage or some version of that."*
>
> **~ Michael Stipe**

Because of the animosity and emotional furor that the Kinsey reports generated, funding was withdrawn. Never again was such extensive research undertaken.

Today, Kinsey's work remains the very best information we have on both male and female homosexuality. His important research lives on in the Kinsey Institute at Indiana University, which is committed to advancing our knowledge about sex and providing information on critical issues regarding sexuality, gender, and reproduction.

Other Research

Since Kinsey, various attempts have been made to assess what percentage of the population is gay, but these forays into statistical significance have met with difficulty. Most surveys have simply asked whether people actually identify themselves as 'gay,' and so have reported numbers lower than Kinsey's one in ten. Some have returned figures as low as one or two percent.

The information obtained from sex surveys is only as accurate as that which is volunteered by the respondents. Their accuracy also depends very much on the way the questions are phrased and the manner in which the particular survey is conducted. Remember that many people who have or who have had relations with the same sex just do not see themselves as being gay. And there is also the undeniable fact that many people are reluctant to honestly report what they do or have done sexually because of a learned sense of shame or guilt.

"You could move." Agony Aunt 'Dear Abby' responds to a reader who complained that a gay couple was moving in across the street and wanted to know what he could do to improve the quality of the neighborhood.

~ Abigail Van Buren

According to researchers at the *Williams Institute on Sexual Orientation Law and Public Policy*, only four percent of adults aged eighteen to forty-five in the US identify as homosexual or bi, which matches a similar number of voters reportedly identifying in this way. However, when gay is defined as having same-sex attraction or engaging in same-sex behavior, the figure shoots up to almost one in ten.

Recently (2015), a survey conducted by YouGov found that almost half of all UK residents aged between 18 to 24 years old describe themselves as being, to some degree, bi-responsive, a sign that the younger generation may be abandoning a monosexual belief system. (Monosexuality means being attracted exclusively to one sex or gender only.)

In the US, the YouGov poll found that about half of America does not believe there is such as thing as bisexuality. And only 39% of US citizens agree with the statement that sexuality exists on a scale. (This compares with 61% in the UK.)

That said, five times as many young people in the US identify as bisexual compared to young Brits, while five times fewer young US people identify as gay than do young people in the UK.

For many men, though, being 'on the down-low' — engaging in same-sex activity but keeping it secret — is far removed from being gay.

Perhaps one of the reasons people are so reluctant to disclose their sexuality is that they do not want to be different, to stand out, or to be seen as 'abnormal' or 'unnatural' — thus suffering the perceived consequences.

Unfortunately, in the eyes of many, being gay is neither normal nor natural.

Isn't Being Gay Abnormal and Unnatural?

For me, being gay is both normal and natural. In fact, it would be decidedly abnormal and unnatural for me to try to be anything other than gay, simply because that is an important aspect of what and who I am. It was not something I chose to be; because I do not believe that people 'choose' their sexual orientation in the way they might choose the music they listen to or the home they live in. People can no more choose their sexuality than they can choose the pigment of their eyes or the color of their skin.

If you were to offer me a magic potion that would change me and make me straight, I would certainly refuse it. I am happy to be me, and happy to be gay. This is true for many other men and women who are gay.

The fear of being different, and of being discriminated against and perhaps victimized because of it, however, is something that almost every gay person has had to contend with at some time in his or her development.

> *"I was always fascinated by people who are considered completely normal, because I find them the weirdest of all."*
>
> ~ **Johnny Depp**

The Oxford Dictionary defines normal as "the usual, average, or typical state or condition." In this sense, being gay is not normal, because gay people are not "the usual" and neither are we "average". But then, what's so great about being usual or average? Is there something inherently wrong or bad about being something other than that — something other than just average? Is gay a "typical state or condition?" For me it is. And if you are gay, then it is normal for you, too. In this sense we can say that being gay is entirely normal — though not average or even usual.

What then about the term 'natural?' Can it ever be natural to be gay?

Let's look again at the Oxford Dictionary and see what is meant by this word 'natural.' Here 'natural' is defined as "existing in or caused by nature; not made or caused by humankind." Does homosexuality exist in nature? The answer is an unequivocal yes.

Homosexual behavior has been well documented in a broad spectrum of animals — more than four hundred and fifty species, in fact. Such activity includes not only sexual contact, but also long-term bonding, displays of courtship, and the rearing of young. From dolphins to deer, geese to giraffes, animals have been observed to prefer animals of the same sex while bypassing possible partners of the opposite sex.

People have been aware of homosexual behavior in animals for many centuries. As science progressed, so did knowledge of animal behavior, but this was largely glossed over, perhaps because researching such a topic could well have meant suspicions being aroused about the researchers' own sexuality. Now, as giant strides have been made in acceptance, social awareness, and civil rights, scientists are investigating this fascinating area in depth.

Such scientific research and the truth it discloses do not sit too well with those who so steadfastly refuse to reconsider their deep-seated abhorrence and prejudice toward being gay, regardless of logic. The prejudiced opponents of gay people conveniently argue that humans should not be compared to animals. Yet it is not entirely unreasonable to suppose that if there were no examples of homosexuality in the natural world, then these same groups and vested interests would be the first to claim this as evidence that being gay is 'against nature.'

One thing is obvious: the nature of prejudice is emotional, not logical, and blind prejudice is nothing if not emotive. Nazi Germany believed gay people to be no more than animals, and this thinking — and the emotion that drove it and which it, in turn, generated — was instrumental in the futile attempt to exterminate all homosexuals.

While it may be dangerous to draw conclusions from the natural world that we extrapolate onto the human, to anthropomorphize, one thing that homosexuality in animal species does demonstrate is that sexuality is a far broader and much more complex subject than many people have imagined.

Animals, of course, have no choice. They simply exist. But human beings, surely, are born with the ability to choose. Indeed, this belief is fundamental to the kind of psychotherapy I practice. If this is the case, then why doesn't everyone choose to be straight? What, exactly, makes a person gay?

What Makes a Person Gay?

Pause for a moment and flip the question. What makes a person straight? Think about it for just a little while and you will find no answer. Ask your straight friends why they are straight — what made them straight, and in all probability they, too, will be unable to come up with any kind of reasonable response, other than "I was born that way." In all probability they have never thought about it before. It's just not something that anyone ever asks. Yet gay people are regularly asked — and often ask themselves — the 'why' question.

> *"I was raised around heterosexuals, as all heterosexuals are, that's where us gay people come from... you heterosexuals."*
> **~ Ellen DeGeneres**

Over the years, there have been many theories as to why someone is gay, and yet no one has been able to provide any suitable, conclusive answer. Many believe that there is a genetic component, an aspect of nature; others think that a person's sexuality has to do with the effect of hormones in the womb; while still others believe that it is the result of conditioning, or nurture.

The American Psychological Association states: "There are probably many reasons for a person's sexual orientation and the reason may be different for different people." And this sounds as near to the truth as we are likely to come for now.

Sexual Orientation

Sexual orientation can be defined in three ways: feelings, behavior, and identity.

It can be based on *feelings* of desire, an attraction to the same sex that engages the emotions. Some people simply find themselves fantasizing about persons of the same sex without actually acting on their feelings. This in and of itself does not necessarily mean that someone is homosexual, although it can be the first stage of recognizing that one is gay or bisexual — though the person may not identify it as such at the time.

Sexual *behavior* means actually acting on desire. It is sexual activity that involves contact or intimacy with someone else — and of course, if you're gay, it means sexual activity with someone of the same sex. This may be masturbation; oral sex using the mouth and tongue; intercrural sex (in which the man places his penis between the thighs of another and thrusts), and anal or vaginal caressing, probing, or intercourse.

Though sexual behavior may be an indication of sexual preference, it does not necessarily make a person gay or bisexual. People in prison or in situations where the opposite sex is just not available — such as in certain cultures or at sea, for example — can experience same-sex relations, returning to heterosexual activity when the opportunity arises. Many young people experiment, especially in adolescence when hormones are running high and opportunity for interaction with the opposite sex is perhaps restricted.

When a person *identifies* him or herself as being gay, then he or she might describe him or herself as such. As mentioned, surveys have shown that many more people report having had sex with a person or people of their own sex as opposed to those who identify as gay — hence the terms MSM and WSW.

This may be particularly significant in non-Western cultures and countries, where people might not necessarily identify as being gay, but nevertheless engage in same-sex activity at least as frequently as those who identify as gay.

Some people believe that being gay is a choice that people make. Nothing could be farther from the truth. Given the many obstacles and opposition that each gay person must contend with and somehow overcome — the scorn of some elements in society, rejection, discrimination, and possible exposure to hate crimes — it is very difficult to see how anyone could initially *choose* such a life. Sexual orientation is so obviously beyond personal choice.

Most gay people who have come to terms with their sexual orientation believe that being gay is not a choice, any more than a person chooses to be straight or elects to have a certain eye color (though they may seek to hide it behind colored lenses).

Once a gay or bi person has accepted his or her sexuality, it is quite rare for anyone to want to change it, even if they could. Most say that they feel much more fulfilled and happy once they have accepted their sexual orientation.

Can Homosexual Orientation Be Cured or Changed?

Ask yourself if heterosexuality can be cured. The answer is a categorical no — though this is a question that quite a few young (and not so young) people who experience an attraction to the same sex sometimes ask. Homosexuality cannot be cured any more than heterosexuality can be cured. Being gay is not a sickness, and neither is it a disease. As a result, no cure is possible nor, indeed, needed.

There was a time when being gay was listed as a mental disorder, when psychologists and psychiatrists tried to 'cure' people of their homosexuality.

Only in 1986 was homosexuality removed entirely from the psychiatric 'bible' of mental illness, the *Diagnostic and Statistical Manual of Mental Disorders* (DSM). In 1993, the slower moving World Health Organization followed suit, removing it from its list of mental disorders, the ICD-10 (*International Classification of Diseases,* 10th revision). This was surely the speediest recovery from 'mental illness' in the history of psychiatry! With a single sweep of the psychiatric pen, a large percentage of humanity was no longer deemed mentally ill.

It was as if psychiatry had paradoxically decided that the only thing disordered about homosexuality was to classify it as a mental disorder.

Yet there remain a few medical people today, some of them psychiatrists, and also psychologists and therapists, who cling to this outdated notion. Such people are almost always influenced by religious beliefs. However, they are in a very rare minority. The vast majority of psychiatrists and psychologists, and all of the main psychiatric and psychological organizations in the UK and the US, unanimously agree that being gay is not a disorder and that attempts to cure it not only do not work, but are far more harmful than anything else.

Today the emphasis is wisely placed on acceptance of one's sexual orientation, and not on any attempt to change it.

In the past, psychiatrists resorted to all kinds of approaches in an attempt to 'cure' homosexuality. Hormone treatment, drug-induced nausea, psychoanalysis, and religious counseling all have been employed. One of the most common 'treatments' was electro-aversion therapy, in which the gay person was restrained and immobilized, and electrodes attached to the body. They were then shown pictures of men or women in various states of undress. A powerful electric shock was then systematically delivered. This painful and barbaric treatment succeeded only in harming, not in converting anyone to a heterosexual orientation. Enormous mental disturbance and actual suicide have been attributed to this misguided 'therapy.'

These inhumane tactics simply did not work. The idiocy of such treatments lies not only in their primitive methodology but in their naiveté. They completely ignored the obvious fact that producing an aversion to one particular thing does not mean that a person is automatically attracted to its opposite. Creating an aversion to carrots does not mean that a person will automatically like broccoli.

A hangover from this approach to human sexuality may be seen today in what is called 'reparative therapy' or 'conversion therapy,' an approach that attempts to convince gay people that their feelings are wrong, unnatural, and can be 'cured.' This is something that has been almost universally contested by the scientific community.

In the UK, the Royal College of Psychiatrists categorically states that:

> *"There is no sound scientific evidence that sexual orientation can be changed."*

Not only is there no real evidence that reparative therapy actually works, but documented evidence shows that the harmful effects of this 'therapy' include depression, social withdrawal, self-harm, and suicide. All of which should serve as clear warning against employing psychiatry and psychology in an attempt to change aspects of human behavior and identity simply because they are in some way disapproved of on social, political, moral, or religious grounds.

Here is what the British Psychological Society (BPS) has to say on the matter:

> *"The BPS believes that people of same-sex orientations should be regarded as equal members of society with the same rights and responsibilities. This includes freedom from harassment or discrimination in any sphere, and a right to protection from therapies that are potentially damaging, particularly those that purport to change or 'convert' sexual orientation."*

Despite clear condemnation from all of the major psychological and counseling societies and associations, sadly, this kind of 'therapy' remains entirely legal in the UK.

Most of this 'reparative therapy', however, is carried out in the US, and in 2007 the American Psychological Association (APA) completed a systematic review of eighty-three studies. Having spent two years examining the available research, it concluded that there was no convincing evidence that sexual orientation could ever be changed, and that attempting to do so could cause severe depression and actual suicidal tendencies.

In 2009, and based on this scientific research, the APA voted overwhelmingly to repudiate reparative therapy.

"To date, there has been no scientifically adequate research to show that therapy aimed at changing sexual orientation (sometimes called reparative or conversion therapy) is safe or effective. Furthermore, it seems likely that the promotion of change therapies reinforces stereotypes and contributes to a negative climate for lesbian, gay and bisexual persons."

~ American Psychological Association

At the time of writing (2015), California, New Jersey, Oregon, and Washington, D.C. have outlawed this discredited practice.

There is no major mental health organization that has sanctioned attempts to change sexual orientation. In fact, virtually all have issued policy statements cautioning professionals and the public about 'treatments' that claim to alter sexual orientation.

As a therapist, I am appalled that 'reparative therapy' continues to be practiced on those people unfortunate enough to enter into it, and I am far from alone in this, with Californian state Sen. Ted Lieu calling it "junk science," and professor of psychology Dr. Mary Strobe asking: "Who are the 'professionals' involved in 'converting' gays, especially given the scientific evidence refuting such practices? All the legitimate professionals involved in therapy would not engage in such behavior; they would consider it unethical."

If a person is unhappy with his or her sexual orientation, the only sensible and wise thing to do is to help him or her come to terms with and accept it.

But in order for a person to accept his or her sexuality, it is necessary to know what that sexuality is.

How Do I Know If I Am Gay?

As we have seen, simply because a person engages in same-sex activity does not necessarily mean that he or she is gay.

For many, it is a simple matter; they are attracted to the same sex and had an awareness or recognition of this long before they ever acted upon that attraction. For them, it just feels natural to be who they are and to feel as they feel. For others, though, it may take longer to discover their true orientation or identity.

Currently, many psychologists think that an awareness of sexual orientation usually emerges in that period between middle childhood and the early teenage years. It is then that patterns of emotional and sexual attraction may manifest themselves, most often without the involvement of any previous sexual experience.

This, however, is simply a generalization, because the human experience is so varied and so rich. Different people have different experiences, and they respond to those experiences in different ways — a fact that is as true for sexual orientation as it is for practically everything else in life.

For some people, the homophobic atmosphere of social discrimination and prejudice becomes internalized, making it very difficult for them to accept their own sexual orientation, and they may spend quite a long time denying to themselves as well as to others where their feelings truly lie.

It is quite natural for a person to question his or her sexuality, especially when young, and there really is no reason to rush or hurry the process of acknowledging which sexual orientation or sexual identity is yours. Knowing what you are can take time, and each person has his or her own particular pace in accomplishing this.

Knowing *who* you are can take much longer. In fact, it is a process that continues throughout a person's life. We are all, in some way or another, in the process of becoming who we are, and this is something that will continue for as long as we live, as new experiences provide new information that we process and incorporate into the multiplicity of aspects we call our 'self.'

> *"I don't remember deciding to become a writer. You decide to become a dentist or a postman. For me, writing is like being gay. You finally admit that this is who you are, you come out and hope that no one runs away."*
>
> ~ **Mark Haddon**

Some people like to experiment and explore with others before realizing what they really like, while others prefer to stand back and see where their desire is most consistently directed. If we find ourselves continually aroused by members of the same sex, to the virtual exclusion of the opposite sex, then it is probably safe for us to assume that we are gay. But it is not quite as clear-cut as that. As we saw with the Kinsey scale, most people are not at one end or the other of the scale. It's absolutely fine if we are, but many just fit somewhere in between.

People who are attracted to both sexes are known as bisexual. This does not mean that they like each sex equally, simply that they have a sexual attraction to both male and female.

If you have had sexual experiences that were against your wishes, or if you have been forced to have sex with someone against your own will, then this does not make you gay — even if you experienced an erection or sexual arousal while doing so. In cases of male rape, for example, it is not at all uncommon for the person being raped to experience an erection, and even to ejaculate. Paradoxically, this is simply part of the natural fear response, and has nothing to do with sexual orientation.

Determining sexual orientation may be a lengthy and confusing experience for some. It may mean long hours, if not years, of deliberation and a good deal of soul searching and possible inner conflict before a person really knows what his or her orientation really is. Here, good counseling can prove invaluable. Working with a counselor or therapist who is experienced in the field of sexuality and sexual orientation can assist in clarifying things and help resolve the confusion. Such counseling is always conducted in the strictest confidence. No qualified counselor or therapist will disclose anything about your sexuality, sexual orientation, or gender identity to anyone else.

Remember that being gay does not mean that you have to fit into any kind of gay stereotype. The vast majority of gay people simply cannot be distinguished from those who are not gay. Being gay does not make anyone less masculine or less feminine. Always keep in mind that you are who you are, and who you are is okay.

> *"No, I've never thought that I was gay. And that's not something you think. It's something you know."*
> **~ Robert Plant**

Eventually, only you can say what your sexual identity is. No matter how a person identifies, as gay or straight or anything in between, it is important to remember that he or she is a valuable human being.

Discovering your true sexual orientation and gender identity can be a wonderful, though not always easy, journey. One thing is certain: once a person has discovered who he or she is, and has accepted and made peace with this, living becomes much easier and life can be even more fulfilling.

In beautiful symmetry, the more comfortable we are within ourselves, the more comfortable other people are with us, and the more comfortable our lives become.

So far we have been talking about sexual orientation, but we have said nothing about gender identity. The questions that we need to answer now are, what is the difference between our sex and our gender, and in what way, if any, do they interact with each other?

Sex and Gender

When we refer to a person's sex, we are talking about that person as male or female. It is a biological term, something decided before birth. A male, for example, has testicles and larger bones than a female, while a female can menstruate, but a man cannot. A person's gender identity, however, can differ from his or her actual biological sex. It is possible for people to be assigned to the male gender at birth, but to feel that they are female, and vice-versa. This is known as being transgender.

Transgender is a term that is used to signify people whose gender identity does not conform to the typical social expectations of their biological sex. There are several different kinds of transgender people, and we will discuss this shortly.

Also, there are those who are bigender or gender fluid, which means that they have days when they identify as fully male, days when they identify as fully female, and days where they feel like a mixture of both. This can cause real confusion, and sometimes downright hostility, in those whose concept of gender is limited and uninformed.

Additionally, there are people who are agender, who do not identify as having a gender at all, binary or otherwise.

And then there are some who may be considered to be pansexual, polysexual, or omnisexual, which means that they are not limited in choice with regard to biological sex, gender, or gender identity, and so feel attraction toward people of any sex or gender identity.

If all of this sounds confusing, it really doesn't need to be. Just remember that, unlike biological sex, when we refer to someone's gender, we are talking about the *concept* of maleness or femaleness — of masculinity and femininity. Though a person's biological sex assignment remains quite stable across different cultures, aspects of gender can differ considerably.

"These names: gay, queer, homosexual are limiting. I would love to finish with them. We're going to have to decide which terms to use and where we use them. For me to use the word 'queer' is a liberation; it was a word that frightened me, but no longer."
~ Derek Jarman

Each of us has a gender identity, even though we might not yet have formed a clear idea of our sexual identity or orientation, and this gender identity is the sense we have of being male, female, agender, or in some way fluid. It does not refer to our gender role — the behavior generally viewed as masculine or feminine by our culture — but to the way that we ourselves identify as male or female. Each person's gender identity is a core value that is held at a very deep and private level of reality; it is something that is treasured to the point of being sacrosanct.

It is believed that gender identity is formed and irrevocably fixed before the first year of life. Though attempts have been made to alter a person's gender identity after this, no valid scientific evidence has ever shown that this is possible, and some attempts to alter gender identity have met with the most tragic consequences.

As we have seen, for some, sexual identity does not match gender identity, and this can create confusion and sometimes even hostility in others who dislike or are uncomfortable with difference.

In most cultures, the way people behave is usually labeled as masculine or feminine. When our behavior and interests are viewed as atypical or unusual for our particular biological sex, then we may be seen as odd. Men who behave in feminine ways may be labeled 'fairies,' 'sissies,' or 'queer,' while women who behave in more masculine ways can be called 'tomboys,' 'lezzies,' or be viewed as 'butch.'

Because a culture labels certain behaviors as masculine or feminine, however, does not mean that they are an actual part of someone's gender or of their gender identity; nor does it mean that the person exhibiting such behavior is necessarily gay.

Care must be taken not to confuse transvestites with transgendered people. Through television, the popular media, and movies such as *The Rocky Horror Picture Show,* most people are familiar with the term 'transvestite,' commonly thought of as a man in drag — though, interestingly, the term is almost never applied to women who adopt men's traditional clothing, donning suits, ties etc. Most transvestites are heterosexual men who enjoy dressing in women's clothing from time to time, and not people who identify as having a gender different from their biological sex. (In fact, research has shown that homosexuality is *less* prevalent among transvestites than in the general population.) I recall one client in my psychotherapy practice, a heterosexual policeman who enjoyed wearing his wife's dresses, describing it as "a clothing option."

The term 'transsexual' is most often used to connote that a person has or would like to have some form of gender affirmative surgery. Transsexual people seek to alter their bodies to bring them in line with their gender identity. This may be done through make up, padding, hormone treatment, surgery, or a combination of any of these. Traditionally, this process of transition is known as gender reassignment, though recently the term 'gender affirmation' has been used because of its positive — and many would argue, more accurate — connotation. (It is important here to distinguish between 'transgender' and 'transsexual'. A person who identifies as transgender may or may not seek gender affirmation surgery, and their identity as a trans person does not depend on seeking or receiving surgery.)

Just like any other human being, a trans person may be heterosexual, bisexual, homosexual, or asexual.

A person may also be intersex. People who are intersex can have physical characteristics that make it difficult to identify them as either male or female (although it is not always as obvious as having the physical characteristics of both sexes). Simply put, they are born with an anatomy that doesn't neatly fit the standard gender definitions.

Sometimes this is surgically altered in infancy, with the intention of raising the child as either male or female — a highly questionable practice that attempts to push a child into a particular gender identity and bypass the person's own developing identity. It is far wiser to leave well enough alone, and allow the child to express and identify what is right for him or her as they grow to maturity.

"Normal is nothing more than a cycle on a washing machine."
~ Whoopie Goldberg

Others do not know of their true gender identity until they reach adulthood, and still others might not ever realize that they are intersex. An acquaintance of mine, who served with distinction as a male soldier in the United Nations peacekeeping corps, did not discover that she was intersex until she was diagnosed with ovarian cancer. In other words, the term 'intersex' is something of a socially constructed category for what is, essentially, true biological variation.

For many people who have no real knowledge or understanding of what it is to be gay, there can be confusion between being homosexual and being trans, and often the two have been equated in the popular imagination. Such confusion has helped neither trans nor gay people.

Today, gay people are linked with bisexual, trans, bigender, and intersex in solidarity because all are minorities that have been, and in many ways remain, discriminated against.

The fight for acceptance and civil rights, and the advances that this struggle continues to bring, cannot be restricted or accorded to one group and not to others. Equality is not something that can be handed out like bread or bonbons to some, yet denied to others who are equally hungry, equally deserving.

Now gay people in various stages of their journey stand shoulder to shoulder with those who are trans, intersex, and bigender; and the acronym LGBTIQ has come to signify this grouping.

LGBTIQ stands for Lesbian, Gay, Bisexual, Trans, Intersex, and Questioning or Queer. (Queer is a reclaimed word, once used as an insult, now used as an umbrella term for anyone who may identify as being bigender or sexually diverse.)

All are human beings of different sexes, sexual orientations, and gender identity who share one thing in common — a wonderful diversity that adds to the spectrum of human experience and to the richness of humanity itself.

Chapter Two

The Ugly Face of Homophobia

"Homophobia is like racism and anti-Semitism and other forms of bigotry. It seeks to dehumanize a large group of people, to deny their humanity, their dignity and personhood."

~ Coretta Scott King
(Widow of Martin Luther King Jr.)

The young man standing opposite me in the sexual health organization office looked desperately unhappy. He said his name was Adam and that he had been thrown out of his home with nowhere to sleep, no money, no job, and no means to earn a living. He was just sixteen years old. And he was gay.

"I knew there'd be trouble when my mom found out that Ricky Martin was gay," he told me, sipping his tea. "She was a big fan. When she heard he was gay she went ballistic, smashing all his CDs... ripping up all his pics."

"Then she found a note I wrote to another boy in my school, talking about what we did and how much I wanted to meet him again. When I came back home she'd put some of my clothes together and just kicked me out." He took a deep breath, as if he were about to dive under water. "She said I couldn't stay under the same roof with my little brother; like I would contaminate him ..."

"Have you given her time?" I asked. "What about calling her?"

"I tried that," he said. "I've been sleeping rough, but I borrowed a mate's phone and called her."

"Good," I said. "And?"

"She asked me why I hadn't done the right thing and killed myself, and then she put the phone down on me ..."

Though perhaps extreme, sadly Adam's story is not unique. In the UK today, it is estimated that around thirty percent of all homeless youth identify as gay. In the US, research has shown that up to forty percent of all homeless young people are gay, lesbian, bisexual, or transgender.

Not every case of LGBTIQ youth homelessness has to do exclusively with sexuality, of course, but the fact that, as a group, we are disproportionately represented is cause for real concern. It is not always easy to be gay in a world where most people are not, and it is even less easy to be gay and homeless. I know this personally, because when I was much younger, I, too, was homeless and found myself sleeping on the street.

> *"It always seemed a bit pointless to disapprove of homosexuality. It's like disapproving of rain."*
>
> **~ Francis Maude, British Parliamentarian**

The UK charity *ChildLine*, the free 24-hour counseling service for children and young people, reports some revealing statistics:

2,725 young people call *ChildLine* every year to talk about sexual orientation, homophobia, and homophobic bullying.

Males account for fifty-five percent of calls made about these issues, but only twenty-five percent of total calls to *ChildLine.*

Young LGBTIQ people reported being triply isolated, with schools, friends, and families being homophobic.

Most feel lonely and completely isolated, with nowhere else to turn.

Many report feeling suicidal.

Homophobia and the discrimination that so often accompanies it can take many forms, from subtle innuendo to outright violence.

(Though this chapter focuses on 'homophobia', much of this information also applies to prejudice and discrimination directed towards LGBTIQ people in general. Sadly, biphobia, transphobia, and bigotry towards those who identify under the umbrella term 'queer' — intersex, bigender, asexual, agender etc. — is still very much with us.)

Prejudice, bullying, and verbal abuse are all too widespread and commonplace in the lives of many LGBTIQ people — the young and those who are no longer young.

Despite all the advances in civil rights, marriage equality, and anti-discrimination law, homophobia is still with us, it is still rife, and it still damages. Though progress has been made, there is still widespread prejudice and discrimination.

Given the power that homophobia has to disrupt lives, foster fear, and incubate hatred, perhaps we need to know a bit more about it if we really do want to be gay and happy. In fact, our ability to be happy as LGBTIQ people is deeply influenced by our ability to deal with homophobia in its various forms.

Origins of the Word *Homophobia*

Homophobia has been around from early times, but only recently has it been given a name, and only in 1994 did it begin to appear in dictionaries.

Prior to the 1960s, it was homophobia, and not homosexuality, that was the *real* sin that dare not speak its name. In 1967, a self-identified heterosexual psychologist named George Weinberg was talking to some other therapists. They were discussing the work of a female friend when he inadvertently mentioned that she was lesbian. Immediately, the therapists' attitude changed and they began to discuss her in negative terms.

"It came to me with utter clarity that this was a phobia," said Weinberg. For him the roots of homophobia were clear. "It is fear, fear, and more fear." Later he would explain: "It is based on the preposterous notion that if you are like everybody else you will be safe, secure, and happy ..."

In 1969, the word *homophobia* appeared in print. The US tabloid magazine *Screw* included it in an article that tellingly referred to straight men's fear that other people might think them gay.

A couple of years later, in 1971, the word *homophobia* was used by psychotherapist Kenneth Smith in an article titled: "Homophobia: A Tentative Personality Profile." The word — and the concept — had arrived.

Today the word *homophobia* is listed in the Concise Oxford Dictionary as meaning "an extreme and irrational aversion to homosexuality and homosexual people." The definition that seems to me to best fit its current usage and application, however, is that of Rachel Krantz and Tim Cusick in the book *Gay Rights*, where homophobia is defined as "Literally, the irrational fear of homosexuals; *used more widely to denote hatred for gay men and lesbians and the view that they are somehow inferior to heterosexuals*." (Italics added.)

> *"You've got to be taught to hate and fear,*
> *You've got to be taught from year to year,*
> *It's got to be drummed in your dear little ear,*
> *You've got to be carefully taught."*
> **~ South Pacific, Rogers & Hammerstein**

As is the case with all forms of prejudice, anti-gay bigotry is something that is learned. It is not something that any child is born with, but a belief-set and attitude acquired from society, the media, friends and family — something known in psychological parlance as an *introjected value*. (The term 'introject' means to incorporate the attitudes, beliefs, or ideas of others. Things introjected are not native to us, but learned from other people, becoming part of our own internalized value system.) However, calling prejudice a 'phobia' can all too easily have the effect of freeing those who are prejudiced from having to alter their behavior and amend their attitude.

Whereas fear may play a part in homophobia for some people, for others it clearly does not. Many homophobic people have a deep-seated and irrational dislike, hatred, or contempt for LGBTIQ people, without necessarily feeling fear. As a neat illustration of this, Britain's Ken Clarke, former Minister of State for Justice, once said: "I am not homophobic, because 'phobia' means 'fear,' and I am not afraid of homosexuals."

The same point has been made in the US by preacher Samuel Frost of Reign of Christ Ministries: "Phobia means 'fear': I am afraid of homosexuals. Well, that's not true, either," he said, before delivering the clincher, "any more than I am afraid of child molesters, rapists, and murderers," neatly and insidiously linking gay people with those others.

Like it or not, though, we seem stuck with this word *homophobia*. It has entered our dictionaries because it has become part of our language. It may not be the ideal word, but it is part of any discussion on being gay and being happy.

Perhaps the chief significance of this word *homophobia* is that it places things within a psychological context that exists in direct opposition to the idea that homosexuality is a disorder. The word homophobia allows us to see that it is not homosexuality that is really the problem, but the irrational, disordered response to it. If we delve deep enough, the one conclusion we can make concerning homophobia is that it has its roots in anxiety and inner discomfort.

In Chapter One, we touched briefly on homophobia, as we discussed where the idea that gay isn't okay came from. Perhaps now is the time to look a little closer at the origins of homophobia.

The idea that gay people are somehow inferior to heterosexuals is inherent within the notion of homophobia. Indeed, homophobia certainly does contain a strong element of *heterosexism* (sometimes called *heterocentrism* or *heteronormativity*).

Heterosexism is the term used to denote the belief, or belief system, that privileges heterosexual values, seeing them as superior, universal, and the best of all possible values. It is, essentially, a system of subtle and not so subtle coercion that insists on heterosexuality in exchange for being accepted as a first-class citizen of society. Such an attitude engenders an "if you're not straight then you don't really matter" approach toward other people.

What Causes Homophobia?

Though the causes of homophobia are complex and profound, one of the interesting things that research has confirmed is that, in general, males tend to be much more homophobic than females.

Part of the reason why the story of Adam's mother, with which we began this chapter, has the power to move us is because it seems so very unnatural, so atypical. Women — and mothers especially — are just not expected to behave in such a heartless, uncompassionate, and viciously homophobic way. Though there are of course exceptions, generally speaking, women seem to be far less judgmental and condemning of homosexuality than men. (Homophobic women may be more rare than homophobic men, but this is not to say that they do not exist — as the American anti-gay campaigner Anita Bryant, the obsessional critic of the Kinsey Research, Judith Reisman, and the leader of the Westboro Baptist Church in the US, Shirley Phelps, demonstrate.)

> *"Homophobia is gay."*
> **~ Frank Iero**

Many gay people sense this instinctively. Young and not so young LGBTIQ people have often felt safer coming out and sharing their secret with a girl or woman than they ever would have with a boy or a man, especially in the early phase of coming to terms with their sexual orientation.

The reason males tend to be more homophobic than females is complex and varied, but the irrational attitude of revulsion that so many males — including gay men — have toward others who are in some way feminine or effeminate may offer a clue.

Homophobia and Masculinity

Anchored firmly in many people's minds, is the feeling that homosexuality is some form of betrayal of one's own sex. And nowhere is this attitude more clearly seen than in some men's and some boys' attitudes toward gay men.

The great psychologist Alfred Adler, a contemporary of Sigmund Freud, believed that society devalues girls, seeing them in some way as inferior to boys, and that this gives rise to a sense of rejection of their femininity. He called this *"masculine protest"* and believed it involves a struggle to dominate.

In males this leads to a sense of superiority and the choice of a masculine ideal in what is termed their "guiding fiction." Because of this "masculine protest," males can see other males who appear to renounce this favored position as traitors threatening the status quo. In this schema, gay men are seen as less than 'real men,' and this can produce contempt and strong, even volatile, emotion. If a man displays feminine traits or engages in what is considered to be feminine behavior — or if this supposition is projected onto him because he is gay — then this may ignite "masculine protest" and trigger visceral reactions that can quite easily be converted into violence.

This is particularly the case in families and social groups that hold more traditional views of gender and family roles and in families where the man is traditionally 'the king' and in which masculinity is defined as essentially or exclusively heterosexual. Often, the fear of being seen as 'queer' leads men to act in hyper-masculine and even aggressive ways and to close down their feelings and emotions because they believe that this would identify them in some way as feminine.

An over-identification with such an internalized masculine guiding fiction can cause some men and boys to seek sexual contact with girls and women in order to prove to themselves and/or others that they are not gay. Such an attitude undoubtedly plays a role in some teenage pregnancies, bringing untold misery into the lives of people who might otherwise have chosen a different partner and a different path.

All this considered, it is perhaps unsurprising that the strong relationship between homophobia and a fictionalized masculinity may also play a role in date rape and other forms of sexual violence.

Other Causes of Homophobia

Homophobia may be driven by other factors, of course. Research into the nature of prejudice — which is what homophobia really is — suggests that homophobia is, in fact, a *combination* of prejudices.

In the minds of homophobes, gay people can be viewed as clannish, as belonging to a tribe or group other than the one to which they themselves belong, and therefore they can be perceived as outsiders who represent some form of threat. Being outsiders, identified by being sexually different, they can also be demonized as predatory and sexually obsessed. Females who are attracted to — and attract — other females can be perceived as competing with men for women.

Homophobia can also be a kind of 'homosexual panic': something caused by the fear of homosexual feelings within the homophobic person him or herself. It is this particular aspect that can cause a person to engage in outward displays of homophobia. Proclaiming a strong dislike for and condemnation of LGBTIQ people can act as a useful red herring or smoke screen. When employed in this way, homophobia is a cover or ruse designed to take the focus away from those who are in fact gay or who have same-sex feelings that they do not want to acknowledge or admit — to themselves or to others.

A clear example of this can be seen, for instance, in the case of Ella Masar, a professional women's soccer player in the United States, who has made comments in the past regarding homosexuality in sport and society. Masar made statements such as 'I am often surrounded by people living ungodly lifestyles, specifically when it comes to homosexuality.' In July 2015 however, Masar married same-sex Houston Dash teammate and Canadian international team player, Erin Mcleod.

One of my clients, a middle-aged man of Afro-Caribbean heritage, related an experience that is a perfect example of this type of homophobic ruse. As a devout Christian, he was struggling to come to terms with his feelings toward men. He was gay and wracked with guilt because of it. One afternoon he visited a public toilet known to be a cruising place for gay men, only to be approached and propositioned by the pastor of his own church who had stood in the pulpit and preached a sermon vehemently condemning homosexuality the Sunday before. The pastor had been using condemnation of gay people as a smoke screen so that no one would suspect that he himself had these feelings and attractions. While he may have felt more secure hiding behind his condemnation of homosexuality, he had used his influence to inflame and worsen the situation for many other gay people.

A series of recent studies conducted by the University of Essex in the UK and the University of Rochester, in conjunction with the

University of California, Santa Barbara in the US, supports the hypothesis of homophobia as a ruse. Using a series of highly sophisticated tests, research teams looked at the discrepancies between what people said about their sexual orientation and their implicit — or actual — sexual orientation. The results were astounding. The people who scored highest on the homophobia testing were those who professed strong heterosexual orientations yet had the strongest undisclosed same-sex feelings. These people were the most likely to exhibit a deep-seated dislike of gay people.

According to Dr. Netta Weinstein, lead author of this study, "Individuals who identify as straight but in psychological tests show a strong attraction to the same sex may be threatened by gays and lesbians because homosexuals remind them of similar tendencies within themselves."

Explaining the homophobia research findings further, Dr. Richard Ryan, professor of psychology at the University of Rochester, says, "In many cases these are people who are at war with themselves and they are turning this internal conflict outward."

Examples of this smoke screen strategy reveal an astonishing level of hypocrisy that can be really shocking when brought to light and exposed as the bigotry that it really is. Here are just a very few examples: former FBI chief J. Edgar Hoover and his partner Clyde Tolson, associate director of the FBI, consistently targeted and persecuted homosexuals as well as groups fighting for gay rights such as the *Mattachine Society*. Both men were rumored to be gay, and there is little disagreement that Hoover had a long and passionate relationship with Tolson.

In the 1950s, United States Sen. Joseph McCarthy targeted gay people as well as suspected communists, persecuting them and causing them to be regularly subjected to police harassment. Gay men were systematically dismissed from public service, and by 1951 federal workers were being fired at the rate of sixty a month. In the military, around two thousand people a year were discharged because they were gay. Many gay men dismissed from their jobs were unable to find other work because of it. Countless lives were ruined, families torn apart, and quite a few took their own lives as a direct consequence of this persecution. Only later was it revealed that McCarthy was in all probability himself homosexual.

The American evangelical preacher Ted Haggard, who often spoke of "the evils of homosexuality" and vehemently opposed gay marriage, was himself exposed in a gay sex scandal in 2006.

The former chairman of the Young Republican National Federation, Glenn Murphy Jr., a rising star in US politics and a vociferous anti-gay campaigner who also strongly opposed gay marriage, was shown to have a history of homosexuality. He was found guilty of sexual assault on a twenty-two-year-old man — a crime for which he received a six-year prison sentence.

Virginia Congressman Ed Schrock, a man who sought every possible means to persecute gay people, opposed accepting gays in the military, protesting: "You're in the showers with them! You're in bunk rooms with them!" He also did his best to block any possibility of gay marriage, sponsoring legislation designed to make same-sex marriage automatically illegal across the whole of the US. Yet in a scandal that has now consigned him to well-earned obscurity, it was revealed that this same man regularly used male prostitutes that were hired from gay dating services.

> *"A huge part of what animates homophobia among young people is paranoia and fear of their own capacity to be gay themselves."*
>
> **~ Dan Savage**

There are countless such examples of homophobia being used as a smoke screen or camouflage for homosexual behavior and orientation.

Of course, one reason a politician might be publicly homophobic and vocally anti-gay is because it is a definite vote-winner, especially amongst right wing and fundamentalist religious voters. Politics has always been an area shot through with blatant opportunism.

As all these examples show, homophobia isn't always what it appears to be on the surface. The thing to remember is that homophobia can spring from many places. None of these explanations of the origin of homophobia exists in exclusivity. None deny homophobia's linkage to the larger world in which we live. It has its connections to the myriad frames through which the homophobic person views the world — social, political, religious, and personal. We live in a world that influences us each day. Just as the homophobe is a product of that world, so too are we.

Let's delve a little deeper now and look at the types of homophobia, because the more we understand it, the better placed we are to deal with it. And our ability to deal with homophobia has a lot to do with our ability to be happy as well as gay.

Types of Homophobia

Homophobia can be divided into four basic categories:

1. Cultural homophobia
2. Institutional homophobia
3. Interpersonal homophobia
4. Personal or internalized homophobia.

We'll start with the general and move to the specific.

First on our list is *cultural homophobia.* This refers to social standards — social prejudices that, as we have seen, have their origins in society's parochial past, in things such as tribalism and religion, which dictate that being gay is morally wrong or reprehensible. Cultural homophobia also encompasses heterosexism, which, as we have also seen, is the belief that being heterosexual is superior. (A classic example of this comes from France, a country generally considered to be permissive in its attitudes toward sex. "Heterosexuality is best," proclaimed French Prime Minister Edith Cresson, speaking in 1991).

We see cultural homophobia each day in the media: in newspaper and magazine advertisements where everyone is heterosexual; on TV shows where practically every relationship is straight and every young person is automatically presumed to be attracted to, and so will grow up and marry, someone of the opposite sex. In those few instances where gay people are identified, they are generally depicted as comedic, neurotic, or dysfunctional — anything other than gay *and* happy.

Cultural homophobia is the reason LGBTIQ people have largely been excluded from history. It is why you probably heard no mention of the fact that Alexander the Great, Leonardo da Vinci, Michelangelo, Tchaikovsky, Hans Christian Anderson, Emily Dickinson, Federico Garcia Lorca, and movie heartthrob James Dean were gay. Why your history teacher forgot to mention that Socrates, Plato, Leonardo da Vinci, Abraham Lincoln, Eleanor Roosevelt, Ralph Waldo Emerson, and Allen Turning — the father of the computer — were attracted to the same sex.

The list of famous and historical LGBTIQ figures whose sexuality has been erased from the history books is almost endless.

This kind of homophobia suppresses LGBTIQ history in the same way that black and women's histories were once suppressed. In its denial of fact it distorts the reality and increases oppression. Because of this, so many young gay people grow up with feelings of worthlessness, or with a terrible sense of difference that can easily turn into a fearful sense of alienation. When the accomplishments of gay people are hidden, then straight and gay receive a distorted view of the world. Learning only about the lives of heterosexuals, gay young people are denied the opportunity of recognizing the worth and validity of gay people.

When you're young and have sexual feelings for the same sex, it's easy to believe you're the only one, that everyone else in the world is straight and that there is something wrong with and abnormal about you. In the suppression of gay people in history, and of the contributions that LGBTIQ people have made to society in all areas — science, medicine, art, literature, politics — generation upon generation of LGBTIQ people have been robbed of positive role models and an accurate perspective. In addition, generation upon generation of straight people have been denied the opportunity to see that gay people can indeed be valuable and valued members of society.

Cultural homophobia is something that hurts not only LGBTIQ people, but damages society itself by minimizing — and so covertly discouraging — the worthwhile contributions that gay men and women have made and can continue to make to society, and pressuring everyone to conform to rigid stereotypes. A society that is based on oppression can never be completely healthy, nor can it ever be fully functional. In denying the rights and identity of LGBTIQ people, the rights and identity of society itself are in some important way also denied and its levels of happiness compromised and reduced.

Institutional Homophobia

This kind of homophobia refers to ways in which governments, religious organizations, schools, business, and other institutions discriminate against LGBTIQ people on the basis of their sexual orientation. Like cultural homophobia, institutional homophobia again encompasses and is based on the belief that straight is superior and best.

Institutional homophobia runs throughout the structure of many organizations. Some institutions, including religious institutions and even governments, take open and explicit stands against being gay. Others are institutions, organizations, and agencies that have negative attitudes or implicit policies toward LGBTIQ people, such as refusing to allocate resources, refusing to give any attention to the needs of gay men and women, or in some less obvious way discriminating against them.

In my role as educator and lecturer, I have delivered anti-homophobia diversity training and workshops and given talks to various organizations, agencies, schools, and universities in the UK. During the course of my work, I have witnessed shocking, deep-seated homophobic attitudes across the board: in the police, the probation service, youth services, education, and other social services agencies.

When pointing out the disproportionate incidence of suicide amongst young gay men under the age of twenty-one, for example, one response was that they should be condemned for being so selfish — totally disregarding the misery that drove them to the drastic action of ending their own lives!

In a room full of policemen who did not know I was both gay and the facilitator, the most awful homophobic banter went on prior to the training; all of which was quickly dismissed when I disclosed who I was. Later, when presenting facts regarding the terrible damage caused by homophobia, I was told, "That doesn't happen these days. You've got a chip on your shoulder. Go back and tell 'your people' that there is no homophobia in this police force!" This despite the fact that the figures I had presented were impeccably researched and current, and that I had heard their anti-gay remarks and witnessed their overtly homophobic behavior just moments before.

Though I have worked in many British schools to help deal with homophobic bullying, the head of one school quickly withdrew permission for me to give a talk about homophobia because teachers feared for their own safety. They were genuinely afraid that parents would surround the school and create a massive disturbance — perhaps leading to physical violence — if it were discovered that I was suggesting that it is acceptable to be gay, but completely unacceptable to bully someone who is gay or is perceived to be. Imagine being young and gay in such a school, such a social environment. What do you think the chances are that you will be gay *and* happy?

So deeply entrenched is homophobia in some institutions, and in some people within those institutions and organizations, that they refuse to acknowledge it, even when they are clearly exhibiting it or when its evidence is staring them in the face. Such is the nature of prejudice.

Those working in a similar field in the US know only too well that institutional homophobia is equally alive and well there, too. Institutionalized anti-gay sentiment and behavior is not confined to the UK and the US, of course, and in fact in many countries it is far worse.

> *"To be raped is to be sexually violated. For society to force someone, through shame and ostracism, to comply with love and sex that it defines, is nothing but organized rape. That is what homophobia is all about. Organized rape."*
>
> **~ Lee Maracle**

Institutional homophobia is intrinsically connected with the concept of power, but not necessarily or exclusively in the sense of the "masculine protest" discussed earlier. As a psychotherapist, I recognize that it was not simply blind ignorance that led those people I mentioned earlier to exhibit such blatant homophobia, though this inevitably played a part, but it was also the desire to 'be someone' within their organization or agency, and to maintain or exert some form of power or powerful opinion that would demonstrate this.

Throughout history, politicians and power brokers have found it useful to use minorities as scapegoats. In Nazi Germany, Jews were rumored to be the minority who poisoned wells, stole children, and ruined the economy; in the USA and South Africa, black people were labeled inferior and ignorant and subjected to segregation; North American Indians in the US and in Canada and native aboriginal peoples in Australia were separated, ostracized, and forced to live on pitiful reservations, their culture and many of their human rights denied; in the UK Eastern Europeans are often marginalized; Romany people (often referred to by the term 'gypsies', a term many of them object to) continue to be discriminated against across Europe; Asians were expelled from Uganda because their industry and acumen had set them apart from the majority; and minority Chinese Malaysians were so blatantly discriminated against that many felt compelled to leave their own country. The list goes on and on.

LGBTIQ people, likewise, have been blamed for all manner of things, from pedophilia (despite evidence that proves the majority of pedophiles are heterosexual men), to being immoral and reckless disseminators of disease (though HIV-AIDS is universally more common and widely distributed amongst heterosexuals than amongst gay people — male or female. In fact, HIV-AIDS is quite rare in lesbians).

Amongst the negative consequences of such institutional homophobia are limitations on job opportunities, parenting rights, and relationship recognition for LGBTIQ people.

In using minorities in this way, those in power — or seeking power — have sought to deflect attention from the real issues, failing to ensure the human rights of at least 10 percent of their people, while abnegating responsibility for failure and injustice and protecting their own privileged position.

The tremendous opposition of the US military to the open acceptance of gay people within its ranks is a classic example of institutional homophobia. The fact that polls showed 70 percent of the US population supported allowing gay people to serve in the military seemed to make no difference. Neither did the abundance of solid research conducted in those countries that had accepted gay people in the armed forces, which clearly showed this in no way affected morale or efficiency and had not negatively impacted the armed forces of those countries. The move to allow openly gay people into the US military met with all manner of resistance, almost all of which was based not on any logic, but on simple prejudice.

Only with the election of President Barack Obama, and his courageous determination to end such discrimination and blatant prejudice, was the 'Don't ask, don't tell' rule done away with; and in 2010 gay people were at last openly accepted into the US military. We had always been there, of course, but only covertly and so forced to live in fear of discovery and the possibility of dishonorable discharge. The lifting of the ban changed all that.

> *"We need somebody who's got the heart, the empathy, to recognize what it's like to be a young teenage mom, the empathy to understand what it's like to be poor or African-American or gay or disabled or old - and that's the criterion by which I'll be selecting my judges."*
>
> ~ **Barack Obama**

In the UK, gay men and women have been officially allowed to serve in the armed forces since 2000. Today, gay people are accepted into the military in more than forty different countries worldwide.

Far from strengthening institutions and organizations, institutional homophobia weakens them, causing friction and discontent between individuals and groups, and preventing the smooth functioning of the organization as a whole. It is something that causes a great deal of unhappiness.

Interpersonal Homophobia

Moving progressively from the more general to the more specific, we come to the category of homophobia called *interpersonal*. As the name suggests, this kind of homophobia signifies the dislike, hatred, or fear of LGBTIQ people that can exist on the interpersonal level. It may be expressed in several different ways, including through verbal or physical abuse or harassment or through discriminatory behavior and an attitude of blatant or subtle disdain and condemnation.

Interpersonal homophobia may find expression in avoiding interaction with, or shunning, gay people, causing them to feel or become ostracized or excluded. Often this kind of homophobia is observed in those whose attitude is: "What's this got to do with me?" It can also take the form of name-calling, and result in various types of assault — verbal or physical, and sometimes both.

Derogatory remarks, telling 'jokes,' whispering, and negative body language can all be employed as interpersonal tactics designed to discriminate against and intimidate gay people. This kind of homophobia can also take the form of physical violence. Sadly, this is something that many LGBTIQ people are forced to contend with. Research in the UK, the US, and numerous other countries has clearly shown that verbal abuse and physical harassment are almost universal experiences for LGBTIQ people — and all for no other reason than the assailant's own homophobia.

> *"All parents should be aware that when they mock or curse gay people, they may be mocking or cursing their own child."*
> **~ Anna Quindlen**

If you are gay, lesbian, bisexual, or transgender, and you experience homophobia in any form, always keep this in mind:

This is not your problem — it's theirs.

The question that really needs to be asked about interpersonal homophobia is why those who are confident in their own sexuality, happy in their own skin, and content with their own life should have any reason to dislike or hate LGBTIQ people.

As our discussion of homophobia has already shown, people who are uncomfortable with their own sexuality or feel threatened by the sexuality of others are much more inclined to be rigid regarding what is sexually 'correct' or 'acceptable' and may attempt to punish others — either in order to distance themselves from them, in their own or in others' eyes, or to force their beliefs upon them.

Research has also shown that people who report having little or no social contact with gay people tend to be much more homophobic than those who do. When heterosexual people have had the chance to talk with and get to know a gay person better, then a greater degree of empathy generally ensues. When people are able to respond to people as people, and not as stereotypes or hostile outsiders, they are generally more accepting of difference.

> *"Homosexuals are not interested in making other people homosexuals. Homophobes are interested in making other people homophobic."*
>
> **~ Stephen Fry**

In my work focusing on homophobia in schools, I regularly met young people who told me in confidence that they did not particularly like to play a homophobic role, but that they felt it was expected of them, either by their peers or by their families, and that failure to tow this line might well result in being targeted themselves. It looks as if homophobia really does have a lot to do with fear, after all.

Interpersonal homophobia has one thing in common with all forms of homophobia: it attempts to restrict and to separate gay people from their nature. It distances them from their birthright — the ability to be gay *and* happy.

Yet the one form of homophobia fed by all the others, that which has perhaps the greatest capacity to cause harm, increase suffering, and separate gay people from our natural ability to feel happy, is the destructive kind known as *personal homophobia.*

It is this that we must turn to next.

Personal or Internalized Homophobia

Personal homophobia is based on the learned belief that being gay is wrong. It perpetuates the myth that gay people are immoral, sinful, sick, and inferior. We have already looked at some of the reasons for this, the origin of such beliefs, and we have seen that they spring from a variety of sources. With these beliefs come feelings of disgust and contempt, fear and hatred. But perhaps the most pernicious thing is that absolutely anyone — straight, gay, lesbian, bi, trans, or intersex — can buy into these beliefs, and so experience some form of homophobia.

When gay people do this it is called *internalized homophobia,* and it works from the inside, from deep within the person, poisoning and damaging as it goes. With internalized homophobia, the worm, truly, is in the heart.

Gay people, like any other, grow up learning heterosexual — and all too often heterosexist — values. Just like so many straight people, we have been taught that being gay is abnormal, unnatural, and that it is a sin. But more than this, we may well have been taught from the very earliest age that being gay is inferior, and so if we are gay then that means that we, too, must in some important way be inferior. And one thing is certain: people who feel inferior have a very difficult time feeling happy.

The feelings of shame that accompany internalized homophobia cause people to hide or devalue their sexuality, lower their expectations of life, dismiss their own abilities and capacity for growth, and even engage in harmful behavior.

The problem is that, living in a society that is in so many ways heterosexist and homophobic, it is easy to internalize these values and to feel that there is something wrong with us for being gay. In my practice as a psychotherapist, I regularly see people who are struggling because of internalized homophobia. Some recognize this but don't know how to remedy it, while others are still in the denial stage, struggling to come to terms with their sexuality and hoping that something will come along to change things and save them from themselves.

Gay people do not always come to me seeking therapy directly because of their sexual orientation, of course; more often they come because of the psychological and emotional problems that homophobia has brought into their lives. Internalized homophobia — like all forms of homophobia — can have some quite dire consequences.

The psychological distress that internalized homophobia can cause may manifest itself in various forms. It can present as depression, anxiety, panic attacks, sexual dysfunction, insomnia, obsessive disorders, low self-esteem, and feelings of self-loathing. Any of these things can lead to behaviors designed originally to distract from or cope with the awful feelings that homophobia has generated: alcoholism, substance abuse, overeating, risky sexual behaviors, and self-harming.

> *"Understand that sexuality is as wide as the sea. Understand that your morality is not law. Understand that we are you."*
> **~ Derek Jarman**

A review of research studies confirms my own clinical experience. A meta-analysis is a systematic method of evaluating statistical data from several different studies that focus on the same subject or problem. Just such a meta-analysis of twenty-five different studies conducted between 1997 and 2004 in Europe, North America, and Australasia show that gay people are at significantly higher risk of mental disorder, substance abuse, depression, and suicide ideation (wanting to commit suicide or thinking about it, without actually making plans to do it).

When we are coerced into rejecting ourselves, we may attempt various strategies in order to deal with this. We might try to conceal our identity — from ourselves as well as from other people; we might try to change our sexual orientation; we might consider or practice self-harming; or we might even attempt or complete suicide. All these responses are displays of self-loathing and its natural outcome, self-disrespect.

Yet no one is born hating and disrespecting gay people or hating and disrespecting themselves for being gay. *Homophobia is not a natural state — it is something that is learned.* Those heterosexist values are not ours; they are *introjected values.* (As previously mentioned, the term 'introject' means to incorporate the attitudes, beliefs, or ideas of others.) It is when our introjected values clash with our own nature and our own innate values that real conflict arises.

> *"Lots of people hate gay people. You can tell who they are because they start sentences with, "It's not like I hate gay people ..."*
>
> **~ Ali Liebegott**

Having internalized those heterosexist values unnatural to us, we can become so confused about ourselves that it is difficult to see where the myth ends and where we begin. Feelings of loathing and inadequacy may permeate our daily lives, acting as a filter for all we see and experience, affecting the way we function and relate to the world — and of course the way we relate to and treat ourselves.

In this state we easily collude with the idea and incubate the belief that there is something desperately wrong with us: that we are bad, sinful, or inferior, and we can suffer because of it. We do not always see that the feelings that this belief causes are the result of myth, of distortion, and of oppression. Because of this, genuine self-acceptance may become difficult — but it is essential. As we move through this book, we will continue to see how the ability to be gay and happy depends very much on a person's ability to accept him or herself.

It is important to remember that researchers and psychotherapists focus on the problems that people experience and on those who are experiencing them. Though the increased risk of anxiety, depression, and other mental and emotional difficulties are certainly there, and though therapists such as myself see a good number of LGBTIQ clients, this does not mean that most LGBTIQ people are desperately unhappy or that they necessarily experience other profound psychological difficulties.

As a psychotherapist, I see a wide spectrum of the human race, gay, straight, trans, and intersex. Despite the various forms of homophobia, internalized and otherwise, the great majority of gay people, like the great majority of straight people, live their lives without developing any kind of psychological disorder. Because someone is gay, and has grown up in a heterosexual world, does not automatically mean that they will develop psychological problems, become neurotic, or be in any way unbalanced, mentally or emotionally.

Each person responds to life and to the experiences they encounter in their own particular way. We know that two different people can pass through a very similar experience and respond in a very different manner. One person might be hurt and almost devastated by the experience, while the other just seems to pick themself up, brush themself off, and get on with things as if nothing in particular had happened. Gay people are human beings, and human beings are immensely resilient, robust, and capable of dealing with all manner of experiences.

Homosexuality harms no one. Homophobia harms many. When we are harmed it is because of ignorance and prejudice. We are also harmed when we buy into this same ignorance, this same prejudice. To such a large degree, we are all products of our environment and of the society in which we grow and live, and so we are all perhaps in some way homophobic. If we start from this basic assumption — that we ourselves are homophobic — then we can begin to accept responsibility for it and actually do something about it. Always remember that you are bigger than any box you have been placed in.

"The only queer people are those who don't love anybody."
~ Rita Mae Brown

We can exchange ignorance for awareness, myth for truth, and though it may take a while to dispel the myths and the ignorance of society, we can change ourselves a whole lot quicker. The surprising thing is that when we change, so does our world.

Homophobia Harms Heterosexuals Too

The sad truth is that there will always be prejudice and so there will always be prejudiced people; people who, for whatever reason, insist on disliking, hating, and persecuting difference — even though some may do it in the name of a compassionate and loving God.

The Oxford Dictionary defines prejudice as "preconceived opinion that is not based on reason" and as "dislike, hostility or unjust behavior deriving from unfounded opinions." And this is exactly what homophobia is. Like love, prejudice is blind, but unlike love, prejudice does not heal; it harms. What many people do not realize, however, is that homophobia does not only harm gay people; it also harms society and those who are not gay.

When men and women are forced into rigid portrayals of sex roles and behavior, it inevitably restricts their ability to fully enjoy emotional closeness. Attempting to fit into any stereotype, gay or straight, prevents people from being their true and spontaneous selves, and this can only place pressure on individuals and strain on relationships. The fear of being seen as gay automatically limits the natural development of intimacy between friends of the same sex. Such fear diminishes personal authenticity by creating barriers that reduce emotional flexibility. These things can seriously harm human relationships.

As we saw with Adam at the beginning of this chapter, homophobia can wreck families, tearing them apart. When a parent discovers that a child is gay, and that parent is homophobic, terrible emotional upheaval and rejection can occur. Surely a better, more loving way would be to support any member of the family who is gay, allowing him or her to be who he or she is, regardless of sexual preference. Perhaps one day those with true love in their hearts will come to see that though the human race may not be one big, happy family, we are at least all part of the family called "humanity," and we are all deserving of love.

Since homophobia causes suppression of the achievements of gay people, not only in history, but also in the present day, the whole of society receives a distorted view of gay people, one far removed from reality. In so many areas it is as if we just do not exist.

One of the areas where we can see this invisibility in action is in the high-profile world of professional sport, where the portrayal of a stereotypical masculinity, especially, is extremely rigid.

American football, in particular, suffers from this negative stereotyping. There are signs, however, that this is changing. After Michael Sam came out as gay, he became the first openly gay player drafted by the NFL, courageously going against a long tradition of denial and deceit. (And though he was never officially signed by an NFL team, Sam was later drafted by the Montreal Alouettes, becoming the first openly gay player in the Canadian Football League, as well.) Recently (2015), the New York Giants became the first NFL team to publicly endorse an anti-homophobia campaign.

In the UK, Welsh rugby football star, Gareth Thomas, had the full support of his teammates and the great majority of rugby fans when he came out as gay; his courage off the field matching his courage on.

The invisibility of gay sportsmen is also evident in the most popular sport in the world — soccer.

For so many sportsmen, the fear of coming out seems too great, so they hide their sexual orientation, shying away from the negative stereotyping of coaches, teammates, and fans — further distorting reality and reinforcing the false belief that 'real men' could never be gay.

The reality is that gay people have contributed and continue to contribute enormously to all aspects, and at all levels, of our pluralistic society — including sports. We always have and we always will.

Perhaps one of the most harmful aspects of homophobia is its effect on basic human rights. From simple dislike to vehement hatred, homophobia runs the gamut of prejudiced emotion. Unchecked, it leads to discrimination, exclusion, oppression, and to an inevitable denial of human rights.

> *"The rights of every man are diminished when the rights of one man are threatened."*
> **~ John F. Kennedy**

History has clearly demonstrated that the denial of rights to some inevitably leads to the denial of rights to others. Governments and dictatorships that have encouraged the oppression of gay people have also oppressed other groups because of ethnicity, race, and religion. The sobering truth is that if we collude in the oppression of one part of society, we will eventually find ourselves colluding in our own oppression.

Nowhere is this better expressed than in the words of the Christian pastor Martin Niemöller, imprisoned in Dachau concentration camp for his opposition to the Nazis:

First they came for the socialists, and I didn't speak out
because I wasn't a socialist.

Then they came for the trade unionists, and I didn't speak out
because I wasn't a trade unionist.

Then they came for the Jews, and I didn't speak out
because I wasn't a Jew.

Then they came for me, and there was no one left to speak for me.

Dealing with Homophobia

The way we approach homophobia depends very much on the way we approach ourselves. When our confidence is high and our self-esteem robust, we are in a much better position to deal with whatever life brings our way — including prejudice. We will be looking at self-acceptance and self-esteem later in this book, as well as how to live more positively and assertively. But for now — and in fact, forever — the one critical thing to remember whenever you encounter homophobia is:

You're not the problem — their views are.

It is *never* acceptable for people to make homophobic comments, overt threats, or repeat false information regarding gay people and homosexuality. To call someone "a fucking queer" or "a filthy dyke" or some such derogatory name is as unacceptable as making racist remarks or hurling racist abuse. Both are hate incidents and neither have any place in a civilized society.

Winston is a young black man who is also gay. "I grew up black," he told me. "Everyone could see what I was. I learned how to handle racism from an early age. I had the support of my family and my community, and most people agreed that racism is wrong, so I had most of society on my side." Things were very different when it came to his sexual orientation, however. "The support just wasn't there," he said. "If somebody called me a 'nigger,' I'd know exactly how to respond, but if someone called me a 'fucking queer' then I'd just turn to jelly and collapse. Not only that, but it was blacks as well as whites who were doing it." Only when Winston could see the similarities between racism and homophobia could he really begin to handle homophobia.

If you are gay and not deeply closeted, then there may well come a time when you are confronted by bigotry and prejudice because of your sexual orientation. There are times when you are going to have to stick up for yourself and who you are. Knowing how to respond to homophobia when you encounter it can mean the difference between walking away with your dignity and self-esteem intact or becoming the victim of prejudice and ignorance. The right response can even cause a homophobic person to question his or her learned beliefs and prejudices and begin the process of re-education that can lead to taking a more human and humane position toward sexuality.

The nature of homophobia is judgmental. It exists in order to condemn, and this condemnation can sometimes take the form of bullying. Like all forms of bullying, its power lies in its ability to intimidate and upset. Nothing is more disarming to a homophobic person than when his or her criticism just seems to bounce off the person at whom it's directed. Bullying is all about identifying weakness and vulnerability in others and then accentuating it. But bullying needs a victim in order to be successful, and when the target refuses to play that role, the bully can soon lose interest and look elsewhere, or even question his or her behavior.

Homophobic remarks and insults are meant to ruffle and are expected to hurt. When they obviously do neither, then it's as if the homophobic person has his or her powder dampened. The fuse thus fails to ignite and so the damaging explosion is rarely forthcoming. A knowing smile and a quick "Yes, but it's completely okay; my mother knows," or "So what else is new" or a yawned "And your point is...?" when spoken calmly and with confidence can steal the thunder from any homophobic bully hurling the "You're gay!" or "You're queer!" kind of remark.

> *"If gay and lesbian people are given civil rights, soon everyone will want them."*
>
> **~ James Howe**

When the target of homophobia lacks any sense of self-condemnation and refuses to roll over and play dead, then it is he or she, and not the homophobe, who generally ends up controlling the situation. This does not mean that the gay person need scream about his or her sexuality (of course, neither is it necessary to hide it). It simply means that when a gay person is confident in his or her sexuality, this greatly increases the chance of deflecting insults or criticism and controlling the situation.

For a gay person to arrive at this level of self-acceptance and social skill usually requires a fair amount of life experience and a good deal of practice. It is often not something that young people, or those who have struggled with their sexuality for a long time, may readily possess. The good news is that, like any skill, it is something that can be acquired — and surprisingly quickly.

In just a little while, I'll list a few quick responses that you can employ when faced with homophobic remarks. Later in this book we'll be looking at a set of assertiveness techniques and strategies that you can learn to use in order to more skillfully negotiate difficult situations.

Handy Retorts to Homophobia

When you stop and think about it, there are a limited number of remarks that a homophobic person can make. Having a swift come back really can diffuse a difficult situation or simply turn ignorance on its head. More than this, it can allow you to take control of the situation, maintain your dignity, and walk away with your head held high.

Sometimes, people who use homophobic language just aren't aware that they are doing so. Quite recently the word *gay* has become something of a vogue word, meaning 'lame' or 'rubbish,' among many young people.

The first recorded use of the word in this way was at the end of the 1970s, and took place among high school students in the US. The same thing has now happened in the UK, and in Germany, where the word for gay (*schwu)* has also become a popular pejorative term among young people.

Today, *gay* is the most popular term of abuse used by children. In one survey of British teachers, 83 percent said that they heard it used on a regular basis, compared to 53 percent for the second most frequently heard term, 'bitch.'

'Gay' has taken on a life of its own, far removed from its meaning of being attracted to the same sex, or from its original sense of joy and happiness.

The strange thing is that the great majority of young people using the word *gay* as an insult do not recognize it as being homophobic. Most often it is used as a kind of throwaway remark that has nothing at all to do with sexual orientation. According to Tony Thorne, compiler of the *Dictionary of Contemporary Slang,* "It is nearly always used in contexts where sexual orientation and sexuality are completely irrelevant." Though this is undoubtedly true, and *gay* is most often used without any kind of malice, the word is also used to bully anyone not conforming or fitting neatly in with the group mentality. A person does not need to like the same sex in order to be labeled gay, as many heterosexual boys and girls have already learned from experience.

The negative effect that this can have on young gay people can be considerable. Growing up in an essentially heterosexist society, *gay* was a word used to signify pride and acceptance of sexual orientation: a word used to encompass not only what people do in bed, but also to describe a more complete sensibility and identity. It is the one word rescued from the language that homosexual people have felt easy in identifying with and using in regards to themselves: a morally neutral, positive word denoting a certain sense of rightness and self-acceptance. To have it used in a negative, pejorative manner easily undermines this. Imagine the uproar that the word black or Asian would produce were it to be used in this way. "That's so black!" or "You're so Asian!" might not meet with quite the same degree of tolerance in most schools or classrooms.

While it is not possible, or even advisable, for teachers and adults to correct every single young person who uses the word *gay* in this manner, the wise thing would be to educate the entire school about the effects that the inappropriate use of the word can have. Many young people today are far more concerned about discriminating against LGBTIQ people, and if they realized the implications of their terminology, they might very well think twice about using the word *gay* in this way.

"Courage lies in being bold."
~ Robert Frost

A good response to hearing the word *gay* used in this negative sense might be:

"You seem like a pretty decent person to me, someone who wouldn't go along with lowdown prejudice and bigotry. But when you use the word *gay* like that, it makes you look like a real homophobic bigot. Are you happy to be seen that way?"

Or you might say something like:

"If you really don't mean it that way, then maybe a different word might be better. Come on, let's get creative here!"

People generally tell homophobic jokes only when they assume that those listening are not gay or will not object. Here is a handy rule of thumb that you can use whenever someone begins to tell a homophobic joke: Whether or not you are gay, ALWAYS object.

"If you are neutral in situations of injustice, you have chosen the side of the oppressor," said Archbishop Desmond Tutu, once more speaking out for sanity and simple human decency.

If it is not right and just to tell jokes about black or Asian people, then it is equally as unjust and wrong to tell jokes about gay people. A simple response might be:

"That kind of joke isn't really funny, is it? When you say things like that, you're saying that you condone prejudice. That isn't really what you believe, is it?"

A good response to the "You just haven't met the right guy/girl yet" type of remark might be:

"And maybe you haven't met the right guy/girl either."

That old chestnut "Why do gay people have to flaunt it?" can be met with a simple:

"If you think that not hiding away is the same as flaunting it, then look around you. You'll see straight people flaunting it just about everywhere."

You can respond to the "It's probably just a phase you're going through" with a quick:

"And maybe being straight is just a phase you're going through," or "The way you know you're straight isn't a phase, is the same way that I know I'm gay isn't a phase."

The "Gay people spread diseases like AIDS" kind of comment may be dealt with by giving a healthy dose of truth, as in "Fact is that HIV-AIDS is primarily a straight disease. But what's with the prejudice? HIV is a virus, not a sin."

Appraise the Situation and Respond Accordingly

Of course, the way we respond to homophobia can vary according to where it's coming from. Each experience is unique and requires sound judgment, instinct, and the ability to assert ourselves. In my work with gay people, many have been surprised to learn how easily these qualities can be developed and honed.

Perhaps the first and most basic thing to do when encountering homophobia is to assess whether the possibility for physical violence exists. If the homophobia is coming from a crowd of drunken thugs who are hurling abuse, then of course the best course of action is to remove yourself from danger. This is not being a coward — it is being sensible.

Straight people who see such incidents taking place need to stand by the person being abused. Remember Desmond Tutu's remark: "If you are neutral in situations of injustice, you have chosen the side of the oppressor."

When there is no real fear of physical violence, the very best thing to do is to respond in a calm but firm manner, one that clearly shows that you will not accept homophobic comments, attitudes, or behavior. Homophobic people depend on the complicity of others in order to succeed, and when they meet with sturdy opposition to their bigotry, they can very soon beat a hasty retreat.

Do your very best to stay cool and collected when challenging homophobia. Being in control of yourself and simply stating your position, without losing out to displays of anger, really can shake the homophobic person's confidence and weaken animosity. Staying more calm and remaining more logical can usually win the day.

Try to remember that they, too, are in their own way victims of a learned belief system that is in so many ways faulty. Your goal is more to educate than to punish — no matter how strongly you feel like hurting those who have hurt you. History has taught us that oppression is seldom ennobling, yet when the oppressed adopt the same tactics as the oppressors, then they become little better than them and things do not move forward.

Homophobia in the workplace is also completely unacceptable and in many places there are now laws strongly opposing it. No one has to suffer in silence when a co-worker, colleague, or boss is making homophobic remarks or picking on someone because of his or her sexual orientation. Should you experience such behavior, it is your duty to yourself and to those like you to do something about it.

> *"Being an American is about having the right to be who you are. Sometimes that doesn't happen."*
>
> **~ Herb Ritts**

This means that you need to be assertive and, as mentioned, we'll talk a bit more about assertiveness further on in this book. Today, many organizations and companies have a budget for staff and employee training and personal development, and regularly invest in diversity and equal opportunities training. Recognizing that a happy workforce is a productive workforce, organizations may also include training designed to increase their employees' ability to express and assert themselves in a positive, constructive way. Perhaps your organization could make specific LGBTIQ assertiveness training available to its employees. If no such training is scheduled, then it's certainly worthwhile suggesting it to the LGBTIQ network, human resources or other department responsible for diversity training and employee advancement.

If pointing out the complete unacceptability of homophobia doesn't bring the necessary change, it is incumbent upon you to talk to someone higher up, a manager or someone in authority. If it is this person who is the cause of the problem, then don't be afraid to seek help elsewhere. Call a gay helpline and ask for advice.

Remember that in many countries, including the UK, Canada, Australia, New Zealand, South Africa, and some parts of the US, it is against the law to discriminate on the grounds of sexual orientation, so you have the law on your side. You are protected in the public and the private sectors, in the workplace, in your job, and you cannot be discriminated against in housing, hotel accommodations, or restaurants because of your sexual orientation.

In the US, however, it really does depend on which state you are in.

At the time of writing (2015), in a majority of US states – 29, to be precise – it is perfectly legal to fire someone because he or she happens to be gay, bisexual, or transgender. It is even possible to fire someone because he or she *appears* to be gay. It seems incredible that in half the US states a person can legally be denied service in a restaurant or refused a lease on an apartment simply because he or she is gay. Just as there was a time when it was legal to refuse to serve a cup of coffee or a plate of food to people simply because of the color of their skin, so it is still legal to do the same because of a person's sexual orientation — or merely their *perceived* orientation.

> *"All men are created equal. No matter how hard they try, they can never erase those words. That is what America is about."*
>
> ~ **Harvey Milk**

It can come as quite a surprise for those living outside the US to learn that the country that believes itself to be the bastion of equality and justice has no federal law that specifically concerns itself with protecting people against discrimination because of their sexual orientation. Though others rightly enjoy the protection of the law, those who are gay so often do not. Not to put too fine a point on it, what this means is that in the eyes of the law, all US citizens are *not* equal.

On the positive side, nearly half of the fifty states *do* have laws that prohibit discrimination on the grounds of sexuality in both the public and the private sectors. (If you live in the US and would like to learn about the protection from sexual orientation discrimination that your city, county, or state affords or denies you, visit the *Lambda Legal Defense and Education* website www.lambdalegal.org)

Though it is an important element in the battle to end injustice, legislation alone is not enough to change people's deeply entrenched attitudes toward LGBTIQ people. In South Africa, where discrimination on the basis of sexual orientation is outlawed by the country's constitution and gay marriage has been legal since 2006, homophobia is rife, and there are, according to the U.N. Commissioner for Human Rights Navi Pillay, "some of the worst cases of homophobic violence," including a lesbian who was found dead after being sexually attacked with a toilet brush.

The first consideration for any LGBTIQ person must be safety. Once this is reasonably assured, perhaps the most important thing to understand is that there is almost always something that can be done to remedy a homophobic situation and to challenge discrimination.

> *"Our lives begin to end the day we become silent about things that matter."*
>
> **~ Martin Luther King Jr.**

This might mean refusing to roll over and play dead when someone attempts to intimidate or insult you or someone who is gay. It may mean speaking up when jokes or derogatory remarks are made about gay people. It could mean being armed with the facts that enable you to correct some of the many myths that abound about being gay.

Each time you do this you will be doing something really positive. You will be standing up not only for your own rights, but for the human rights of so many others.

Chapter Three

Myths About Being LGBTIQ

"In the absence of facts, myth rushes in..."
Stacy Schiff

There are so many myths regarding being gay. Sadly, gay people themselves believe some of these. After all, the great majority of us have never been educated in this area. We, like most other people, had to figure things out as we went along, and so we, too, may have bought into some of the distortions that abound about being gay.

Friends and acquaintances can make homophobic remarks or express anti-gay opinions. Such occasions are opportunities for you to challenge their prejudice and help them understand how hurtful they are being. Many people don't realize where their opinions are coming from and how damaging they are for LGBTIQ people. When they (and we) are forced to reconsider, it becomes an opportunity to change thinking and behavior.

Until our preconceived ideas are challenged and we are made aware that our assumptions are incorrect, we may too easily assume that being heterosexual is the only valid way to be, and that anything that deviates from this is wrong, abnormal, or unnatural.

If we are knowledgeable about the many myths that are perpetrated regarding LGBTIQ people, then we will be in a much better position to challenge those false beliefs in a logical and confident way.

Challenging Myths and Faulty Beliefs

Let's take a quick look at the beliefs and at some of the faulty reasoning that fuels and maintains homophobia — and at the reality of same-sex orientation.

Being Gay Is a Choice You Make

This is perhaps the most common misbelief that people have about being gay. The evidence now points to the fact that LGBTIQ people have no real say in the matter. We do not choose to be gay any more than we can choose our skin color. Similarly, you cannot choose to be attracted to the opposite sex — you either are or you aren't.

"Gender preference does not define you. Your spirit defines you."
~ P.C. Cast

So many factors seem to contribute to our sexuality, and the probability is that no single explanation will answer the riddle of its origin.

Extensive research on identical twins has demonstrated that almost all share an identical sexual orientation — gay or straight — indicating that there is probably a genetic or biological element to a person's sexuality. (This is not to say, however, that gay parents automatically mean gay children.)

Sexual orientation and gender identity are complex subjects and there is no clear-cut answer to why some people are LGBTIQ and others aren't. But the more we understand about human sexuality, the clearer it becomes that something as basic as sexual orientation and gender identity is not a choice. It really does appear to be a combination of biology, genetics, and social influences that finds expression in sexual preference and gender identity.

It's Just a Phase You're Going Through

Being gay isn't something that is outgrown, and it's not a phase any more than heterosexuality is a phase.

This myth probably stems from a reality that crosses gender and sexual orientation lines. It's not uncommon for young people to experiment sexually or to feel great attachment to friends of the same gender. This is less about sexual orientation and more about curiosity. In our homophobic culture, it's easy for young people to confuse admiring physical attractiveness in someone of the same gender with homosexuality.

None of these behaviors is necessarily connected to homosexuality. It's not unusual to have different types and levels of attraction as we mature. With time, our sexual preferences become clearer and more distinct.

Over the years, therapists have tried to 'straighten' out gay people. Even when the 'patient' has fully wanted to change, no therapy has succeeded in doing any more than temporarily suppressing sexual feelings. (As we saw in chapter one, 'conversion' or 'reparative therapy' has been thoroughly disproven and condemned as useless and even harmful by *all* major psychological and psychi-atric associations.)

Homosexuality isn't a phase, and it's not something that will be outgrown any more than a person will outgrow the color of their eyes.

Gay Men Abuse Children

Another truly pernicious myth, based entirely on blind prejudice, is the misguided idea that gay men are attracted to children. Such a belief is in direct contradiction to the facts — not that the facts have ever really stood in the way of genuine prejudice.

Every respected mental health and medical organization, both in the UK and in the US, completely refutes the claim that there is a connection between being gay and sexually abusing children. Many studies have looked at pedophilia, and the evidence is conclusive: the vast majority of those who engage in pedophilic behavior are heterosexual men.

One such study conducted by the University of Colorado surveyed 269 cases in which children were sexually molested or abused by adults. Out of the entire 269 abusers, only two were gay; all the rest were straight.

Having conducted a comprehensive review of research on the subject, Dr. Gregory M. Herek, professor of psychology at the University of California at Davis, categorically states, "The empirical research does not show that gay or bisexual men are any more likely than heterosexual men to molest children."

Another myth bites the dust.

Gay People Make Bad Parents

This is another subject on which there is an abundance of research. And this research proves conclusively that children — both biological and adopted — raised by same-sex parents are as well-adjusted and as psychologically healthy as those from homes where both parents are heterosexual.

An extensive review of research on children raised by same-sex parents by sociologist Dr. Bridget Fitzgerald found that "the sexual orientation of parents is not an effective or important predictor of successful childhood development." Professor Judith Stacey of New York University confirms this finding, adding, "Rarely is there as much consensus in any area of social science as in the case of gay parenting ..."

In fact, one 2010 longitudinal study found that children of lesbian mothers did better than children of non-lesbian parents. In the same year, the first large-scale study based on US national data found that "children raised by same-sex couples have no fundamental deficits in making normal progress through school."

Despite myths to the contrary, science clearly demonstrates that children raised by gay parents do at least as well as children raised by heterosexual parents.

The truth is that good parents are good parents — regardless of sexual orientation.

Being Gay Is Just about Sex

Like other humans, most gay people are looking for relationships that are more than one-night stands. Of course there are LGBTIQ people who are more sexually active than others or who prefer the single life, and this is equally true for heterosexuals. But for most, being gay is about having a full and complete relationship with a partner with whom we are happy and compatible.

The idea that all gay men are sex-crazed satyrs has led to the myth that HIV-AIDS is a gay disease, caused and perpetuated by the gay community. While having multiple sexual partners and unprotected sex certainly increases the potential spread of HIV-AIDS, this is true for the heterosexual community as well. HIV-AIDS is a global health issue, not a gay disease.

Being gay is not simply about having sex. Many gay people do not, in fact, have sex. They may be between partners, or are uninterested in sex for some reason, or have made a conscious decision to be celibate. Some couples might no longer be sexually active, but are still deeply in love and very much gay.

The fact is that we may have sex only a few hours a week – if that – but we are gay 24 hours of every day.

Gay Relationships Never Last

Another popular myth is that gay relationships just cannot last, or are not as long-lasting as heterosexual ones.

In today's world, with its fast-paced lifestyles and rapidly changing social values, relationships of all kinds are in the process of transformation. In the USA, around half of all marriages end in divorce, while the UK now has the highest divorce rate in the European Union. And this in spite of the fact that society at large actively supports marriage and the heterosexual lifestyle.

Gay relationships, however, have had no such structural support, and only relatively recently have civil partnerships and same-sex marriage been available in a very few countries.

Denmark was the first country to allow gay people the right to registered partnership in 1989, with the Netherlands sanctioning gay marriage in 2000. Gay marriage is now legal in twenty-one countries, including the UK, Ireland, and all of North America. Civil partnership, which affords many of the same rights as marriage, is now recognized in several other countries.

> *"Gay marriage won't be more of an issue twenty-five years from now than interracial marriage is today."*
>
> **~ Jared Polis**

In direct contradiction to the myth that says that gay relationships don't last, there are long-term research studies indicating that gay relationships are as stable as straight ones.

Professor John Gottman, emeritus professor of psychology at the University of Washington, conducted one such research project. Collecting data from gay couples over a period of twelve years, Gottman and his team found that eighty percent remained in the relationship, with only twenty percent ending their relationship over this time. This rate, when projected over a lengthy forty-year period of time, is lower than the divorce rate for heterosexual first marriages over the same time span.

Commenting on the research, Professor Gottman said, "The overall implication of this research is that we have to shake off all of the stereotypes of homosexual relationships and have more respect for them as committed relationships."

The report cited one interesting reason for the enduring quality of gay relationships: the gay couples' ability to resolve conflict and encourage positive emotions.

LGB People Are That Way because of Abuse

This is as silly as saying that a left-handed person is that way because of abuse, or that people who prefer coffee to tea do so because of past trauma. The fact is that there is no direct correlation between sexual abuse and sexual orientation, and there is absolutely no evidence to suggest that past abuse is associated with being gay.

There are straight people who have had abusive childhoods and there are gay people who have had wonderful childhoods. The reverse is also true. Abuse is clearly not the origin of sexual orientation or gender identity.

Heterosexuals Live Longer Than Gay People

This is yet another piece of nonsense. Gay life expectancy is similar to straight life expectancy. Both depend on living healthy and happy lives. Unsafe sex practices are as dangerous for straight as they are for gay people. There is no correlation between being gay and a decreased life span.

Gay People Try to Recruit

Just as it is not possible to turn a gay person straight — despite the ridiculous claims to the contrary — so it is not possible to turn a straight person gay. The fact is that most gay people, like most straight people, are far more interested in living their own lives and developing their own strategies for happiness than in recruiting others or attempting to turn anyone gay.

In research conducted by one major online dating website, it was found that a minuscule 0.06 percent of the service's gay male subscribers had ever searched for straight male matches, and a mere 0.1 percent of lesbian members had done the same. The idea that there is some 'agenda' to recruit non-gay people into becoming gay is simply another myth.

Gay people cannot procreate, so gay sex is wrong because it is unproductive. As a society, we long ago learned that sex is about far more than procreation. Sex is not only pleasurable, but it is also a means of forging deeper, more intimate relationships. Infertile couples, older couples, and those who are delaying procreation through the use of birth control are not considered to be wrong or bad — we have no problem with their continued sexual activity. Furthermore, many animal species are known to engage in mating behavior with the sole intention of pleasure, not procreation.

The misguided notion that sex is solely for procreation and not for pleasure has been responsible for the horrific practice of female genital mutilation, still practiced in certain cultures.

Sex really isn't only about producing offspring, and there's no reason to hold LGBTIQ sex to a different standard than heterosexual sex.

Myths about Gay People within the Gay Community

Human beings are social animals. We have a need to belong, to fit in, and to be accepted by others, especially those with whom we have a common interest. It's in our nature to form groups, tribes, and communities where we feel safe and comfortable.

As with any community — gay, straight, bisexual, construction workers, or doctors — we tend to profile people for ease of identification. If we belong to a particular community, we can find ourselves perpetrating traits that are commonly associated with that community. We may model our behavior, our attitude, and even our look on what we believe to be the community's identifying aspects.

Of course, not all members of a group or community act a certain way, dress a certain way, or think a certain way. Not all construction workers have a tool belt hanging below a potbelly, and doctors don't always walk around in white coats with stethoscopes dangling from their necks. People are people, and there's a wide range of traits and styles to be seen among all communities within the human family. The LGBTIQ community is diverse.

But if we are unsure of ourselves, and of our place in the scheme of things, then it's quite easy to believe that we need to conform to a certain image, life-style, and behavioral pattern. Young people, especially, can find themselves adopting some stereotypical traits and behaviors as a way of becoming part of the community.

The problem here is that in doing so, they risk becoming a parody of a gay person, a non-authentic version of what they think they ought to be because they are 'gay.'

Because of this, it is important to remember that some LGBTIQ people exhibit these traits, and that others do not. If this is how you feel most comfortable, that's fine, but simply because others act in or look a certain way does not necessarily mean that you are compelled to do so.

> *"The first gay person I ever met was surely not the first gay person I ever met."*
>
> **~ Mary Schmich**

Not all gay men like showtunes, wear make-up, or sport moustaches; not all lesbians wear Birkenstocks, have bulging biceps, or have close-cropped hair. A stereotype is simply a stereotype. Again, only a person can really be a person.

Myths will always abound, and education, science, and common sense will continue to debunk those myths that hold no truth. But even though we will need to continue our effort to counter the harmful myths, the important thing to realize and remember is that being gay can actually be fun.

Despite all of the myths, LGBTIQ people will continue to be LGBTIQ people. The great majority, like the great majority of straight people, will do no harm to others. We want what we are entitled to — to live our lives unharmed by ignorance and prejudice. Just like everyone else, we have the right to be happy.

Chapter Four

The Powerful Voice of Religion

"All religions have something to say about sex, and it rarely coincides with scientific knowledge of sex and sexuality."
~ Dr. Darrel Ray

There is no doubt that our ability to be gay and happy is influenced by society's religious attitudes. Religion has a powerful impact on culture, and vice versa. Because of this, it can be helpful to understand what religions have to say on the matter of same-sex relations.

In virtually every argument, religion can and does offer an opinion on what is morally or ethically right or wrong. It's also possible for people of the same religious persuasion to have drastically different interpretations of scripture.

Despite the claims made by many that all religions condemn homosexuality, this is not entirely true. Not all religions condemn homosexuality — though many religions appear to do so. Like many other religious and moral rules, texts on homosexuality are a product of the culture and the times in which they were written. Respected religious scholars and laypeople alike have differing interpretations on what those texts say to the people of this century.

There are mainstream Christian denominations that appear to have no problem with homosexuality, just as there are Jewish, Buddhist, Hindu, and other believers who affirm that being gay is not a sin, but rather a different way of having been created. Even within given denominations, there are congregations that are open to, even geared toward, LGB believers.

The thing to remember is that religions are not monolithic; they are most often a collection of denominations, beliefs, and perspectives. Christianity, Judaism, Islam, and Buddhism all have their different divisions and versions. Dogma and a literal reading of ancient written texts bind some almost entirely, while others follow a less rigid, and often more compassionate, path.

> *"All religions are true, but none are literal."*
> **~ Joseph Campbell**

It's easy to forget that because something is written, it means only that it is written. The *meaning* we give to what is written is what really matters. And it is the *interpretation* of what is written that produces its meaning.

The Christian Church

In the dark days when human beings could be openly bought and sold as chattel, Christian ministers regularly defended the practice of slavery by quoting scripture and claiming that because 'it is written' in the Bible, then it was approved by God; there could be no dispute and that was the end of the matter. Typical of this approach were dogmatic conservatives such as Richard Furman, a prominent Baptist minister at the time, who claimed that: "The right to hold slaves is clearly established in the Holy Scriptures, both by precept and example." And he had no difficulty in showing where those examples were written in both Christian and Jewish scripture.

Fortunately, times have moved on, and most people no longer attempt to justify the unjustifiable idea of slavery simply because it is referenced in an ancient text — no matter how sacred they hold that text to be. Sadly, the same cannot be said for the unjust treatment meted out by many religious people to those who are gay. And these zealously anti-gay individuals and institutions get most of the attention in the press, leaving some who are gay to believe that there is no room for them in the faith community, and that all people of faith condemn homosexuality.

In truth, Christian scripture is less clear on the matter than some would believe. It is also true that scholars continue to study and to interpret the sacred texts even today. For these scholars, God is still speaking; and they are trying earnestly to listen to what God is saying, and not rely solely on the church's past interpretation.

The actual meaning that any religion has in people's lives is not static, of course, but something that can and does change according to geography, history, and the impact of social struggles, movements, and attitudes.

> *"If someone is gay and seeks the Lord with good will, who am I to judge?"*
> **~ Pope Francis**

In the Christian Bible, homosexuality is mentioned twice in the book of Leviticus (Chapters 18 and 20), which cites it as an "abomination" (in some translations) for a man to lie "as with a woman." Leviticus also includes prohibitions against eating shellfish and wearing garments of two different fibers, amongst many other things, rules that have long ago been relaxed for even the most literal Christians, although they are still upheld in many orthodox Jewish communities.

Also, in the Bible it is written that if a man discovers on his wedding night that his bride is not a virgin, he must stone her to death on her father's doorstep (Deuteronomy 22:13-21). Fortunately, this is yet another biblical injunction that is no longer observed. Once more, because something is 'written' in scripture, this does not mean that it has to be followed verbatim, or that it is literally true.

Gay Christians and their supporters also point out that the gospels, the four accounts of the life and teachings of Jesus, have nothing to say about homosexuality. The New Testament letters of Paul, specifically Romans and Corinthians, do seem to speak to homosexual acts, but interpretations and translations vary from scholar to scholar. Some contend that Paul's writings speak not against gay sex, but rather against sex without commitment, which is a generally accepted Christian view of sex: a gift from God within marriage, and sinful outside of marriage. (The Bible also calls for the stoning of those caught in adultery, another biblical injunction no longer practiced by Christians.)

> *"I would not worship a God who is homophobic and that is how deeply I feel about this. I would refuse to go to a homophobic heaven. No, I would say sorry, I mean I would much rather go to the other place."*
>
> **~ Archbishop Desmond Tutu**

Others in the Christian faith use these passages to make a distinction between being gay, which they accept as inborn, and acting upon gay impulses. They see gay sex as a perversion of the gift of sex, akin to violations like rape and pedophilia. If you're gay and a Christian, they contend, celibacy is your only option. "Be a eunuch for Christ," they urge. Others chastise the gay community for 'endorsing' a promiscuous lifestyle, which is outside of Christian teachings.

Under the best conditions, what each biblical author intended can be difficult to determine, given that texts are written in ancient languages, in and about a culture far removed from today, by human beings with biases. Homosexuality, like the rights of women, slavery, and dozens of issues before this, is currently at the forefront of issues in the church and culture, and a matter of much (often heated) conversation and debate.

In *Bible, Gender, Sexuality: Reframing the Church's Debate on Same-Sex Relationships,* theologian James Brownson contends that Christians should reconsider biblical strictures against same-sex relationships. Says Brownson:

"Issues of sexuality in Scripture are complicated — not only issues related to homosexuality and gay unions, but a wide range of issues on the meaning of marriage and celibacy, the significance of procreation, the acceptable place of divorce in the church, the roles of men and women, and so on. In the face of such complexity, the temptation is either to revert to simple answers from the past or to avoid the particularity of the biblical texts and simply focus on broad principles such as justice and love. Neither approach will help us move beyond the current impasse in the church."

Although the few biblical passages against homosexuality seem clear-cut to some, Brownson analyzes each of them in light of ancient beliefs and contemporary understandings, and presents a compelling argument for committed same-sex relationships.

> *"Men never do evil so completely and cheerfully as when they do it from religious conviction."*
> **~ Blaise Pascal**

Evangelical Christianity, in particular versions imported from the US, profoundly influences the current attitudes toward gay people in much of Africa. Most African countries have laws that attempt to accomplish the impossible, to stop gay people from being gay — a remnant of their Colonial past that they seem unable or unwilling to shake off. In a recent 'Commonwealth Games' international sporting event held in the UK, forty-two of the fifty-three participating commonwealth countries had laws that criminalize homosexuality.

In Russia, a country ruled by the iron hand of ex-KGB operatives, the government embraces the anti-gay attitude and homophobia of the Russian Orthodox Church in an attempt to win favor and shore up its shaky popularity.

History teaches that despots fall and tyranny eventually ends, and so we can expect that one day the change that is long overdue in human rights in these countries will become a reality.

Judaism

Within Judaism, the oldest of the Abrahamic religions, change is also coming. While traditionally Judaism has forbidden homosexuality, again citing the texts from Leviticus, less conservative branches of Judaism have moved away from this position. Even among Orthodox Jews, change is taking place. In 2010, after months of discussion and input, a group of Orthodox rabbis issued a joint statement that affirmed the worth of LGB persons in the Jewish community and called for compassion and acceptance, stating, in part:

"Jews with homosexual orientations or same sex-attractions should be welcomed as full members of the synagogue and school community. As appropriate with regard to gender and lineage, they should participate and count ritually, be eligible for ritual synagogue honors, and generally be treated in the same fashion … as any other member of the synagogue they join. Conversely, they must accept and fulfill all the responsibilities of such membership, including those generated by communal norms or broad Jewish principles."

"We do not here address what synagogues should do about accepting members who are openly practicing homosexuals and/or living with a same-sex partner. Each synagogue together with its rabbi must establish its own standard with regard to membership. Those standards should be applied fairly and objectively."

There is growing openness to gay leadership in the Jewish community, as well as openness to same-sex marriage. Of course this openness doesn't apply to every Jewish community, but there is little doubt that greater acceptance is developing within Judaism and its leadership.

The World of Islam

Let's look now at Islam, the second largest religion in the world.

Islam is more than a system of beliefs. In some countries such as Iran, Iraq, Saudi Arabia, and Pakistan, it also functions as a strict legal system — called *Sharia* — creating an intertwining of the two. The majority of Muslim countries, though, adopt only a few aspects of Sharia law.

Orthodox Islam, like Orthodox Judaism and Orthodox Christianity, considers homosexuality to be a sin and so condemns it. The overwhelming opinion of Islamic clerics is that homosexual activity is a punishable offence, although no specific punishment is stated in the Muslim holy book, the Qur'an.

> *"Those who can make you believe absurdities, can make you commit atrocities."*
> **~ Voltaire**

The Qur'an contains seven references to "the people of Lot," the same people in the Bible's story of Sodom and Gomorrah. In both sacred texts, God appears to destroy the towns because of their sexual practices, which included homosexual rape. And the prophet Muhammad is purported to have stated, "If you find anyone doing as Lot's people did, kill the one who does it, and the one to whom it is done."

Such a reading is not completely without its dissenters, however. The gay South African imam (an imam is a religious leader, considered by the Shiite branch of Islam to be divinely appointed and an infallible successor of the Prophet Muhammad) Muhsin Hendricks believes that "the story was really about economic exploitation, inhospitality to guests, rape, molestation, and homosexual practices that were related to idolatry".

And another gay imam, Daayiee Abdullah, told the *Washington Post,* "If you have any same-sex marriages, I'm available."

Yet another Muslim scholar, S. Siraj al-Haqq Kugle, who teaches Islamic studies at Emory University in the US, blames Islamic hostility toward homosexuality on a misreading of sacred texts by ultra-conservative mullahs.

In *Reading the Qur'an,* a 2011 book by Muslim intellectual Ziauddin Sardar, it is argued that "there is absolutely no evidence that the Prophet punished anyone for homosexuality." According to Sardar, "the demonization of homosexuality in Muslim history is based largely on fabricated traditions and the un-reconstituted prejudice harbored by most Muslim societies."

Dissenting voices, however, are only a tiny minority. The great majority of mainstream Muslim scholars consider homosexuality to be a grave sin.

For some time now, various Islamic revivalist movements (especially within the branch of Islam called Sunni) have called for the death penalty to be carried out on those who engage in male homosexual acts, claiming this to be the authentic Islamic position. Currently, nine Islamic countries carry the death penalty for homosexual acts. In the Islamic country of Kuwait, homosexuality between females is legal but between males is illegal. Meanwhile Lebanon, a country with both Christian and Islamic influences, is discussing the possibility of legalizing gay marriage.

The way Muslims in the UK feel about homosexuality appears to be changing. In 2009, a Gallup survey of five hundred followers of Islam reported that all participants had zero tolerance for homosexuality. But two years later, a poll found that more than seventy-five percent of UK Muslims agreed with the statement: "I am proud of how Britain treats gay people." In the US, seventy-one percent of Muslims oppose gay marriage.

Ironically, Indonesia, the largest Muslim country in the world, on the whole exhibits a proactive acceptance of gay people, where there are even mosques for homosexuals.

It would be wrong to see Islam as a violent religion that spews hatred, despite the attempts by a minority of radicals to argue and act otherwise. It is a religion of great beauty and benevolence. In all but one of the one hundred and fourteen chapters in the Qur'an, Allah, the God of Islam, is referred to as a God of mercy and of compassion. And there are many who believe that if such a God exists, surely He would show His mercy to all people — gay and straight.

Looking East

While the Abrahamic religions — Judaism, Christianity and Islam — have influenced our culture, so often condemning homosexuality, other Eastern religions — Hinduism and Buddhism — have long histories of accepting same-sex love.

Hinduism is the third most popular religion in the world. Sexuality is rarely openly discussed in Hindu society, and homosexuality is a taboo topic, although this is a fairly recent cultural development. However, same-sex attachments and desire were known and tolerated in ancient and medieval India. As early as 1700 BCE, Hinduism acknowledged a "third gender," those born with mixed male and female natures or who were sexually neuter. It was under Christianity's influence on Hinduism during India's years of British rule that laws against homosexuality were passed.

> *"If there is any religion that could respond to the needs of modern science, it would be Buddhism."*
>
> **~ Albert Einstein**

Buddhism, the religion with the fourth largest number of followers, sees the key distinction as being not between bad homosexuality and good heterosexuality, but between celibacy and sexuality. Celibacy is seen as the religious ideal, but because most cannot achieve this, the goal is to avoid sexual misconduct, a concept that is undefined. Therefore, many Buddhists do not consider the issue of homosexuality to be a religious matter. Today, Buddhist appraisal of homosexuality takes its cues from its host culture. In areas that are more accepting of gender variance and homosexuality, same-sex connection and relationships are more likely to be seen as permissible.

> *"What is your companion's opinion? If you both agree, then I think I would say, if two males or two females voluntarily agree to have mutual satisfaction without further implication of harming others, then it is okay."*
>
> **~ Dalai Lama XIV**

Tibetan Buddhism is a religion based on acceptance, finding a place for, and seeming to embrace, all things — including gay rights. The Dalai Lama, its spiritual leader, is noted for his human rights activism. A spokesman for the Office of Tibet states, "His Holiness opposes violence and discrimination. He urges respect, tolerance, compassion, and the full recognition of human rights."

Sikhism

In the Sikh religion, there are no specific laws against homosexuality. Though some Sikh religious teachers have taken it upon themselves to speak out against it, others find nothing wrong. Homosexuality itself is not mentioned in the *Guru Granth Sahib Ji*, the holy scripture of the Sikhs.

One thing is made clear, however, and this is that Sikhs are not meant to have animosity or harbor hatred to anyone, regardless of color, race, caste, creed, gender, or sexuality.

Religion and the Global Divide

There is no doubt that religion strongly influences people's views on homosexuality, and attitudes are also powerfully affected by geography and economics. Research conducted by the Pew Research Center (2013) in thirty-nine countries among 37,653 respondents found that homosexuality is far less accepted in poorer countries with high levels of religiosity. It is much more widely accepted in more affluent countries where religion plays a less central part in people's lives.

The Bottom Line

The bottom line is, in spite of what you may have been told, God — if he, she, or it exists — doesn't hate gays, and neither do all religions or religious people. Through the centuries, religions have changed their collective minds on many things, and it seems likely that, in time, those who have adopted an anti-gay stance will change on this issue, too. Indeed, in many places, the change has already taken place.

Religion and Life

As we have seen, religious attitudes toward homosexuality have influenced culture, and as far as being LGBTIQ is concerned, generally in negative ways. But it's also true that culture is influencing religion, and that many scholars and believers alike are willing to reconsider their religion's historic beliefs on the matter.

It is not your job to answer questions of theology regarding homosexuality. Great theologians of every religion have wrestled with myriad issues over the years, and even with their deep thoughts, intense research and sincere prayer they don't agree on much of anything. As a gay person, you do not need to be a theological expert on the matter.

It is, however, helpful to have a thoughtful response if the issue comes up, a response that is truthful to who you are. 'True believers' have used scripture as a weapon since Day One, and while it's never appropriate to use the Bible as a club, it can be a helpful shield. If people quote scripture to you, remind them that Paul, the New Testament author who seemed to speak against homosexuality, also wrote, "Nothing can separate us from the love of God."

The Qur'an also offers passages of assurance and hope: "Those who believed and those who suffered exile and fought (and strove and struggled) in the path of Allah, they have the hope of the mercy of Allah: And Allah is oft-forgiving, most merciful."

If you're a believer, you can say something like, "I believe that God (or Allah) created me exactly as he wanted me to be," or "I think perhaps the authors of scripture had something else in mind when they wrote those passages."

If you're not a believer, consider saying something like, "I cannot believe in a God who would create such a large percentage of people who are predisposed to something he considers sinful. It's one of the reasons I want nothing to do with organized religion."

There's no reason to respond with hostility; be honest and assertive. And if you choose, walk away. There's no need to engage or to defend yourself.

Can You Be Gay, Religious, and Happy?

Numerous studies have indicated that people of faith tend to be happier than those that are not a part of a religion. "Regular and frequent religious attendance does seem to be one of the significant predictors of less stress and more life satisfaction," says Scott Schieman, a professor of sociology at the University of Toronto. "It just puts people in touch with like-minded congregants," he says, and thus produces many of the benefits of a strong social network.

"It's a period of time when you can actually connect with others and you're not alone in your beliefs."

While organized religion has definitely played a large role in propagating homophobia over the years, there are a growing number of congregations that are open to and affirming of gays. If being part of a faith community is important to you, there are options, although it might take a bit of searching to find one that's a good fit. (This is also true for straight people!) If you can connect with a group that is accepting and open, a place where you can meet people who share your values and appreciate your contribution to society, a place where you can get support while wrestling with life's spiritual questions, there is great potential for happiness in being a part of a worshiping body.

> *"The whole purpose of religion is to facilitate love and compassion, patience, tolerance, humility, and forgiveness."*
> **~ Dalai Lama XIV**

If, however, belonging to a traditional faith community isn't your cup of java, it's still possible to be a spiritual person. Religion has done much to damage people's ideas on spirituality, and so many are not the least bit interested in being part of any organized religion. There are other ways to connect to your spiritual side. Consider exploring an Eastern religion or philosophy, or pursuing a spiritual discipline that works for you: Chi-kung (Qigong), meditation, fasting, journaling, or charity work. All have the potential to help you feel connected to the universe and to assist you in self-awareness, both of which are linked to happiness.

There are also organizations that provide the happiness benefits of religion without all that doctrine. Connecting with an organization that works toward a cause you believe in will provide you with the connection and social interaction that will help you to cultivate relationships while making the world a better place. Great organizations that feed your spirit while letting you explore your gifts can be spiritually enriching without being the least bit religious.

In summary: you were created with a body, a mind, and also with something intangible, an aspect of your self that is capable of responding on a deeper, 'spiritual' level. You have thoughts and emotions, and all of this makes you unique. It's good to pay attention to all aspects of yourself.

Finding a way to nurture your inner self through meaningful relationships with common connections and goals can be an important component in your long-term happiness.

Chapter Five

Coming Out

"It takes a lot of courage to show your dreams to someone else."
~ Erma Bombeck

For some of us, the path to understanding and accepting a sexuality that veers from the norm is a long and uneasy journey. The many pressures placed on LGBTIQ people through heterosexism and various kinds of homophobia can cause us to disguise our true feelings, persuading us to keep our sexuality or true gender identity hidden — sometimes even from ourselves.

The fear of being different, of not fitting in, or of being rejected can so distance us from our true nature that we become strangers even to ourselves. Such fear can turn an otherwise quite happy life into an anxious existence full of falsity and never-ending compromise.

Others are more fortunate. We may have been aware of and comfortable with our sexual or gender identity from a fairly young age. Though, like everyone, we will have encountered our own difficulties, we knew who we were and this understanding acted as a buffer against whatever narrow-mindedness came our way. More often than not, people accepted us as we were, and we somehow seemed to flow and fit into the scheme of things.

A great many of us found ourselves somewhere between these two apparent poles, making whatever adjustments we felt necessary as we grew up and moved out into the world.

Once we accept and acknowledge who we are, things become clearer within, and it can be wonderfully liberating to end the pretense and share information about this important part of ourselves with others.

Straight people rarely feel the need to tell anyone about their sexual orientation because heterosexuality is the norm and expected, so others simply take it for granted. For gay people, coming out can be an important milestone on the road to a genuine sense of healthy self-esteem and greater happiness. It is a way of affirming the person that we are.

> *"You are not a mistake. You are not a problem to be solved. But you won't discover this until you are willing to stop banging your head against the wall of shaming and caging and fearing yourself."*
>
> **~ Geneen Roth**

Only a few years ago, gay celebrities kept their homosexuality a closely guarded secret, so many assuming that if it were publicly known that they were gay their careers would be over. Movie heartthrob James Dean's publicist even choreographed tiffs with young starlets in restaurants that fed the gossip columns of the time and assured his public that he was indeed straight. When Dean died in an automobile accident returning from a gay bar, the news sent tidal waves of shock through his army of devoted fans.

Another film superstar, who starred next to James Dean in the classic movie *Giant,* the Oscar-nominated actor Rock Hudson, reigned as the king of romantic comedies in the 1950s and '60s. It wasn't until he died of HIV-AIDS in 1985 that the public became aware of the many ways his homosexuality was closeted and covered up during his career.

It is certain that today, too, there are celebrities — major movie stars, actors and entertainers — who remain in the closet, their publicists carefully orchestrating the myth of heterosexuality.

Singer Ricky Martin vehemently denied being gay for years, finally coming out in 2010. The first American woman in space, Sally Ride, had a long-term relationship with another woman, Tam O'Shaughnessy, though this did not become known until her death in 2012, when O'Shaughnessy was listed as a survivor.

Actress, director, and Hollywood icon Jodie Foster came out to the public in 2013 after decades of speculation about her sexuality. Although fully 'out' in her personal life, Foster — like many other gay celebrities — kept her private life private until she was ready to go public. US actress and talk show host Rosie O'Donnell's television career took a nose-dive after she came out in 2002, although since that time she has become a powerful advocate for gay rights.

As culture, especially youth culture, has changed, in many ways homophobia has softened. Though it may still persist in certain areas and amongst certain people, broadly speaking, in Western society being gay is no longer seen as something really strange and abnormal. Research has found that young people today are more likely to disclose their orientation than young people in previous generations. These days, the act of coming out does little to tarnish the reputation of those who choose to do so.

Few people blinked an eyelid when Apple CEO, Tim Cook, came out in 2014 saying, "I'm proud to be gay, and I consider being gay among the greatest gifts God has given me."

George Takei, famous for his role as Sulu in the Star Trek series is openly gay and a vocal proponent of LGBTIQ rights. Likewise, Oscar nominated British actor Sir Ian McKellen, widely regarded as one of the world's finest actors, is out and confidently gay, as is UK actor, writer and presenter, Stephen Fry. When Fry announced in 2015 that he intended to marry his partner, Elliott Spencer, he was inundated with good wishes and expressions of support. Both Brits enjoy tremendous popularity internationally, and both are active supporters of LGBTIQ rights.

Comedian and talk show host Ellen DeGeneres enjoys enormous popularity more than fifteen years after coming out, and country star Ty Herndon is openly gay.

> *"I would advise any gay person that being out in the real sense can never happen too soon."*
> **~ George Michael**

Actor Neil Patrick Harris has been out for years and continues to work in the television industry, and when Olympic diver Tom Daley came out in 2013 at the age of nineteen, it did little to impede his massive following — in fact, the overwhelming response from his fans was one of support, and even of admiration. Indeed, it seems that what most bothers people today is hypocrisy. Being out, even in very public professions, appears to be a far better choice than lying about sexual preferences, to which any number of outed politicians can attest.

Coming Out to Yourself

Being gay in a world that assumes everyone is straight means that gay people have an additional layer of identity to unpack and assimilate, particularly during adolescence.

Acknowledging that we are gay can be an enormously empowering and freeing experience ... eventually. For some of us, admitting our sexual orientation is the culmination of a long and frustrating process. Yet once we've realized our true sexual identity, we can initially feel alone, isolated, and sometimes ashamed. Recognizing who we are sexually is the important first step to recovering our self. This is the springboard that will allow us to leave those confused, negative feelings behind and learn to embrace our wholeness. From this point on, we can learn to assert ourselves as happy and secure members of the human family.

Gay people almost universally say that they felt 'different' from other people at an early age, although many didn't connect it to sexuality. As hormones began to surge, they began to recognize that their sexual awakening didn't match the way things were shown on TV or was very different to the ways that their friends were responding. It was then that they began to ask the question, "Am I gay?"

Said Annabelle, "I was in denial for the longest time. I foolishly thought that being gay would bring shame on my family or make me stand out from my friends and everyone else. I just wanted to be 'normal'. It was only after I found myself head over heels in love with a girl that I came out to myself. I knew what I liked, what I felt, and just couldn't keep on denying it anymore."

If you're wondering if you might be gay, the Internet provides a wealth of information to help you navigate your questions, as well as excellent resources to help you with the process of understanding your sexuality. (A couple of sites to explore: www.ucl.ac.uk, www.yoursexualorientation.info, www.hrc.org, www.pflag.org.) The website www.gayteens.about.com offers some helpful questions to ask yourself as you consider your next move.

You may also be able to find a sounding board within your family or among your friends. Or perhaps, like so many others, for you it will be a 'light bulb moment,' when suddenly and with great clarity you understand that you're gay, and with that realization, things just seem to fall into place. Remember that it's your call if, when, and to whom you come out.

Finding the courage to be appropriately open about your sexuality can contribute enormously to a deeper sense of self-esteem and self-acceptance. Some things are simply too important to keep secret. Making the decision to come out, and choosing whom to come out to, allows you to have control of the situation, which is a powerful tool in the disclosure process.

Many gay people wrestle for years with issues of sexual identity, and so determining and acknowledging our own sexual orientation — coming out to ourselves — must be accomplished before we are really able to come out to other people.

Once we have come out to ourselves, coming out to others can be a significant step in solidifying our sexual identity and an important step in the process of becoming gay *and* happy. That being said, coming out to others is not absolutely essential in order to accept yourself and live a happy life. Some people choose to keep these details private, and that's perfectly okay.

> *"The most terrifying thing is to accept oneself completely."*
> **~ Carl Jung**

For most, coming out is a surprisingly simple process, and many people report wishing they had done so earlier. But for some, coming out can be difficult, stressful, and even traumatic.

With every change in relationship — even changes like marriage or the birth of a child — there are elements of loss, whether these are expressed or not. When a person comes out as gay, a relative or friend can initially feel that they have lost the person they believed they knew.

Although most people will be naturally accepting and supportive, others may need time to reach this point. Be aware that there may be those who will never come to accept or support your sexuality. No matter the response of other people, always remember that it's your life, and it is your opinion of yourself that really matters.

Teens

For many people, gay and straight, some form of identity confusion is common during adolescence. Our teenage years, especially, can be a time of great uncertainty and insecurity as we struggle to understand more about who we are and how we can best fit in and respond to the world about us. We are busy trying to develop and establish a sense of self, questioning everything we have been told, and testing things for ourselves. It's not uncommon for teens to 'try on' different personalities in an attempt to find their true selves.

For many teens, sexual awakening begins around age twelve, although of course there is considerable individuation in this. Children around this age usually become more keenly aware of their sexual feelings. Sexual attraction and arousal can start to exert themselves quite powerfully and gay teens usually begin to develop romantic feelings for those of the same sex or gender.

Although most gay teens may have felt 'different' for a long time, for many their sexual identity is confirmed when someone who has been a same-gender friend, or person they have admired, becomes an object of sexual attraction.

School counselors have come a long way in their ability to be helpful in sorting out sexual feelings, and if you feel that you can confide in such a person, this may be a good starting point. You may also be able to talk with another trusted adult — your parents, a teacher or someone from school, or an adult connected with any clubs in which you participate — or perhaps you have close friends with whom you feel comfortable discussing your sexuality.

Your local LGBTIQ support agency may have counselors available to help you sort out your feelings, or a qualified therapist can also be helpful — not because you are 'damaged' or need 'fixing,' but in order to help you better understand yourself and your sexual desires. Websites such as the Trevor Project (www.trevorproject.org) have online materials that can also be helpful in this area.

Though most people who care about you will be understanding and accepting, it may be that not everyone will immediately react in this way, and for some unfortunate young people, this might include family members.

Before the age of eighteen, use caution if you think your parents or guardians will be unwilling or unable to accept your sexual identity. Until this age, parents and guardians still have primary responsibility for you.

Some US parents who believe that homosexuality is a sin or a form of mental illness have committed their children to institutions or enrolled them in programs to 'cure' them — despite all evidence that such programs do not work.

Parents may even throw their gay child out of the house. As we have seen, in the US, it's estimated that forty percent of homeless people are LGBTIQ teens. In the UK, estimates put it at around thirty percent in urban centers. Such figures, however, may well be on the conservative side, because of under reporting and lack of proper monitoring.

> *"Everyone has people in their lives that are gay, lesbian or transgender or bisexual. They may not want to admit it, but I guarantee they know somebody."*
>
> ~ **Billie Jean King**

Organizations such as the *Albert Kennedy Trust* (www.akt.org.uk) in the UK, and *Forty to None* (www.fortytonone.org) in the US can be helpful if you find yourself in this situation.

These wonderful organizations provide help and assistance to homeless LGBTIQ young people. (If you live in other countries, check online for 'LGBT homeless help,' which should bring up the contact details of an organization near to you.)

If you have reason to believe that your parent or guardian may be powerfully opposed to the fact that you are LGBTIQ and you do want to come out, then be sure to come out to a respected adult — a teacher, guidance counselor, or family friend — and gain their support. Rehearse with them, and perhaps even ask them to be present when you speak to your parents. It's also good to have a back-up plan in case things get too heated. Try to prearrange a safe place to stay for a few days while allowing things to cool down or finding permanent housing. These possible consequences are not meant to scare you from coming out to your parents. Many teens are happily surprised when parents who seemed to be unaccepting offer real support, despite apparent previous lack of understanding.

Overwhelmingly, though, most people who come out report a sense of relief and a greater degree of life satisfaction for having done so. Many LGBTIQ people feel that, although coming out may have its difficulties, being out gives them more freedom to be who they are. And the ability to be who we are is a key factor in our ability to be happy.

> *"The single best thing about coming out of the closet is that nobody can insult you by telling you what you've just told them."*
>
> **~ Rachel Maddow**

Bullying

Out or not, the sad fact is that LGB teens can be the targets of bullying, teasing, and harassment, with social media and technology making this kind of nastiness even more prevalent. If this is your experience, it's imperative that you consult with a trusted adult. No one should have to tolerate abuse. Don't assume that you can manage this on your own. Consult a teacher or administrator at your school, and include your parents in the conversation. Most schools have strict anti-bullying policies. Unfortunately, not every school is equally adept at implementing them, and some schools turn a blind eye to LGBTIQ harassment. If your school is unable to protect you, or if the harassment happens off school grounds, it is well within your rights to contact law enforcement for assistance, and this may well be the most sensible thing to do.

Private schools present a different set of problems. Some such schools prohibit homosexuality on religious or other grounds, which may make it impossible for a young gay person to be out and to stay in that school. There are no easy answers here. If you enjoy your school, or if the benefits of being there greatly outnumber the drawbacks, it may be important to keep your sexual preferences a guarded secret. In some schools, secret support networks form among gay students, and this kind of support can be invaluable during your high school days. There may also be other schools with equal or greater quality education that are perfectly accepting of being gay, so research is important when deciding whether or not to come out at school.

No matter the school or circumstance, it is important to find supportive friends as you grow and mature into your sexuality. Connecting with a support group for gay teens, or teens who are questioning, is a helpful first step. If your school doesn't have such a group, the Internet can help you to find a group that meets your needs, so check online for the one nearest to you.

> *"One's dignity may be assaulted, vandalized and cruelly mocked, but it can never be taken away unless it is surrendered."*
>
> **~ Michael J. Fox**

The Internet can also provide support in other ways. For stories of support for gay young adults, check out *It Gets Better* (www.itgetsbetter.org), or look at *PFLAG*'s site (www.pflag.org) for US support options. In the UK, *Get Connected* provides a similar service (www.getconnected.org.uk).

Exercise care when connecting with strangers on social media sites such as Facebook, and also on gay cruising sites such as *Gaydar.net* Remember that not everyone online is exactly as they say they are, and profiles can sometimes be fronts for pedophiles or gay stalkers; so only ever arrange to meet people through such sites after you get to know them and have seen and talked to them on camera. If you do meet, be sure to do so in a public place where there are plenty of people around and never go anywhere private with anyone you feel at all uncomfortable with — no matter what they say. For anyone under the age of 18, telling a parent, guardian, or other trusted adult about conversations and planned encounters is also very important. They can provide advice and protective support to ensure no harm comes to you.

Sadly, suicide rates among LGBTIQ teens are high. Yet no matter how difficult life may feel, there is always, always, always a reason to keep living. If you find yourself thinking about ending things, reach out and ask for help. This really is a brave and positive thing to do. It takes more courage to admit you need help than it does in trying to face things on your own.

Organizations such as the *Trevor Project* in the US (Call: 866-488-7386, website: www.trevorproject.org), and the *Samaritans* in the UK (Call: 08457 90 90 90, website: www.samaritans.org) can be really helpful here. Remember that, no matter how bad things seem, there are those who are available to help and support you. Do what you can to get the help you need, and stay strong! It really does get better. Know that you can — and decide that you will — have a happy life and nothing and no one can stop it from happening.

As LGBTIQ people are being portrayed in more positive ways in the media and as anti-discrimination legislation continues to be passed, homophobia *is* decreasing, especially within younger generations. This will make it easier to be out and to assert yourself as a LGBTIQ person, a person with the right to live, to love, and to be happy.

Owning our sexual preferences is just the beginning of the journey. Current research indicates that gender identity — a person's sense of maleness or femaleness — is fixed very early in life. Yet, as people change and mature, their understanding of their gender identity may change and mature as well. It's not unusual for people of all genders and sexual preferences to experiment sexually during adolescence and beyond. Just as teens try on different hairstyles and clothing types in order to figure out who they ultimately are, teen relationships are an opportunity to connect with different people in different ways in order to figure out what feels right.

Unlike clothing and hair dye, though, people have emotions, and it's not fair to them, or to you, to use them indiscriminately and then discard them. So be careful as you 'try people on.' Beware of treating sex too casually. Recognize that, no matter how 'uncomplicated' the relationship, sex inevitably has an emotional component, and in your quest for self-discovery, you and others can get bruised. Even if you're careful, it may be impossible to get through adolescence without being hurt or without hurting others romantically. Just as your feelings need to be respected, always remember that so do the feelings of other people.

Along with the emotional side, taking physical precautions to protect yourself from sexually transmitted infections (more on this in a later chapter), unwanted pregnancies etc., are also important.

Bisexuality

Accepting yourself as gay can be a journey from confusion into clarity. And the same is true for those who are bisexual. As we have seen, the sex researcher Alfred Kinsey clearly delineated bisexuality more than fifty years ago. There *are* those who are genuinely attracted to both men and women; these people are bisexual.

We know now that sexual attraction happens on a continuum, so it's no surprise that many people experience bisexual leanings and may or may not act on these feelings. Of course, having the occasional fantasy doesn't mean that someone is bisexual. Those who identify as 'bi' may well have a preference for one gender or the other, and preferences may vary over time, demonstrating the fact that sexuality *can* be fluid.

It is not uncommon for bisexuals to have an apparently 'straight' public life and a less than straight private life. Statistically, bisexual people seem to be less accepted by both the gay and the hetero populations. In fact, a 2002 survey conducted at the University of Iowa's nursing school indicated that sixty-one percent of heterosexuals found bisexual men unacceptable and fifty percent found bisexual women unacceptable.

> *"We all do better when we work together. Our differences do matter, but our common humanity matters more."*
> **~ Bill Clinton**

One of the myths in the gay and straight community is that claiming to be bisexual is just a way to hide being gay. For some who are just discovering or struggling to come to terms with their sexuality, particularly teens, claiming to be 'bisexual' may be a way to bridge to homosexuality, a means of feeling somewhat 'normal' while coming to terms with their sexual preferences. But true bisexuality is more than a phase or a form of denial.

People who are bisexual can feel conflicted and may be reticent to make their sexual preferences known for fear of being labeled indecisive, unable to accept their homosexuality, or simply promiscuous. Bisexuals are as capable of having lasting relationships as any other human. Remember that long-term relationships are about far more than sex.

One client of mine, Laila, said: "For me, being bisexual is not about shagging everything that moves, or leaving one gender for another at the drop of a hat. I love people. I fall in love with a person, their personality, not their gender. If I'm in a relationship, I'm in it with that person. It will or won't last on its own merits."

Trans

Understanding and acceptance of trans people has been a long time coming. Sadly, transgender and transsexual people continue to be regularly discriminated against, not only by society in general, but also within the gay community. LGB people can easily be less than welcoming to trans people, some even adopting a superior stance.

Trans people, even more than LGB people, may well have to face issues of identity confusion and body image on their journey to acceptance and greater happiness. Some, but certainly not all, may choose gender affirmation surgery in order to bring their body more in line with their gender identity.

Among people who are transgender, conversation with a properly trained, certified, and empathetic counselor may be critically important to combating depression and bolstering self-esteem. A 2011 survey of nearly 6,450 transgender and gender nonconforming people conducted by the *National Center for Transgender Equality* and the *National Gay and Lesbian Task Force* found that as many as 63 percent of respondents experienced discrimination due to bias about their gender identity. Forty-one percent had attempted suicide, compared to an estimated thirty to forty percent in the LGBT community as a whole.

> *"I think ... if it is true that there are as many minds as there are heads, then there are as many kinds of love as there are hearts."*
>
> **~ Leo Tolstoy**

On the bright side, in some areas, things are improving for trans people. For citizens of the UK, gender affirmation surgery is available without cost on the National Health Service, the NHS. Advocacy groups are working to eliminate discrimination in the US, calling on insurance companies to cover the cost of gender transition if prescribed by medical professionals. Universities such as Brown, Harvard, and Princeton are now offering insurance plans that include hormone therapy or gender-affirmative surgery for transgender students.

In the work world, HR departments are learning more about trans persons and how to be supportive. Sadly, many trans persons (along with other LGBIQ people) discover that there is no legislation that requires an employer to hire them in the first place.

The need for continued understanding and advocacy for transgender people continues.

Organizations such as *GLAAD* (www.glaad.org/transgender) and the *Human Rights Campaign* (www.hrc.org/issues/transgender) offer support and education, and there are also support groups that specialize in helping transgender people, specifically, such as *Laura's Playground* (www.lauras-playground.com).

In the UK, *The Gender Trust* has been set up to support all those affected by gender identity issues (www.gendertrust.org.uk). In the US, the *Transgender Law Center* 'provides basic information about laws that affect trans people, including employment, health care, civil rights, family law, and identity document changes'.

Also in the US, trans people in crisis can contact the *Trevor Project*'s hotline at 866-4-U-TREVOR (866-488-7386). In the UK, the above-mentioned *Gender Trust* can be helpful. Their number is 01527 894 838.

Again in the UK, the *UK Angels* (www.theangels.co.uk), and the *Beaumont Society* (www.beaumontsociety.org.uk) provide useful information and services, while *Press For Change* is a key lobbying and legal support organization for trans people in the UK. Be sure to check online for trans organizations if you live in another country.

An online digital magazine that focuses on trans and genderqueer news, advice, and entertainment is *META* (www.pocketmags.com and type Meta into the search bar).

It is especially important for trans people to find a supportive, accepting, and understanding community in which to process ideas and issues.

Intersex

For those who are intersex, things can be even more complex. Self-acceptance and the ability to hold your head up high and openly be who you are in a world that is full of standardization have their own particular challenges. Because of this, the intersex person may experience a roller coaster ride of expended emotional energy.

It is the birthright of every intersex person to feel good and to claim their share of happiness. Again, it is essential that intersex persons have support on their journey and an appreciation that though they may not be part of a majority there is absolutely nothing wrong with them.

The UK based *Organisation Intersex International* (OII) has helpful advice, and also has a '*Handbook for Parents*' that many might find useful (www.oiiuk.org).

The *Intersex Society of North America* (ISNA) has an excellent website that provides much useful information (www.isna.org). The ISNA "is devoted to systematic change to end shame, secrecy, and unwanted genital surgeries for people born with an anatomy that someone decided is not standard for male or female."

> *"The first step in the evolution of ethics is a sense of solidarity with other human beings."*
> **~ Albert Schweitzer**

Also, *Accord Alliance* has an extremely useful and comprehensive '*Handbook for Parents*' that can be very helpful not only for parents of intersex persons, but for intersex people themselves. It is available as a free download on the Alliance's website: www.accordalliance.org.

Inside you is the strength and the courage to be who you are. Use this, together with the strategies you learn in this book to create and claim the abundant happiness that you deserve.

LGB Acceptance of Trans and Intersex

It is important for the LGB community to embrace and support persons who are transgender or intersex. Equality is not something that can be given to some and not to others; there can be no real equality until each of us has it. We have begun to pave the way together; we should not abandon or leave any of our brothers and sisters behind in our quest for understanding, acceptance, and equality.

Gay, lesbian, bisexual, trans, or intersex, once you are out to yourself and begin to form friendships and create relationships, you'll begin to feel more secure in your sexuality and more comfortable coming out to others. But while being out to yourself is the first step toward a happier life as LGBTI, there may well be other challenges that come up as you learn to embrace your sexuality. Recognizing the issues and managing them early and appropriately will be important in your quest for ongoing happiness.

Why Come Out?

Coming out is a huge step toward self-awareness and honesty, with yourself and with those around you. It is an act of personal empowerment; an affirmation of your right not only to exist, but to be yourself and to be comfortable with who you are. The restrictive confines of the closet may offer respite and a sense of security for a while, but it isn't meant to become a permanent abode. As untold numbers of out LGBTIQ people have found, it is so much better to open the door and walk out into the great big world, your head held high, feeling good about yourself.

As a psychotherapist, I sometimes find myself reminding people that they really are only as sick as their secrets. I have found this to be true in so many areas of life, and none more so than in the area of sexuality. When we cease apologizing for our existence and stop hiding away in shame, life becomes so much more meaningful and fulfilling. More importantly, we sit more comfortably in our skin and so we begin to enjoy life, becoming happier in the process.

In recent research (2013) conducted by Montreal's *Centre for Studies on Human Stress*, it was found that people who were out and open about their sexuality experienced lower levels of anxiety and depression than those who were closeted to family and friends. Moreover, gay and bi men not only had lower rates of depression, they were found to be more physically fit than heterosexual men.

All of this, of course, is not to say that coming out doesn't carry with it a certain risk. The nameless, faceless 'public' is not the same as your family and friends. Coming out to those you love or are friends with can be difficult. Friends, too, might walk away from your relationship; though it's safe to say that anyone who stays away probably never really was a friend, or not the kind of friend you'd want in your life.

The great majority of people who come out to their family and friends are often happily surprised at the acceptance and support they find. Most report that it was one of the best things they ever did, and that their lives became so much easier when they ended the charade. One 2003 study found that very few young people believed their relationship with their parents had changed as a result of their disclosure.

Remember, though, that it may have taken you years to get to the position where you understand things enough to want to come out, so be prepared to allow a little time for those near you to get their heads around it, too.

One man I worked with, Ajay, a young lawyer from India, had twice been married and twice divorced before he was able to admit to himself that his real attraction was to the same sex.

For years Ajay had hidden this, keeping it as the darkest of secrets, afraid of what might happen if he were to come out of the closet and simply be himself. Something within kept insisting that marriage could cure him of his 'unnatural' feelings. When, eventually, he found the courage to admit the truth and then come out, he met with enormous resistance from his family. His sister in particular had a great deal of difficulty in accepting the fact that her brother was gay. Yet Ajay knew his only possibility of happiness was to be true to himself and to his feelings; he could not continue to live a lie, regardless of whether this unsettled those around him.

> *"We judge people on the basis of their character, and not their sexual orientation."*
>
> **~ Barack Obama**

When his family came to see that this was who he was and that he was not going to change, they learned to accept him. He was their son and brother and nothing could ever change this.

While fear of family disapproval of our sexual orientation is often far worse than the reality, some family members may react strongly to any suggestion that you are gay.

Intuitively, you may be aware of your own family's opinion on being gay, but it's wise to be prepared for a number of potential responses and to remember that those responses, whatever they might be, are not your responsibility. You are gay; the opinions of others will not change that. And, ultimately, your happiness does not really depend on their acceptance of who you are, but on your acceptance of yourself.

Says gay rights advocate Ash Beckham, "You may feel so very alone, but you are not. And we know it's hard, but we need you out here, no matter what your walls are made of, because I guarantee you there are others peering through the keyhole of their closets, looking for the next brave soul to bust the door open, so be that person and show the world that we are bigger than our closets and that a closet is no place for a person to truly live."

Should Everyone Come Out?

Though, generally speaking, those who have come out find the experience liberating and empowering, it is fair to say that not everyone would be wise to disclose their sexual orientation. The gains of opening the closet door and coming out do not always outweigh the potential losses. Research from the UK *Safra Project*, for example, shows that Muslim women may experience a range of negative reactions from family and friends including domestic violence, intensified pressure to marry, and outright rejection.

> *"I remember how being young and black and gay and lonely felt. A lot of it was fine, feeling I had the truth and the light and the key, but a lot of it was pure hell."*
>
> **~ Audre Lorde**

For others, members of socially marginalized racial groups and cultural communities, there may well be a need to manage the values and expectations of those circles or risk being ostracized. If you are a member of such a group or community, this might mean performing a discreet balancing act in order to erect a safe boundary between your background and your identity as an LGBTIQ person. You might choose to come out to certain trusted people while maintaining your privacy with others. Or you might feel it best to remain discreet in order to protect yourself and continue to function safely within your community.

The decision to come out is an immensely personal one, and is best taken when we are reasonably sure that we will be able to handle the outcome. There is no need to rush, so take the time to consider your options.

Racism

Sadly, racism continues to exist in the world, and this is something that crosses gender and sexuality, occurring in LGBTIQ people as well as in straight. Despite laws and declarations of human rights, and though perhaps less overt and openly discriminatory than before, prejudice against people simply because they belong to a different race persists to this day.

If you belong to a racial minority then you may already have experienced this kind of prejudice in one form or another. Here, to be LGBTIQ is to be a minority within a minority, and this can make it even more difficult to come out.

Remember that most people are not racist, nor are they prejudiced. Never allow anyone to tell you that you do not matter, or that you are not as good as them because you do not belong to the majority — racial or sexual. No matter your race, in or out of the closet, hold your head up high, allow your dignity to shine forth, and claim your share of the happiness pie.

Trust

It is wisest to choose a trusted friend or family member for your first coming out. Nervousness and some degree of fear are natural, but taking the plunge can be an enormously freeing experience.

"When I was twelve, I started coming out to my friends," says Sam, a student in his first year at university. "I started with my best friend. I wrote him a note, passed it to him, and he was fine with it. After that, I started coming out to other friends in the same way."

Other LGBTIQ persons choose to bring up the issue of sexual orientation in conversation and gradually lead up to the announcement.

It might arise casually in group conversation, or it might be part of a one-on-one conversation. Some people have an intentional plan and wording worked out, but for others, the information comes out spontaneously. If the time is right, don't hesitate; take advantage of moments to express who you are.

> *"My only regret about being gay is that I repressed it for so long. I surrendered my youth to the people I feared when I could have been out there loving someone. Don't make that mistake yourself. Life's too damn short."*
>
> **~ Armistead Maupin**

When Sherry came out to long-time friend Gina, Gina was initially annoyed at herself for not having any idea that Sherry was gay. She also felt hurt and betrayed that Sherry had waited so long to come out to her. As the conversation continued, Gina, who is straight, asked if Sherry had ever been attracted to her. When Sherry assured Gina that their relationship had always been about friendship, not sexual attraction, Gina seemed somehow offended. But as they continued to talk, they were able to easily get past the awkward first conversation, and they continued to be friends.

Most friends will be as supportive as they can be, but initially they may be at a loss for words, or perhaps have difficulty finding the appropriate words. Remember that for them, as well as for you, this is probably new ground, and they, too, need to find their way. There will be friends who 'knew' or who at least suspected. They will take the information in their stride, and will likely be happy you felt comfortable coming out to them. There will be others who had no idea and so will be caught off guard. They might go quiet or fall silent. Don't automatically interpret this as disapproval; it's more likely they are attempting to respond in an appropriate and helpful manner and are just trying to figure out a way to do so.

Some may use inappropriate humor in order to mask their discomfort. Others might be so flummoxed that they resort to some form of verbal hostility. We may have pushed a button that has triggered someone's self-doubt or other unprocessed issue.

When the response is disrespectful, there is no shame in pointing this out, politely and firmly, as we would any inappropriate remark: "I know that you are trying to be funny, but it's hurtful and disrespectful to me when you make jokes about 'dykes'." Or "I guess you're feeling pretty uncomfortable with yourself, having to come out with things like that ..."

Not everyone will appreciate being called out on their homophobia, but if you can manage to be assertive in these situations, you'll do a lot to educate your friends and elevate their thinking, as well as to increase your own self-esteem. And if their behavior doesn't change, you'll know it's time to move on.

Parents

For many who are gay, it's important to come out to their parents, if not first, then at least early on. "I just wanted to tell them before someone else did," said one young man, asserting control and taking responsibility for a potentially complicated situation.

Talking to parents about matters of sexuality is difficult for almost everyone; so coming out to your parents, no matter your relationship or their views on homosexuality, might not be a picnic. But it is best if they hear it clearly from you. Don't assume they know or suspect. Parents don't generally see their children as sexual beings — a huge blind spot for most parents, regardless of their children's orientations. So the fact that you've been thinking about or participating in sex, let alone gay sex, may well shake up even the most enlightened parents.

Jake came out to his parents at age fifteen, through an email he sent while on a trip. "I figured my parents would be okay with my sexuality, but it was still easier to send them an email than to talk to them in person," he said. "Their response was amazing. They just said they loved me, and it started a conversation so we could talk more when I got back home. It looks like they'd kind of suspected for some time, so my coming out wasn't a total surprise. But it was good to tell them, and to know they were on my side."

Coming Out Later in Life

Not everyone who comes out does so when still young, and coming out later in life has its own particular challenges. Many older gay people grew up in a world where being gay was punishable by imprisonment, forced registration as a 'sex offender,' loss of employment, and the most terrible ridicule. It was a time before the Internet and journals such as *The Advocate* and *Gay Times*, a time where the few gay bars operated under the cover of darkness, much as the 'speakeasy' bars of the US prohibition era.

Many older gay people felt that remaining in the closet was simply a matter of survival in a world where they had little or no support and where they would face a great deal of condemnation and the harshest of consequences if the truth of their orientation were known. Now, in their mature years, society has changed in so many ways, and they may well want to end the secrecy and come out.

> *"I like to think that if I were gay I would be out. Rupert Everett-style."*
> **~ Ben Affleck**

Charles was a mature man who consulted me because of difficulties he was having with anxiety and depression. Now well into his seventies, he had at last decided to come out and live the remaining years of his life free of subterfuge. "All those wasted years," he said. "And now in the winter of my life I just feel it's time."

What Charles had not anticipated was the ageism that he would encounter from within the gay community itself. "Everything revolves around youth," he told me. "I've even been blamed for not having had the guts to come out when I was young, but they don't understand; I just wasn't able to."

Older LGBTIQ People

Research is really only beginning to uncover what it means to be older *and* LGBTIQ. Because many older LGBTIQ people felt unable to be open about their sexual orientation and preferences earlier in life, some may experience even greater difficulty adjusting as they continue to age.

Rutgers University professor, Dr. Michael C. LaSala, believes that aging may be particularly difficult for gay men because historically gay culture has focused on youth and beauty, and as sexual attractiveness diminishes, so does self-esteem. (If this describes you, be sure to read the chapter on accepting yourself – Chapter 6).

Aging can be difficult if we are overly dependent on one aspect or dimension of our self, but when we remember that there is much more to us, and that we have far more value than mere physical beauty, then growing older can be better accepted and handled with dignity.

In 2010, the UK organization *Stonewall* conducted a survey of LGBT people over the age of fifty-five. The data, intended to assist in planning for long-term housing and medical support for the aging LGBT population, revealed that older gay and lesbian people are more likely to be single and to be living alone than their straight counterparts. LGBT people are less likely to have children and they tend to see their conventional families less often. This is sometimes due to the family's rejection. People who came out later in life, or not at all, also have less time to build up lasting relationships within the LGBTIQ community.

If this makes you feel blue about your golden years, don't be! Remember that you have control over many things, and this includes a huge part of your own happiness. With a little planning, your later years can be absolutely amazing. Many older LGBTIQ people manage to find wonderful, long-lasting relationships, even in later years. The same rules that apply to youthful relationships apply to relationships in later life. As long as each partner is loving and supportive, the relationship can be healthy, regardless of age.

In many other ways, aging LGBTIQ people share the same concerns as others involved in the aging process. We may have concerns about finances, health, and death. Some of the health needs and concerns of LGBTIQ people are unique and require further study, but many are not.

As we age, it is important that we learn to assert our rights in terms of the kind of care we receive. If you find this difficult, then read the chapter on assertiveness and follow the principles outlined there.

Unfortunately, homophobia continues to be an issue for older adults. Not every senior community or gerontological physician is knowledgeable or prepared for LGBTIQ seniors. Don't be afraid to ask questions or to assert your rights in order to help educate these health care professionals. If necessary, shop around to find the right doctor and the right community for you. They are out there, and they can be found.

In the coming years, the LGBTIQ community will continue to increase in visibility and in power. As society changes and becomes more open and accepting, it is likely that life for aging LGBTIQ people will change for the better as well.

One US association that offers support to the mature gay person is *SAGE*, the country's largest and oldest organization dedicated to improving the lives of older LGBTIQ people. *SAGE* offers numerous services to gay people nationwide, and their website gives much useful information. The address is www.sageusa.org.

In the UK, *Age Concern* is an organization that does much to support and improve the lives of older LGBTIQ people. Simply type 'ageconcern.lgbt' into the address bar and click on the link.

Other countries may have similar organizations, and a quick search on Google or other search engine will let you know what is available in your area. You could also email *SAGE* and check if they know of a helpful organization in your country.

Jenny is a middle-aged woman who had been living on her own for more than a decade when she came out to her elderly parents over the phone. The conversation was brief, and she opted to give them space to come to terms with it.

> *"We all must be allowed to love each other with honor."*
>
> **~ Archbishop Desmond Tutu**

"When we met again face to face I was really nervous, but it was almost as if I hadn't said anything. My parents aren't the type to want to talk about things like this. So over time I would gradually bring the parts of my 'gay' life into the conversation: my thoughts on gay marriage, my work with gay advocacy groups, and, when I became involved with Judy, things about our relationship.

My parents love me, and they're very fond of Judy, but it's taken them quite a while to come to this point, and I think they're still a bit uncomfortable with my homosexuality."

Uncomfortable or not, there is little doubt that coming out when it is safe to do so, at any stage in life, is beneficial and healthy. According to University of Rochester professor of psychology, Richard Ryan, "Decades of studies have found that openness allows gay people to develop an authentic sense of themselves and to cultivate a positive minority sexual identity." In direct contrast to this, research has confirmed that remaining in the closet carries some serious psychological risks.

Ryan, co-author of a study published in *Social Psychology and Personality Science,* which included people from eighteen to sixty-five years old, found that age actually made little difference in who does and who doesn't come out. The key factor in revealing a gay orientation turned out to be the supportiveness of the environment.

Family and Friends

Family and friends are the single most important element in any person's environment. With the support of family and friends we can much more easily be ourselves, and therefore increase our experience of happiness. Sometimes, though, we can forget that those who support us may also benefit from some form of support themselves.

A really good organization that provides information and support to parents, family, and friends of LGBTIQ people in the US is *PFLAG*. With more than three hundred and fifty local chapters located across the United States and in Canada, this is the largest organization of its kind. Information and additional resources are available through its website: www.pflag.org.

In the UK, the organization called *FFLAG* — friends and family of lesbians and gays — offers similar support and services. Its informative website is at www.fflag.org.uk.

"My folks stressed out when I told them I was gay," said Phil. "I thought they were trying to protect their 'reputation' by encouraging me not to come out too far, but looking back, I think they were just trying to protect me. Among my friends, my sexuality was never an issue, so it didn't occur to me that hate crimes against gays were real, or that my own grandfather, who I was always close to, might disown me — which he did. They could see that being gay isn't easy. They didn't want me to change, but they did want me to be careful."

Sometimes coming out can have some unexpected results. After Jim came out in high school, friends who were wrestling with their own sexuality sometimes discreetly sought him out to talk. When Dave confided in Jim that he thought he was gay, Jim encouraged Dave to tell his parents, but it didn't go well. Dave's father told Dave, emphatically, that he wasn't gay, and he forbade Dave from spending any more time with Jim. "I wanted to help him," said Jim. "Instead, I lost a friend who probably could have really used my support. I don't know how things turned out for him. I hope he found the courage to be himself."

Another consideration is what might be termed 'logistical.' If you are financially dependent on parents or guardians, it really is wise to consider how they might respond to the news that you are gay. Do not allow imaginary fear to hold you back, and let nothing and no one stop you from being yourself. Understand that some people might react in negative ways, however, and in extreme cases withhold financial support. They may even ask you to leave. You know your parents quite well by now, and should be able to judge realistically. If you have genuine reason to believe this might happen, it may be wise to wait until you are financially independent or able to support yourself before sharing your news.

Siblings

If you have sisters or brothers, you already know that sometimes they are your biggest nemeses and at other times your staunchest allies. Coming out is no exception. Some siblings are initially confused, frustrated, and angry, and a few never get past this. For others, it becomes an opportunity to learn, to grow, and to advocate for you and others who are LGBTIQ. Tell them your story and give them a chance to be on board. Don't rely on your parents to talk to them, although if they are young check with your parents; it might be good if you and your parents talk with them together.

Coming Out When You're Married or Partnered

If you've been in a heterosexual marriage, or in an unmarried but lengthy relationship, the first conversation should be with your spouse or partner. This will likely be difficult for both of you, but clear communication will be important as you plan your future, either apart or together. Be clear, be honest, and be respectful, of your spouse or partner and of yourself.

Perhaps you thought your spouse or partner suspected your orientation, but often this is not the case. Your spouse or partner may very well feel angry, betrayed, rejected, and confused — and it's likely that many of these emotions will be directed toward you. Be compassionate, but stand your ground. It is also important to reassure them that it is not their fault, as some partners might feel they are in some way responsible, or believe that they may have 'turned you gay'. It's possible your spouse or partner will have a lot of questions; it's also possible that she or he will need time apart to process the many ways this will change life for both of you. It may take several conversations to work through all the issues that your revelation will create, and it may be helpful to schedule a few joint sessions with a counselor or therapist. Remember that you've taken some time to figure out who you are; your spouse or partner will need time, too.

> *"I've got nothing against gay men, but I wouldn't want my brother to marry one."*
>
> *Response: "Better your brother than your sister."*
>
> **~ Playboy Forum**

Many will choose divorce or permanent separation as the way forward, and this can be a difficult process for all concerned. The best possible outcome is that, though divorced or separated, you remain friends with your ex-spouse or ex-partner. For some, this will not be possible, and a clean break may be best. If this is the case, do your best to separate as amicably as possible.

Not all couples choose to separate or divorce immediately, or at all. They may choose to stay together in order to better care for their children, for the companionship that they already share, or even for sex. Provided couples are looking for the same things and are clear on the parameters of the revised relationship, divorce is not necessarily mandatory. But staying together isn't easy, and doing it in order to linger in the closet or to spare you or your spouse embarrassment are unhealthy reasons to remain married or partnered, and unfair to both of you. This is another time when an outside professional can be extremely helpful in determining the best, most honest way for both of you to move into the future.

If children are involved, your second conversation might be with them, depending on their ages and what you as a couple decide is most helpful. Although divorce has become, sadly, commonplace, this doesn't mean that it's not difficult for children, so focus on them, on the ways your family will change, and on the things that will remain the same, including your love for them. This is a life-changing announcement for all of you, and emotions are bound to run high. If you as a couple can present a united front, your children will fare better in the long run. It may be a conversation that stretches over days, weeks, or months, one that will demand respect for the feelings of everyone involved.

It is also important to remember, especially for those who are knowingly struggling with their sexual or gender identity, that heterosexual marriage will not 'cure' this. Much like the discussion of teenagers 'trying out people', other people are not meant to be used in a futile attempt to convert or to hide a lifestyle. It is not fair or healthy to use another person in this way.

Coming Out at Work

Discrimination and bias can exist in any environment, so use caution when coming out at work. Depending on the culture in your workplace, it is always wise to consider the impact that coming out could have on your career. Knowing your employer and your rights is important in making decisions on whether or not to come out in the workplace.

When you're at your job, your sexuality is no one's business. In fact, there are few, if any, work environments where it's appropriate to discuss one's sexual activities, even over drinks after hours. What you choose to disclose and share is your own business and no one else's.

There are work environments that will affirm your sexual identity, and if you are fortunate enough to work here, there should be little or nothing to lose by coming out. Even in these environments, however, inviting your significant other to the holiday party might raise eyebrows, either from the higher-ups or some co-workers. But there are worse things, after all, than raised eyebrows. Again, discretion is important here. If you truly love your job and feel that coming out might jeopardize your work, you might choose to err on the side of caution. If, however, you feel you can help your co-workers to get past their homophobia and are willing to take on those conversations, go for it.

> *"No matter how far in or out of the closet you are, you still have a next step."*
> **~ Judy Shepard**

As we have seen, in the UK it is against the law to discriminate on the grounds of sexual orientation, while in the US it really does depend on the state in which you live and work. Only 18 of the 50 US states explicitly protect LGBT people from discrimination in the workplace.

Before coming out, be sure to check the laws in your area. It might be wise to also review company policy on things like 'morality clauses' and same-sex benefits. These will give you an indication of the level of acceptance and protection you might expect.

It should be clear by now that coming out isn't a one-and-done event, but rather an ongoing process. Each day, each new relationship, each old acquaintance will provide you with the option of how and whether to come out. You'll have plenty of opportunities to practice! If you do choose to come out, eventually, it will become so much a part of who you are that it will no longer be a big deal. You're gay; those who are important to you already know it, and new friends will know soon enough.

Getting Support

In addition to the organizations already mentioned, support is available from a number of sources, and the Internet puts all of that support at your fingertips.

The *Human Rights Campaign* (www.hrc.org) provides online information and offers publications for purchase, including a resource guide to coming out.

The *GLBT National Help Center* operates a US-wide toll-free hotline, providing information and speaking with callers of all ages about coming out issues, relationship concerns, and sexual health. It also has a large resource base with over 18,000 worldwide listings, providing information on social and support groups, as well as gay-friendly religious organizations, student groups, etc. The toll-free number is 1-888-THE-GLNH (1-888-843-4564). Hours are Monday through Friday from 1:00 p.m. to 9:00 p.m. Pacific Time; 4:00 p.m. to midnight Eastern Time; Saturday 9:00 a.m. to 2:00 p.m. Pacific Time; noon to 5:00 p.m. Eastern Time. Its web address is www.glnh.org/hotline.

The *Gay Straight Alliance* hosts another helpful website that also contains an extensive list of organizations in numerous countries which offer help to students and those in education, as well as to their family and friends. Its address is www.gaystraightalliance.org.

In the UK, the *Lesbian and Gay Foundation* (www.lgf.org.uk) offers support for those coming out and those already out.

The *Albert Kennedy Trust,* also in the UK, provides mentoring, advice, and housing support for young LGBT people. This immensely helpful and valuable organization supports young LGBT 16-25 year olds who have been made homeless or are living in a hostile environment. The web address is www.akt.org.uk.

In the US, the *Ali Forney Center* (www.aliforneycenter.org), a wonderful nationwide organization, is dedicated to assisting homeless LGBTIQ youth. It is located in New York but has branches in several other states.

> *"A ship is safe in harbor, but that's not what ships are for."*
> **~ William G.T. Shedd**

For Muslim LGBT persons residing in the UK or other countries, a very helpful website is *Imaan,* which provides information for gay people of the Islamic faith. Its web address is www.imaan.org.uk

Check online for other LGBTIQ helplines and organizations near you.

Friends, family, guidance counselors, and therapists can also be enormously helpful in the process. Once you're out, you'll know pretty quickly who can be helpful and who is not. Don't hesitate to ask for help and support.

Advice for Family and Friends of LGBTIQ people

When someone comes out to you, what he or she really wants and needs is support and affirmation. They are putting their trust in you and are very likely to need you now more than ever. The process is not always easy, but neither is it extremely difficult — provided there is love and kindness in your heart. It is okay if you need time to collect yourself before responding, as long as you can convey this message in a caring, supportive and respectful manner.

Here are a few ways that you can support someone who is LGBTIQ while still being true to yourself.

Listen

Pay attention to what is being said, and don't be in too big of a hurry to respond. Being a sounding board is the easiest way to be supportive, especially at first. Ask nonjudgmental questions ("Who else have you come out to?" "How can I be helpful?"). It's also fine to ask for time to process the news, and to set a time for further conversation.

Learn

Learn the vocabulary. Ask your loved one or friend to help you with this. Know the acronyms and the definitions. Being able to converse on the topic will allow you to be more supportive.

Research. The Internet is a rich resource of valuable information, and even your local library probably has a few things worth reading. Check out the materials offered through organizations geared toward LGBTIQ families. And don't be afraid to seek support for yourself also.

In the UK, *FFLG* (www.fflag.org.uk) – Friends and Family of Lesbians and Gays — offers support and information, and Pink Parents (www.pinkparents.org.uk) also provides support for LGBT parents and families, while also providing a telephone helpline. Their number is 08701 273 274. The helpline is open from Monday through Friday 9 a.m. to noon (excluding bank holidays).

The previously mentioned *PFLAG* (www.pflag.org) – Parents, Families, and Friends of Lesbians and Gays — is an excellent resource for information and support in the US.

If you live in a different country, be sure to check online for organizations in your part of the world.

Know the community

A really good way to get to know the LGBTIQ community is to join a support group and connect with other parents and family members. There is tremendous power in partnering with others. Meet your son or daughter's gay friends, and let your children know it's safe to bring them home and introduce them. Make your home a welcoming, 'homophobia-free zone.' Familiarize yourself with the issues that LGBTIQ people confront so that you can be supportive of your loved one should they encounter them. Know the law, locally and regionally.

Remember it's about them, not you

Nothing you have done, nothing you could have done, and nothing you can do now will change the fact that someone is gay, lesbian, bisexual or trans. You can, however, help their transition to being gay and happy. Keep the focus on them, not on your feelings. If you need to, process your own emotions later with someone else such as a trained counselor, therapist, or good friend. Do not argue, do not offer alternative interpretations ("You're just confused"), and above all, do not judge.

Don't worry

In a homophobic, judgmental world, the news is all too full of stories and incidents of bullying and hate crimes committed against LGBTIQ people. Gay men are seen as being at higher risk of contracting HIV-AIDS, and as we have seen, any number of sensationalized stories portray LGBTIQ people as sad, lonely, outcast members of society, or as flamboyantly over-sexualized caricatures.

Coming out will not change you or your loved one into someone different. We LGBTIQ people are just regular people with a different sexual preference or gender identity. This might put us at greater risk for some things, but with your support and acceptance, much of that can be avoided. LGBTIQ people have to find our own paths to happiness. Walk with us; it will make a huge difference in the long run.

When TV's *Glee* series regular Kurt Hummel came out to his father, initially it was awkward, of course. But then in a show of support, father Burt went to the free clinic to get information for himself, as well as gay-specific pamphlets that covered the mechanics. Rather than talking to him about that, however, Burt spoke to Kurt about the emotional side of sex.

Women, he said, understand that there is 'one,' while men are more likely to think of it as just something fun to do. "With two guys, you got two people who think that sex is just sex. It's going to be easier to come by. And once you start doing this stuff, you're not going to want to stop," Burt said. "You got to know that it means something. It's doing something to you, to your heart, to your self-esteem — even though it feels like you're just having fun ... When you're ready, I want you to be able to ... do everything. But when you're ready, I want you to use it as a way to connect to another person. Don't throw yourself around like you don't matter. Cause you do matter."

'What's a fuck when what I want is love?'

~ Henry Miller

The bottom line for those of us who happen to be LGBTIQ is that there is absolutely nothing wrong with us and we really do matter. Keep this as your internal mantra when you come out to anyone:

"There is nothing wrong with me and I really do matter."

Never allow anyone, even those you love, to stop you from believing and living this truth.

Chapter Six

Accepting Yourself

"You yourself, as much as anybody in the entire universe, deserve your love and affection."
~ Gautama Buddha

There can be no doubt: accepting yourself is the key to inner balance and emotional harmony. Without the ability to accept ourselves, we block an essential component of happiness — self-esteem.

Valuing yourself and having a robust self-worth is the basis of successful relationships — whether with other people or with yourself. And if your relationship with yourself is out of sync, then so, too, is your relationship with happiness.

Yet my work as a psychotherapist has demonstrated that for many gay people, as well as for many straight people, developing self-acceptance and a healthy self-respect is one of the biggest challenges to be faced. This is particularly true for LGBTIQ people who have grown up in a culture that considered gay to be wrong, sinful, or sick.

The good news is that regardless of what you have been taught or made to feel, whatever your lifestyle, interests, or sexual orientation; short or tall, male, female, fluid, or intersex, slim, medium, or rotund, it is possible to accept, appreciate, and even like yourself. And it *is* possible to be happy. It might take work, as anything truly worthwhile does, but this is something you can learn to do and be.

Self-Esteem and Self-Acceptance

Without self-acceptance and self-esteem, life becomes a battle raged from within, a never-ending struggle to comply with other people's ideas of what your life should be and how you should live it.

Though often linked together, self-acceptance and self-esteem are a little different. With a healthy self-esteem, we are able to appreciate ourselves; we can recognize our positive qualities and use our valuable abilities to propel ourselves forward. This helps us to achieve and accomplish, which in turn enhances our sense of self-esteem, adding to our sense of self-worth. Through self-esteem we validate our being and know that our life is somehow worthwhile.

> *"Often, it's not about becoming a new person, but becoming the person you were meant to be, and already are, but don't know how to be."*
>
> **~ Heath L. Buckmaster**

Self-acceptance denotes something even broader, and perhaps more profound. With it we are able to encompass and adopt all aspects of ourselves, even those darker parts that rankle and sometimes feel awkward — the 'shadow' parts. With self-acceptance comes the ability to acknowledge our limitations and weaknesses, to accommodate our inner darkness — as well as our moments of blinding light — without allowing these aspects to destroy our balance or eclipse our sense of self-esteem. And it is possible to do this while still committing to a lifetime of personal growth, but this means taking whatever harsh self-judgment we might have been passing on ourselves and transforming it into understanding and compassion.

Almost all of us, gay and straight, arrive at adulthood carrying some form of baggage from our early years. For LGBTIQ people especially, the negative bias and messages of disapproval generated by a homophobic environment, by religion, or by myth, are likely to have planted seeds of unworthiness and self-doubt deep within. Our journey may have left us with feelings of fear, not only toward others, but toward ourselves.

These things are the enemies of self-esteem. In order to be happy, we need to feel safe. We need also to trust ourselves enough to believe that we can experience happiness. But more than this, we need to believe that we are *worthy* of happiness. The greater our self-acceptance, the more we allow ourselves to recognize and accept happiness in our lives.

We human beings come into the world in a state of need and dependence. We are born helpless and in need of protection. As infants, instinctively we know the importance of pleasing and, if necessary, placating those with power over us – the adults. We need them to like us, and so we submit to their judgmental authority. Failure to accomplish this might mean that they will stop providing us with what we require: protection and the love that fulfills our needs.

As we grow and move into the greater outside world, we carry this need with us to some degree as we seek to demonstrate our worth to others who might judge us. We try our best to win their approval. Being gay, we have been exposed to homophobia on many levels, which may well have shaken our faith in ourselves and damaged the belief in our full rights as people. Because of this, many gay people become caught up in an endless cycle of seeking approval from others by being super good, super nice, or super accommodating and likeable. After all, the reasoning goes, if people like us, then they might even forgive us for being gay.

Though we may not recognize it, our approval-seeking behaviors are a continuation of our need for the validation we may not have been able to generate from within. They are an extension of our own lack of self-acceptance and damaged self-esteem.

Only by understanding how this happened and releasing ourselves from the belief that we are neither 'guilty' nor 'not guilty' of being gay – we simply are gay – can we reclaim our lives and enter into a balanced relationship with ourselves, one that might previously have eluded us.

It takes courage and a good deal of persistence for anyone to become themself – the person they were born to be. It is an ongoing process for all of us, one that will continue until we die.

> *"It takes courage to grow up and become who you really are."*
> ~ **e.e.cummings**

Becoming yourself requires you to revisit old beliefs and the emotions that they generated, recognizing that though you are responsible for your sexual behavior, you are not to blame for your sexuality. Sexuality and sexual orientation have nothing to do with guilt or innocence. They simply are.

Living with the Past

Just like straight people, so many LGBTIQ people have been hurt in the past, and this hurt may have caused us to act or react in ways that we regret, perhaps even hurting others in the process.

In order to move forward with life, it's important to recognize that whatever thoughts, feelings, or actions we have engaged with in the past were driven by a combination of personal history, what we might call experiential 'programming,' and perhaps also of biology.

The mistakes we have made can now act as fuel for our journey into greater growth. They were the product of our younger selves' perspective — what we believed about the world and ourselves at the time — and that perspective had been influenced by the messages we received from a society that was judgmental, unaccepting, and largely homophobic.

In other words, no matter our past, we acted as best we could, given our 'programming' — the information available to us back then.

Guilt and shame are painfully common among LGBTIQ people. There is a difference between the two. Guilt is the feeling we get when we perceive we have violated some 'moral code'; it is remorse for what we have done or failed to do. Shame is different; it is the feeling of remorse we get not because of what we have or have not done, but because of what and who we believe we are. Because of this, shame can be even more difficult to deal with than guilt. For gay people, these emotions are so often the result of homophobia, particularly the internalized homophobia we discussed in Chapter 2. Usually, they stem from the mistaken belief that homosexuality is both morally wrong and a choice.

Society has been telling this tale for so long that, even after coming out and affirming our sexual identity, though we know in our heart that these things are not true, some part of us may still believe it. Tell people that they are wrong and bad and sinful often enough and for long enough and it is difficult for them to remain unaffected. Homophobia, like so many other cultural norms that we have learned, can linger within us, and we may continue to judge ourselves as though we have somehow committed the ultimate societal taboo.

Carrying these emotions will negatively impact our relationships — with others and with ourselves — and block the road to the abundant happiness that we deserve, so it's important to acknowledge these feelings, and find ways to work through and overcome them. Getting past guilt and shame may require quite a good deal of internal work. It has taken a lot to anchor these feelings in us, and it will take effort to shake them loose and free ourselves from their grip, but it can be done. Be patient with yourself, be compassionate, and be vigilant. Once you've identified the enemy, don't allow it to sneak up on you again.

To move past guilt, ask yourself, "Have I really done anything wrong?" Answer honestly. If you answer in the affirmative, then identify specifically what it is that you believe you have done wrong, and consider how you might behave differently in the future. There is nothing to be gained from endlessly punishing yourself. Be gentle and forgiving. You are human, and like all human beings you will have made mistakes. Learn from your mistakes and allow yourself to move on.

Remember that being born gay is not a choice, and while it's not the norm, neither is it wrong any more than being left-handed is wrong. Knowing this and believing this will be an important step in putting guilt and shame behind you and moving forward into a much happier life.

More than anything else, self-compassion and still more self-compassion is needed as we correct the misunderstandings and release the faulty beliefs that we have consciously or subconsciously accrued and through which we have viewed our lives and ourselves for so many years.

If it is safe to do so, coming out and owning your sexuality publicly is the ultimate shame-buster (see Chapter 5). So many who find the courage to come out report feeling relieved, clean, whole, and happier, even if those to whom they come out don't take it well at first.

Yet even those who have been completely out and open for years can inexplicably feel shame and guilt on occasion due to the deeply ingrained teachings of society. Remember that you hold your own set of morals and standards, and as long as your behavior isn't harmful to others, you are not bound by society's norms for love and intimacy. By embracing and reflecting your true values, it will become easier to set aside the opinions of others and to embrace your own sexuality guilt-free.

Many LGBTIQ people have been unduly hard on themselves, and many excel at self-criticism. Now is the time to treat yourself with kindness. Try to understand that you have been doing the best you could under the circumstances, and in the future you will do better because you are more experienced now. As more information becomes available to you, so your understanding will deepen and your vision will become clearer.

"If you begin to understand what you are without trying to change it, then what you are undergoes a transformation."
~ Jiddu Krishnamurt

Depending on your upbringing and current level of support, it isn't always possible to overcome guilt and shame without some professional help. If you're unable to move past your guilt or feelings of shame, it may be helpful to work with a therapist or counselor skilled in this area. The right therapist will help you let go of such negative feelings and move on into a happier future.

Self-Acceptance

As we have seen, self-acceptance is a major player in our efforts toward mental and emotional wellbeing and happiness. Accepting ourselves requires an honest, although admittedly subjective, understanding and acceptance of our own strengths and weaknesses. It means that we are essentially okay with who we are, while understanding that we are not perfect and can still make positive strides toward improvement.

Self-acceptance also differs from self-esteem in that esteem relates to a person's sense of self-worth, while self-acceptance is a more global affirmation of who we are — there is no judgment. A self-accepting person recognizes and accepts all the facets of his or her personhood: sexual orientation and gender identity, of course, but also strengths and weaknesses, past mistakes as well as successes. Real self-acceptance means we like ourselves, warts and all.

Happiness and self-acceptance go hand in hand. In 2014, psychologists from the University of Hertfordshire surveyed more than 5000 people and found that self-acceptance was the habit that most strongly predicted people's level of happiness and overall satisfaction with life. It also revealed that acceptance was the habit people practiced the least.

"Everything that happens to you is a reflection of what you believe about yourself. We cannot outperform our level of self-esteem. We cannot draw to ourselves more than we think we are worth."

~ Iyanla Vanzant

Note that word 'habit.' Self-acceptance is a habit that can be developed through continued practice. Developing a loving attitude toward self will greatly increase our capacity for happiness. Far from trying to gain the world's approval, self-acceptance – and so a great deal of our capacity for happiness – lies in recognizing our own worth.

We know that bias against being gay may well have conditioned a shame or guilt response, and that some LGBTIQ people choose or feel obligated to hide their sexuality. But those who are unable to accept and like this important component of their identity will struggle with self-acceptance. In doing this, they have erected a significant barrier to their own ability to experience real happiness.

If this describes you, either in the past or in the present, it might take a concerted effort to learn to appreciate who you are.

Self-acceptance might require you to retrain your brain. This can be a challenging journey, especially if so many of the things that you've ever heard about being LGBTIQ have been negative. Remember that although this is your own journey, you are not alone in having to unlearn what you have been taught in order to become self-accepting. Many other LGBTIQ persons have traveled the road before you and are symbolically traveling with you.

Lock securely in your mind the fact that being gay is not a defect. It is simply the way you are. Just as you did not choose your parents or your eye color, this is the orientation you happen to have. It is one of your unique characteristics. It does not make you somehow less than others. Being gay is another way of being, and there is no reason to feel guilt or shame. You have the right to exist — in fact you have the right to thrive, to live a life full of the expression of the person that you are. You have the right to know happiness in your life. You certainly have the right to love and be loved, and you do not owe it to anyone to have to explain your preferences, any more than you owe them an explanation of why you like chocolate rather than vanilla ice cream.

Being gay really isn't a curse. In fact, with time, you may come to see it as a blessing. Generally, however, it's like every other characteristic: neutral. It's what we do with it — how we apply it in our lives — that makes the difference.

Asserting Self-Acceptance

Self-acceptance is an intensely personal journey, and while a strong support network and a good therapist can be extremely helpful, it is up to you to take the responsibility for this, no one can do it for you. The vast majority of the work is internal. It has to take place within.

Self-criticism and self-doubt sabotage self-acceptance. To curtail their negative impact, we need to cultivate a spirit of self-forgiveness.

Treat yourself as you would treat your best friend. You wouldn't allow your best friend to be beaten up or to wallow in negative thoughts; you'd do what you could to help, to bolster his or her mood with loving honesty. And you wouldn't let someone else hurt or speak negatively about your best friend; you would be quick to step in to defend him or her. Asserting your self-acceptance is learning to do these things for yourself. It means becoming your own friend.

A crucial first step in asserting self-acceptance is to interrupt negative self-talk. When you hear yourself saying, aloud or in your head, something like, "Why did I say that? I'm so stupid," immediately interrupt the thought and counter with a more forgiving thought: "I probably could have handled that better, and I'm learning to do that."

> *"Dare to love yourself as if you were a rainbow with gold at both ends."*
>
> **~ Aberjhani**

Instead of, "I'm an idiot in social situations," consider, "I'm a bit introverted/extroverted and something of a flirt/wallflower, and sometimes I get carried away/hesitant when I'm with new people. But I will make the effort to smile/think before I speak and talk to people at tonight's party." Keep in mind that your mistakes are not who you are, and find a way to leverage and appreciate your innate traits.

And instead of, "I wish I weren't gay," remind yourself, "Being gay makes me different, not flawed." Trust yourself: you *are* capable of handling whatever challenges life might bring your way.

Unapologetic

The way we think is greatly influenced by habit, and habits are the product of repetition. Get in the habit of repeatedly thinking positive things about yourself.

Tell yourself over and over again that you are okay, that you're doing the best you can, and that your best is plenty good enough. Accept that you will make mistakes — after all, you are human. We all make mistakes, and with very few exceptions, most of our mistakes aren't fatal. With some effort, we can learn from our missteps and move on in some meaningful way.

It really is best to avoid using the words "I'm sorry" as the introduction to, or a filler in, every conversation. There's no need to apologize for making a contribution to a discussion, and this prelude to speech has a negative impact on your self-worth and may also diminish you in the eyes of others. Plus, these important words lose their true power if used too frequently. If this is your habit, stop it! Choose your words before you speak, and edit out words that sound apologetic. Practice speaking gently and calmly, but with authority.

> *"To be what we are, and to become what we are capable of becoming, is the only end in life."*
>
> **~ Robert Louis Stevenson**

If, on the other hand, you've done something that truly warrants an apology, make it promptly and sincerely, and then let it go. Don't beat yourself up over things that cannot be changed.

Another important step toward healthy self-acceptance is to learn to appreciate your past without dwelling on it. All you've seen, done, and experienced has helped shape the person you are. While no one would choose to be bullied in school or rejected by friends after coming out, even such difficult life experiences as these have the potential to strengthen our character and to deepen our empathy and understanding.

Experience is a wonderful teacher — provided we allow ourselves to learn from it. Once we have learned, then we can allow whatever has happened in the past to be consigned to the past. Celebrate the fact that you have survived this far. And whatever you had to do in order to survive, you did because you felt you had to do it. You did the best you could with what you had at the time. No need to second-guess. Accept it and move on.

Be content with who you are. It is enough. You are enough.

Accepting responsibility for our actions as we move forward, we can continue to work on our self-acceptance, and as we forgive ourselves, so too, we can perhaps learn to forgive others — even those who have hurt us — realizing that they too, in their own way, were as much the product of their conditioning, their introjected values, and learned belief systems as we were.

> *"There comes a time in each life like a point of fulcrum. At that time you must accept yourself. It is not any more what you will become. It is what you are and always will be."*
>
> **~ John Fowles**

The work of self-acceptance is mission critical to a life of happiness. It's a long-term, on-going effort, but with practice it will become second nature. Even those who have a highly cultivated sense of self-acceptance have times of sadness and moments of self-doubt. At times such as these, interrupt your negative self-talk and give yourself the pep talk, or ask a friend to do it for you. Remember that each day you have the right to exist, to live, and to love. You are not a mistake. You are a human being, and you have the right to know real happiness.

As we become more self-accepting, we can begin to appreciate that we are not to blame, and that we never really were. The fortunate among us — and each one of us is as fortunate as we allow ourselves to be — might even arrive at that place where we can access the profound understanding that just as there is nothing wrong with us, so there is nothing really to forgive.

We were always innocent; we just did not know it. And with this understanding comes the realization that we can accept and like ourselves — and still commit to a lifetime of personal growth.

Chapter Seven

Assertive Living

"We are injured and hurt emotionally, not so much by other people or what they say and don't say, but by our own attitude and our own response."

~ Maxwell Maltz

Self-esteem and assertiveness go hand in hand. When our self-esteem is high, we can more easily ask for what we need or want from others, and we can do it politely and firmly. An assertive person isn't demanding or pushy, but can be forthright with opinions and stand up for his or her rights calmly and with dignity.

If you feel you lack assertiveness, take heart. The good news is that assertiveness skills can be learned. And by learning to be assertive, you'll also boost your self-esteem.

So much of our behavior, and the responses we have to other people, are learned. Because of this, it is possible to relearn, or to learn alternative ways of responding and behaving, ways that help us take more control of our lives and our interaction with other people. Being assertive allows us to exert our own rights, without denying the rights of others. With it, it is we, and not other people or our past that choose the way we are and the way we react and interact with others.

Being assertive is often difficult for gay people, since most of us have received messages from the culture that we are somehow inferior and not deserving of respect. So many of us have lived with the belief that "the nail that sticks up gets knocked down." Because of this we can too easily acquiesce and surrender our personal human rights.

Lesbian, bisexual, and trans women have also had to contend with society's prevailing sexism, something that can seriously compromise their confidence and affect their lives personally and professionally.

As LGBTIQ people, we may have become accustomed to acquiescence, to "go with the flow" and "not make waves," even when our rights are being violated or when someone is treating us unreasonably. As a group and as individuals, we might sometimes allow others to treat us in disrespectful or overly demanding ways.

Having pent up our frustration for so long, we may find ourselves crossing the line into aggression, venting our anger in a desperate attempt to be heard or to get what we believe we need. But this is a flawed strategy that can come back and bite us quite severely.

Aggression is all about winners and losers. With it we create conflict. We boss and bully, demand and manipulate, and in doing this, we not only expose our insecurity, we demonstrate that we have no real choice — we are not really in control of our emotions. And when we are not in control of our own emotions, then we are not really in control of the situation.

Though aggression might sometimes achieve our ends, it does so in the worst possible way. Few people like to be treated in an aggressive manner, and so aggressive people can easily alienate others. Consequently, aggressive people usually have few real friends.

Unlike aggression, assertiveness means that we do have a choice. With it we are in control. When we are assertive, we can express our views and articulate our needs directly and with confidence. We communicate effectively and are able to stand up for ourselves. We can challenge discrimination while considering the views and respecting the rights of others.

In asserting ourselves appropriately and consistently, we foster good relationships and enhance our own self-esteem.

Aggression has nothing in common with assertiveness; they are poles apart. In fact, assertiveness can be the antidote to aggression.

Barriers

Many LGBTIQ people struggle to be assertive because we believe we do not have the right to assert ourselves. Others of us have felt anxiety or fear when attempting to be assertive in the past, and this fear has become a sort of 'conditioned response,' an anxious feeling that is triggered when others are demanding or confrontational. This may have prevented us from asserting ourselves when we really should have.

> *"Never be bullied into silence. Never allow yourself to be made a victim. Accept no one's definition of your life, but define yourself."*
> **~ Harvey Fierstein**

One of the biggest reasons we fail to be assertive is fear of the consequences we might incur by standing up for our rights. We're concerned we will be seen as selfish, demanding, or unlikable. We might also fear others' judgment, anger, and rejection.

These are all concerns we might have, but all are based in myth. Failing to stand up for our rights helps no one. It teaches others that they can treat us in disrespectful or demanding ways and that it's all right to do so. But it is not all right. You are a person and so you are entitled to be treated with respect. You have rights, and those rights need to be acknowledged and claimed.

Our own belief system plays an enormous role in our ability to be assertive. If we believe that we are somehow inferior because we are gay, then we need to take a long hard look at why we believe this. The previous chapter on self-esteem and self-acceptance speaks to some of these concerns. As with issues of self-esteem and self-assurance, if assertiveness is too difficult to master alone, you may benefit from working with an assertiveness trainer, counselor, or therapist who is experienced in this area, perhaps someone who is also LGBTIQ.

If we believe that people will only accept or like us on the condition that we go along with what they want, we need to look at why we believe this. If we think that being assertive would make no difference because no one would listen to us anyway, we need to examine the source of this fiction. Each of us has a right to live with dignity and self-assurance.

Becoming truly assertive takes work, patience, and yes, a certain degree of courage. And courage comes with the doing. In the beginning, being assertive can feel strange and even uncomfortable, but with practice it becomes increasingly easier. Practice enough, and it becomes second nature.

There are times in life when each of us needs to assert ourselves, times when we need to express our needs, wants, beliefs, and feelings. When we do this in an honest, direct, and clear way — without violating another person's rights — we affirm our rights, we grow in self-esteem, and we increase our own ability to be happy.

Our Rights

Understanding our rights is a central factor in our journey to becoming more assertive. And being able to assert ourselves is an essential aspect in the process of becoming gay and happy.

We have all heard the term 'human rights,' and we all recognize their importance. The concept of rights has existed for a long time and was enshrined in the United Nations Universal Declaration of Human Rights in 1948, shortly after the atrocities of the Second World War.

This declaration contained what were considered to be the basic principles necessary in order for people to live their lives with dignity and decency. In its preamble, the UN declaration describes human rights as "the foundation of freedom, justice, and peace in the world," and affirms: "All human beings are born free and equal in dignity and rights."

Most of us have little difficulty in acknowledging that people should be treated decently and fairly, regardless of such things as race, ethnicity, religion, or gender. Some of us might even have found ourselves helping others to assert their rights, individually or corporately, but we may have been less ready to stand up for our own rights.

> *"Freedom from fear could be said to sum up the whole philosophy of human rights."*
> **~ Dag Hammarskjöld**

We might have unnecessarily acquiesced, or let things pass in an attempt to conform to other people's wishes or expectations — even if those things were in some way contrary to our own desires, needs, and feelings. In doing this, we have sold ourselves short.

The first step in living assertively — and so happily — lies in clearly establishing what rights we have. If we do not know what our rights are, then how are we to know if someone else is violating or disrespecting those rights? When we are completely clear about our rights, it becomes a great deal easier to stand up for and claim those rights.

What follows is a Bill of Rights that can be used by anyone who is LGBTIQ — or, indeed, by any right-thinking human being — as a useful framework going forward.

Bill of Rights

- **I have the right to be myself.**

  Even though this may be different from others, different from what they think you should be, or different from what they would like you to be.

- **I have the right to be treated as an equal human being regardless of sexual orientation, race, gender, age, mental or physical ability, ethnicity, or religion.**

  There are several groups that do not always receive equal treatment in our society, and we could expand this list. As LGBTIQ people, we may have allowed others to treat us unfairly because of our own self-doubt.

- **I have the right to needs and wants that differ from those of other people.**

  Simply because your needs and wants differ from those of other people, this does not mean that you — or they — are wrong. When we respect this fact, we are better able to be ourselves and live in harmony with our nature.

- **I have the right to express my feelings.**

  So often our culture devalues emotional intelligence while exalting intellectual logic. Yet feelings are an important part of the human experience, and we have the right to ask for support or a change in behavior based on the way we feel.

- **I have the right to express my opinions and views.**

  Just as we have a right to our values, we also have a right to our opinions. Moreover, we have the right to express these in a calm and clear way without feeling responsible for the feelings that this may elicit in other people who may not agree with us.

- **I have the right to be human and make mistakes — provided I accept responsibility.**

  The right to make mistakes can seem contrary to many of the things we have been taught, especially as children. Yet the fact is that we *are* human, and so we sometimes make mistakes, and we need to accept responsibility for this. It's been said that the only real mistake is to fail to learn from our mistakes. When we allow ourselves to claim this right, we allow ourselves to be more fully human — and this can help us to be more understanding and forgiving of other people's mistakes.

- **I have the right to ask for what I want.**

  Asking for what we want in a clear, direct, and honest manner is the very best way to achieve it.

- **I have the right to interact with others without depending on their approval.**

  Many gay people have developed a strategy of 'people pleasing' in an attempt to be accepted and liked in spite of the fact that they are gay. In doing this, we turned our 'locus of control' outward, giving other people the ability to control the way we felt about ourselves. In developing a more robust sense of self-esteem, we are able to rely on ourselves for approval, and so become more secure in ourselves and of our place in the world.

- **I have the right to offer no reasons in order to justify my behavior.**

  If we behave in a way that others do not understand or like, and we do it in a way that is not intended to harm, then we are under no obligation to offer reasons for our behavior. Though others may not approve, and may demand that we justify our behavior, it is up to us whether we choose to or not.

- **I have the right to decide if I am responsible for solving other people's problems.**

  As gay people, others may expect us to be their 'Agony Aunt,' picking up the pieces and providing solutions to their personal problems. This is a role that we may have adopted in order to ingratiate ourselves and to feel accepted. You are under no obligation to solve other people's problems, and you have the right to decide whether to accept or decline this responsibility.

- **I have the right to say "no" or "yes" whenever I choose to.**

  Saying "yes" when what we really mean is "no" complicates life and relationships in unnecessary ways. Saying "yes" when we want the opposite forces us into a position where we either fail to follow through and thereby disappoint others, or we do what is asked while harboring feelings of resentment. Neither of these positions is healthy.

- **I have the right to change my mind.**

  As people, we change and grow according to the experiences we encounter and through our ability to reflect and reconsider. As greater awareness and new information is incorporated into our thinking, we may well change our mind on matters.

- **I have the right to say "I don't understand" and to seek clarification.**

  There is no shame in admitting we don't understand and in asking for another explanation or for more information so that we can. Failure to do this can result not only in further confusion, but in some serious misunderstandings.

- **I have the right to ask — and expect — others to respect my rights.**

  Rights are not favors — they are your rights. Each of us is entitled to have our rights respected, and we have the right to ask this from others.

> *"In order to carry a positive action we must develop a positive vision."*
> ~ **Dalai Lama**

- **I have the right to assert or not to assert myself.**

  We are under no obligation to do anything that we do not want to do, provided we are willing to take responsibility and accept the consequences of this.

  And, of course, other people have the same rights as us. It's important to respect others when they clearly and respectfully express their needs, opinions, and feelings. It's not necessary to agree or to comply, but always remember to value the person and the person's right to communicate.

Four Characters

When we look at assertiveness, there are essentially four basic behavioral types — three unassertive and one assertive. We'll use different fictional characters to represent each one. Notice how all except the assertive character are governed by low self-esteem.

Aggressive Arthur

Arthur's behavior and reactions to other people have their roots in a diminished sense of self-esteem for which he is constantly trying to compensate. He doesn't really believe in himself, and secretly believes that no one else does, either. Because of this, he feels compelled to grab what he needs, even if this means pushing others out of the way in order to get it. He feels that he has to win, at all costs. Failure to do so would confirm his worst fears. He can shout, bluster, and bully in an attempt to intimidate, and he can easily become a zealot in his beliefs. He likes to humiliate his opponent in order to shore up his sense of personal powerlessness, and is often seen as belligerent and confrontational. Aggressive Arthur is not one to easily forgive and forget. He constantly overreacts and tends to bear grudges. He often gets his way because other people are fearful of his volatile reactions and simply want a more quiet life, but they usually feel resentful and angry because of it. Aggressive Arthur has few real friends.

Passive Pamela

Pamela gets through life on the principle of acquiescence — she gives in to almost everyone and practically everything. Like aggressive Arthur, her behavior is a result of low self-esteem. She doesn't like to make waves and sees herself as a victim. She is constantly painting herself into a corner by agreeing to things that she really doesn't want to do and making promises that she cannot keep. She is the kind of person Aggressive Arthur loves to connect with. With Passive Pamela, there is almost always a "but." There are always reasons why she cannot move forward; why she has to stay stuck. Try to help her take control of her life, and you'll hear things like: "I see your point, but I can't do that because..." or "I only wish I could, but..." No matter how hard we try, Pamela will almost always have a reason why she cannot be in the driver's seat and take responsibility for her circumstances. She insists that she just doesn't have the resources — inner or outer — that would allow her to change things. She is poor at making decisions, and often leaves them to others or to chance. Her expectations are low, and people tend to give up on her — which only confirms her own image of herself as one of life's losers.

Indirect Ian

Ian cannot bring himself to be straightforward and direct. What he fears more than anything is rejection. He rarely asks directly for what he actually wants or needs, most often relying on manipulation to get his own way. He frequently falls prey to mood swings and can sulk until he gets what he wants. He may sometimes use a form of emotional blackmail, hone in on feelings such as guilt, and give people the cold shoulder for no apparent reason. Indirect Ian can be a stranger to himself as well as to other people, because he lies to himself and to others — especially about his feelings. His sense of humor is frequently based on sarcasm, and he is not above coming out with jibes, innuendo, and veiled threats. He can appear almost overly friendly to your face, but then turn around and gossip about you. His behavior can create confusion and hurt feelings as others wonder what they've done to upset him this time. People often don't know where they stand with Indirect Ian, and so find it difficult to trust him.

Assertive Angela

Angela feels good about herself. She didn't always feel this way, but she has worked on understanding her feelings. She's learned strategies to help her be more assertive in her life. Now her self-esteem is anchored within herself and doesn't depend on other people. She knows she's doing the best she can, and although she doesn't always succeed, she sleeps well at night because of it. She likes other people and seems to get along well with them. She respects them, and they, in turn, respect her. She has long ago given up any unreasonable demands for human perfection, either from herself or from other people, and is happy to live with her shortcomings while continuing to work on those things she can change. She learns from her own mistakes and is able to forgive others when they make mistakes, too. Angela has learned to ask for what she wants in an open, direct, and honest way, and is able to cope when things don't go her way. She takes responsibility for herself and her actions and encourages others to do the same. People can talk to her without fear of manipulation, attack, or deceit. You know where you stand with Angela; she is who she says she is, and her actions suit her words.

> *"To know what you prefer, instead of humbly saying Amen to what the world tells you you ought to prefer, is to have kept your soul alive."*
>
> **~ Robert Louis Stevenson**

Of course, people being people, anyone can be a combination of any of these characters. Very few people are exclusively one type. A person can be a mixture of passive-aggressive, for example, or choose to be assertive or otherwise at any given time. It's not difficult to see which kind of person we ourselves would be most likely to respect and trust. And most of us are much more likely to accommodate the assertive person's wishes and needs than we are any of the others.

Do you see yourself in these types? If you resemble Aggressive Arthur, Passive Pamela, or Indirect Ian, then perhaps it's time to shed your bad habits and claim the assertive personality that's been hiding away inside you.

An assertive person communicates from the perspective of being equal to others. The first step toward assertive communication is to remind yourself that you are fine just the way you are. You are not broken, so you don't need mending. You have certain inalienable rights. Your goal in being assertive is to express your wants, needs, opinions, and feelings in a clear, direct, and honest way.

A Few Tips on Body Language

Remember that being assertive has to do not only with what you say, but how you comport yourself as you say it. Your body sends a message, so make it congruent with the message contained in your words.

When feeling confronted or cornered, our body language can shift. We draw in, as if trying to shrink in an effort to present a smaller target for the perceived attack, or we tighten up as if about to become aggressive. Remember that in the majority of situations, the person is not attempting to attack or belittle (more on those attack situations a little later). So relax. Take a breath and release, and as you exhale, let go of some of your tension. It's a conversation, not a fight, and you have a right to participate, to hear and to be heard.

An open, relaxed posture will be helpful in asserting yourself. Uncross your arms and loosen your shoulders. Keep your palms open and avoid gestures that symbolically put a barrier between you and the other person. Don't jab the air or point, which are gestures of accusation and blame. Sit or stand firmly, but not rigidly, preferably at the same level as the person you're addressing. It's always best to avoid fiddling and shrugging shoulders, since these gestures convey a sense of acquiescence or passivity.

When we are feeling anxious, there is a tendency to clench the jaw and tighten the lips. There is no need to smile unnecessarily or unnaturally in an attempt to ingratiate yourself, just breathe deeply, articulate slowly and naturally, and let your mouth relax.

Use positive gestures like nodding to underscore your point and to assure that you are listening. And do listen; be careful that you're not mentally preparing your rebuttal instead of paying attention.

Eye contact should be regular and appropriate, neither fleeting nor aggressive. It can be helpful to use a mirror to practice this. Be sure to maintain friendly, relaxed contact at all times.

Slow down your speech and keep your tone of voice moderate and smooth; don't allow the pitch to go up, which can indicate nervousness. Don't yell, and don't whine. Make sure you talk calmly, without raising your voice or shouting. Be sure to avoid conveying a sense of anger or pleading when speaking, and stay away from sarcasm at all costs.

Breathe, breathe, and breathe again. As we breathe deeply, it really does help to calm us down. When you're ready to speak assertively, speak as you exhale, calmly and steadily, expressing yourself in a clear and direct way.

Remember that confidence is often quiet, while insecurity is all too often loud. Relax your body and convey a sense of confidence by allowing it to shine quietly through your body language.

Assertive Skills

In order for us to get what we want, we need to know what we want, and then be able to communicate this to others. People, even those closest to us, are not mind readers. It just isn't realistic to assume that someone intuitively will know what we need or how we feel. And even if they do and they choose to ignore our requests, we do not have to be the helpless victim of their negativity. The very best way to get what we need or communicate how we feel is to express ourselves in an honest, clear, and respectful manner.

Here are some ways that you can develop your assertiveness skills. With practice, these techniques will become second nature, and you'll learn to assert yourself in a variety of situations.

Think Before You Speak

Assertiveness requires some preparation and some organization. When faced with a confrontation, take a moment to prepare your response. What is it you want? A change in behavior? Your feelings respected? Create a brief outline in your head of the points you wish to raise. Even if you are caught off guard, think before you speak. You're always allowed a few moments to collect your thoughts. Don't try to rush in and fill time or space with weak words or stammering. Take a deep breath, speak clearly as you exhale, and project an air of confidence.

Be Specific

Decide exactly what you want or how you feel, and communicate this as clearly and directly as possible. Keep your statements simple and brief. If someone is speaking to you in a disrespectful way, for example, you have every right to do something about it. Choose a short, clear statement that lets the other person know how you feel and what you want, and speak to him or her in a calm voice. "When you tell jokes like that I feel uncomfortable, and I'd like you to change the way you talk when I'm around."

Repeat

Having chosen your clear and direct statement, repeat it as often as necessary until the other person has acknowledged it and responded appropriately. Don't worry that you sound like a broken record. Keep calm and repeat it until you get your point across and are heard. This works particularly well in situations where you feel anxious, or when encountering someone who is aggressive or trying to manipulate you.

Be prepared for the other person to try some kind of strategy in order to take you off message and get his or her own way. No matter what he or she may say, remain calm and simply repeat your statement until you get the response you're looking for. Do not allow the other person to draw you in and divert you from your statement or request.

Acknowledge the Response

Just as you want your voice to be heard, so the other person needs to feel acknowledged, too — even if you disagree with what they are saying. In order to show that you have listened and acknowledged, all that is necessary is that you repeat what they have said and again repeat your own statement. For example, "I understand that your friends don't have a problem with that sort of thing, *and* I feel uncomfortable with those remarks, so I'd like you to change the way you talk to me."

Own Your Statements

It is always best to take responsibility for your own feelings and not blame or label others, no matter how their behavior impacts on or affects you. Own what you say. Your statements come from *your* perceptions, so acknowledge this by using "I" and avoiding "you," which feels more confrontational. For example: "I feel very uncomfortable when that language is used..." Or: "I don't find that joke amusing, and I'd appreciate it if you didn't repeat that kind of thing in my presence."

When we blame others, it can provoke resistance rather than encourage a spirit of cooperation and compliance. Using the personal pronoun "I" shows that you have taken ownership of yourself and your statements. "I don't agree with what you're saying" is much more assertive, and less aggressive, than "You're completely wrong."

Arrive at a Workable Compromise

Sometimes we encounter situations in which there is a genuine conflict of interests. This does not necessarily mean that one person has to lose and the other win. In these situations, it's possible to reach a workable compromise by negotiating from a position of equality, while considering both people's needs and wants. When each person achieves a suitable degree of what they want, resentment is minimized, and both feel better.

Share your Feelings

Being human, we feel and we experience a mixture of different feelings. We might not like what a person is saying or how they are behaving, but still want to remain on a friendly basis with them. When we allow ourselves to communicate the way we are feeling through clear disclosure, we gain a greater degree of control of ourselves and lessen our inner confusion and anxiety. "I'm really anxious not to spoil our friendship, *and* I'd like you to stop making that kind of remark around me."

> *"Speak the truth, even if your voice shakes."*
>
> **~ Maggie Kuhn**

Change if necessary

Negative assertion is particularly useful when dealing with criticism. Remember that not all criticism is meant to hurt or be unhelpful — it might simply be feedback that we can use as we go forward. In this case, acknowledge the behavior, and if necessary, agree to change things. "I can be spontaneous and impulsive, and I kind of like that quality in myself. If that's really a problem for you I guess I could look at toning things down when I'm with you."

Ask for critiques

This is a skill that would appear to swim against the current of our competitive society, because it invites criticism. In the past, we may have been trained to cover our missteps, defend our mistakes, and deny our errors. Negative enquiry stands this on its head and so can be quite disarming. When we communicate honestly, we open the door for change — in ourselves as well as in others. When we are criticized, and treat the criticism as feedback, then we can identify our errors and learn from them. If the criticism is valid, we can accept it, and if it is not, then we can reject it. "I see what you mean, and it looks like you have a good point here. Could you give me a bit more of a breakdown on how I might correct things so we can move forward?"

Practice, Practice, Practice

Practice being assertive with the people you trust most, and begin with smaller, noncritical issues. When you're deciding on dinner or going out to a movie, for example, express an opinion, clearly and without waffling.

Making Requests

As LGBTIQ people, we have the right to communicate our needs, wants, and feelings, and we also have the right to make requests. Though asking for what we want does not necessarily ensure that we will get it, the fact is that we are a good deal more likely to do so than if we do not ask.

> *"There are four ways, and only four ways, in which we have contact with the world. We are evaluated and classified by these four contacts: what we do, how we look, what we say, and how we say it."*
> **~ Dale Carnegie**

In order to be clear and to avoid being misunderstood, we need to ask for what we want openly and directly. We need to be specific. You may feel that there should be no need to ask or to explain because what you are asking for ought to be evident and obvious to the other person. If this is the case, remember that you are dealing with a human being, not a machine, and we human beings don't always work on logic and rationality. What's obvious to us may be less so to someone else.

A good strategy is to assume that the person you're talking with simply does not know or understand what it is you want. This does not mean that they are stupid or that you need to be condescending when talking to them. If emotions are involved, then calmly and clearly let the other person know how you're feeling, and explain what you would like them to do. Keep your request simple, brief, and direct. Be as specific as possible, and calmly repeat your request until you get an appropriate response.

Learn To Say No

Just as we have the right to request things of others, so others have the right to ask things of us. This does not mean that they or we always have to say yes. There are times when people ask us to do things that we just do not want to do. Being able to refuse such requests is a skill anyone can learn.

Our immediate gut reaction will usually let us know whether we want to comply with a request or not. If we really do not want to say yes but do so anyway, something inside us will probably find a way to say no indirectly. This will simply complicate things and gain us a reputation for being undependable or untrustworthy.

There are times, however, when we do need to break a promise. When this happens, it's best to contact the person promptly, explain things, and offer an alternative that will allow the promise to be fulfilled, or allow them to clearly understand why this is not possible.

Remember when you say 'no' to a request that you do not wish to grant, you are also saying 'yes' to yourself as a person — and so enhancing your sense of self-esteem. In refusing a request, make sure that the person you are talking with understands that you are not rejecting them, their friendship, or their role.

Nonassertive people tend to say yes with greater frequency than is healthy. They may fear rejection by others, so they take on additional projects in order to curry favor. This lack of discernment can also lead to saying yes to things like drugs or sexual activities when pressured. Assertive people can find a way to say no to things they'd rather not do. It's your right to make choices on these matters, and you should feel free to express this right.

As you've probably figured out by now, a simple, clear "no" is your best tactic here: "Thank you for thinking of me; my plate is really full right now. I don't believe I could give the project the attention it deserves." If the person persists, simply repeat yourself until the message is clear. You needn't answer every objection raised.

The same is true in other situations: "I'm not into drugs, but I'm happy to be your designated driver," or, "I'm not comfortable with that" are perfectly acceptable, assertive responses. No need to apologize, to feel guilty, or to backpedal, and there's no reason to fear losing out on a relationship. Solid relationships can withstand a little honesty, and real friends shouldn't require you to compromise your principles. If relationships become strained over these issues, it's probably time to move on and find friends with whom you have more in common.

Assertive people also know that while they may ask for things from others, the answer won't always be yes. By all means, make your best pitch; prepare what you want to say, being as clear and relaxed as possible. You might even want to practice in front of a mirror. But if someone says no to something you've suggested or requested, remember that their "no" is not personal, nor is it a rejection of you as a human being. It's merely the other person being assertive, as is their right, just as it is your right.

A sincere "no" is far better than a reluctant "yes." It needn't ruin a friendship or relationship, and it shouldn't prevent you from making requests in the future. Though it might feel awkward and uncomfortable at first, saying no without feeling guilty gets easier with practice.

Whatever you say, though, *make sure you mean it.* Match your actions to your words. Never promise anything you have no intention of honoring or little chance of delivering on. When our actions are congruent with our words, we earn the respect of others, and enhance our own self-respect, our self-esteem.

Be who you say you are and people will know where they stand with you.

Giving and Taking Criticism

There are times when it can be hard to listen to even the most well-intentioned criticism, but with the right attitude, hearing someone's honest evaluation can be helpful. Do your best to see criticism as feedback and not as an attack on you as a person. Rather than immediately rushing into denial or justification mode, try to listen calmly, without jumping to conclusions.

> *"The opposite of self-assertiveness is self-abnegation — abandoning or submerging your personal values, judgment, and interests. Some people tell themselves this is a virtue. It is a 'virtue' that corrodes self-esteem."*
>
> **~ Nathaniel Branden**

Criticism that is obviously intended to hurt says a good deal more about the person making the criticism than it does about us. There is no need to retaliate in kind. In refusing to engage with the other person's game, you remain above the fray and maintain your dignity; you control your emotions and so have a much better chance of commanding the situation. In such instances, calmly state your position. "I do not agree with what you're saying. I am an honest and fair person, and nothing will change that."

Remember that your perceived weaknesses have the potential to become your strengths, depending on how they are leveraged.

So if you're identified as being 'too picky,' keep in mind this can be interpreted to mean that you have high standards. If someone describes you as stubborn, it likely also means that you're persistent. There is a positive side to virtually every attribute if it is reframed with confidence and kindness. An assertive person with a healthy degree of self-acceptance can find value in an honest evaluation and be able to use the information to improve not only the self, but also relationships with other people.

When it's your turn to broach a touchy topic — to mention something that's bothering you or blocking your potential — remember the guidelines for assertive communication. Own your statements. Use "I" language, and sometimes it's helpful to introduce the negative with a positive: "I really appreciate all the good work you've done, and it frustrates me when you promise to do something and then don't follow through. Can we find a solution?"

Few people enjoy confrontation, but until the problem is identified, it's not going to be solved. By stepping up and expressing the issues, everyone has an opportunity to move forward in a healthy way. We often get worked up about the encounter, but once the conversation begins, it's usually not nearly as difficult as we imagined.

It's not necessary to become defensive, even if the other party escalates things. Remain calm and clear, and while you certainly don't want to get pulled off topic, remember to listen. Stay on task and develop a solution. If other issues are identified in the course of the conversation, hold them until the presenting issue is resolved, and then take on the next point.

The other side of this coin is that assertiveness also gives you the ability to deliver compliments and affirmations. The same principles for assertiveness apply here: relax, be clear, and be sincere. When we take the time to notice something we like about a person, be it simply to comment positively on something they are wearing, a new hairstyle, or their manner of handling an issue, we improve our relationships. We not only make the other person feel good, but we may even learn something about our self by paying attention to those things we appreciate and perhaps might like to emulate.

Each of us has a level of responsibility for every relationship. Whether at work, at home, or with the people we encounter every day, a part of every human connection is up to us. By learning to express our self clearly, calmly, and assertively, each encounter will be improved.

Harassment

Choosing to behave in an assertive way will not necessarily guarantee that people will stop being difficult, that all of your problems will be solved, or that you will be happy. But being assertive will certainly increase your chances that these things will happen.

There are situations, however, where assertiveness will not result in resolution. If you feel that your safety is in danger, do what you can to remove yourself from the situation.

Unfortunately, for some people, encounters with bullying don't end when we graduate from school. Aggressive, anti-gay behavior is inexcusable, but it's not your responsibility as an individual to sally forth and personally confront it at every possible opportunity. You may well choose to join an LGBTIQ organization or movement that does this and to lend your support and energy in this direction, but if you find yourself in a situation that has the potential to lead to violence against you, discretion really is the better part of valor.

By all means, stand your ground when you can. Use assertive language to counter abusive or homophobic language. Once you've said your piece, feel free to walk away; depending on the situation, you might even allow your opposition to have the last word. Not everyone will be swayed by your opinions, your logic, or your feelings, but if you've said all that can be said, let it go and recognize that it's time for you to move on.

If the situation threatens to turn physical, don't hesitate to contact the police. This is equally true if your partner or a family member resorts to physical violence. Part of being assertive is asking for professional help in these situations. No one has a right to abuse you. No one. Assert your right to safety by whatever means necessary, and never apologize for protecting yourself.

Self Defense

Today, more and more members of the LGBTIQ community are learning self-defense techniques in order to enhance their personal safety and improve their self-confidence. This does not necessarily mean enrolling in traditional martial arts, karate or judo classes, but taking advantage of the many other options available. In larger cities, self-defense classes designed specifically for LGBTIQ persons are now being taught. In addition to increasing self-confidence and equipping a person to better deal with possible physical danger, self-defense classes also provide an excellent form of exercise, and the opportunity to meet new people and make new friends. As an LGBTIQ person, why not check out what classes are available in your particular area?

Make It a Habit

If you've been caught in situations where you've been less than assertive, use it as an opportunity to learn. Briefly replay the conversation in your head and rewrite the script. Imagine what you could have said that would have been truthful, respectful, and assertive. There is no need to constantly rehash. Look at the situation, analyze it and learn, then let it go and move on. If a similar situation comes up again, you'll be better prepared to respond appropriately. Take a breath and go for it.

Like any skill, assertiveness improves with practice. You may find real benefit in working with an assertiveness trainer or therapist with experience of the special issues faced by LGBTIQ people. In addition, there are plenty of useful print and Internet resources. Whichever path you choose, the only really effective way to become assertive is to learn by doing.

As you work on your assertiveness skills, remember to set realistic goals, and be sure to monitor your behavior and responses. Becoming assertive is a process that takes patience and persistence, but assertiveness skills really can be learned by anyone prepared to put in the effort. With practice, you might be amazed at the difference it will make to your interactions with other people — and to the way you feel about yourself.

Keep in mind that being assertive means that you can express not only feelings of frustration and disagreement, but also of endearment and affection. When you feel comfortable expressing these feelings, it can deepen your relationships and make them more satisfying for you and for those you care about.

The Big Picture

In this chapter we have touched on only a few basic assertiveness skills. I would encourage you to continue to develop your ability in this important area, perhaps taking a course in assertiveness specifically designed for LGBTIQ people. If no such course is available in your area, then perhaps you could petition the HR, training division, or LGBTIQ network in your company or organization to bring such training in. If this is not possible, then a general assertiveness course would also be helpful. Such courses are not usually expensive, and it is well worth checking around to see what is or might be available.

Another way to both practice your assertiveness and put it to work is to speak up for others. You'll learn to communicate clearly, making requests not only for yourself, but on behalf of others. Sometimes this makes the asking easier, because it is less personal and so feels like less of a risk.

Many organizations advocate for the rights of the LGBTI community. Practice your skills by volunteering with one of these organizations, or an organization that advocates for another group. Making phone calls, attending rallies, conferences or conventions, and writing letters on behalf of others can reinforce your newfound confidence. It also provides you with an opportunity to support others and to give back to the community.

"Respecting diversity of sexual orientation and gender identity should be recognized as a matter of strategic importance to every company competing in the global market for talent."

~ Lord John Brown, BP former CEO"

Developing your skills as an assertive person will give you the confidence to live as a happier LGBTIQ person. You are a person of worth, and you have the right to express your needs, desires, and feelings. You have the right to assert your opinions and to live your life. There is very little risk in being assertive, but there are great rewards.

Put aside your fears, embrace your self-worth, and forge ahead. You'll be glad you did.

Chapter Eight

On the Road to Happiness

"Happiness is not something ready made. It comes from your own actions."
~ **Dalai Lama XIV**

Let's begin this chapter with a simple question: if your goal is to be happy, how will you know when you've achieved it? If you awoke tomorrow and things had changed and you knew you were happy, what would be different? What would tell you that you were happy?

And now for the biggie: what steps do you need to take to make this happen?

We will be looking at these important questions, at what it takes to be happy — and strategies we gay people can use to help accomplish this — much more closely in this chapter. But before we begin our discussion on happiness, we first need to decide just what it is we are talking about. Let's look a little closer at what this thing we call happiness really is, this thing so many gay people want, but somehow seldom seem to have enough of.

In this chapter, we'll see that happiness is a state of mind, one of contentment and wellbeing, which allows us to feel relatively secure and unworried. We'll see that happiness is an attitude rather than an occasion, a verb rather than a noun. It is something we do much more than something we are. And we'll look at how you can 'do' more of it — at how you can bring more real happiness into your life.

Happiness Is an Art — But Also a Science

No matter our sexual orientation, no matter our past, no matter our genetic make-up, it *is* possible to achieve deep, enduring happiness. And what is more, as LGBTIQ people and as human beings, we are entitled to it.

The truth is, we have far more power over our own happiness than most of us realize. Research conducted by Dr. Sonja Lyubomirsky, Professor of Psychology at the University of California, Riverside, offers scientific evidence to support this. In each of us, some of our happiness level is inborn. It's true: some people are just born happier, and they have an innate tendency to find the sunny side of things. This inborn level of happiness accounts for about fifty percent of our happiness ranking.

Lyubomirsky and her team of researchers also discovered that ten percent of happiness comes from circumstances: a good marriage, good health, food on the table, a job that we enjoy. But overall the rich are no happier than those earning much less. Of course, enormous stressors like poverty, homelessness, and abusive relationships can be massive barriers to happiness, but as long as people are safe and earning enough to cover basic living expenses, the research shows that their happiness level does not fluctuate with income level.

Paradoxically perhaps, being in a fulfilling relationship or working at a job you enjoy are great gifts, but these things only account for a relatively small percentage of overall happiness.

If approximately fifty percent of our happiness level is predetermined at birth, and ten percent is dictated by circumstances, we are left with about forty percent. That's the percentage of happiness over which we *do* have influence. And that forty percent is more than enough to make a huge difference in our lives.

Lyubomirsky's research indicates that all of us can develop proper attitudes and cultivate happiness habits that will allow us to live happier lives. In so many ways, *happiness is a choice that we can make.*

I believe this to be so important that I'm going to repeat it:

Happiness is a choice that we can make.

It *is* possible to create our own happy-ever-after. It takes some effort, because cultivating happiness is an active, ongoing endeavor, but a happier life is well within the reach of every single LGBTIQ person. Happiness is within *your* reach!

Why It Matters

Forty percent is less than half; so perhaps at first glance this number doesn't seem as significant as the fifty percent of our happiness quotient that's innate. But it's certainly a larger percentage than the ten percent dictated by circumstances. Yet circumstances are the things so many people blame for their lack of happiness.

How would you feel if you owned forty percent of the entire world's gold? Wouldn't that be an awful lot of gold bullion? Wouldn't it make you rich beyond your wildest dreams? What if you owned forty percent of the world's happiness? Would that be enough for you?

The point is that you *do* own forty percent of the world's happiness — forty percent of *your* world's happiness. That really is a big piece of the happiness pie!

And it's something that we ourselves can control, so it makes sense to use it to our own advantage.

Think of it this way: we are all born with certain genetic strengths and weaknesses. Perhaps you have a family history of diabetes. There's nothing you can do to change your genetics, but there are many things you can do to lower your risks: watch your diet, exercise, avoid smoking, work with a physician to make sure you're getting the proper screenings, and so forth. So it is with happiness. You're wired a certain way, certainly, but when it comes to enjoying life, genetics are not destiny, and there is much that you can do to increase your own experience of happiness.

One of the greatest myths about happiness is that it is found, stumbled upon, or discovered: that it happens *to* us. The truth is that it is cultivated. Happiness levels may spike when something great happens, but without effort they tend not to change in the long term. If you are truly happy today, you'll probably be equally happy tomorrow — even if your circumstances change.

Just like every other emotion, happiness is not an all-or-nothing proposition. Even happy people get the blues, and even the most morose of us laugh from time to time. Often, those who have faced seemingly insurmountable, crushing circumstances are able to find happiness. Some of their resiliency might be innate and attributable to the level of happiness they were born with, but this certainly isn't the whole story. For so many, *happiness is chosen.*

Overcoming Barriers

For gay people, perhaps the biggest single barrier to happiness is homophobia, a subject we discussed in Chapter 2. Living in a culture that discriminates and sees sexual orientation as an excuse to bully and persecute creates an additional layer of stress that can have long-term implications, including damage to self-esteem and self-acceptance (see Chapter 6). Add to that other life stresses that generally occur within the population, and we might begin to imagine that true happiness is next to impossible for anyone who is gay.

Nothing could be further from the truth.

While living in a world that discriminates and oppresses has its challenges, you *can* still choose to be happier, and you *can* develop ways to increase your happiness quotient.

Think back to the opening questions of this chapter. Do you have an idea of what makes you happy?

Most of us are actually not that good at predicting what makes us happy. Often we focus on the future and on specific events that we believe will bring contentment: "Once I get that promotion ..." or "When I've met the right person ..." or "When I no longer face discrimination... then I will be happy."

> *"Learn to value yourself, which means: fight for your happiness."*
>
> **~ Ayn Rand**

Rarely is this the case. Many people consistently overestimate the level of happiness a given event will bring. By focusing on the 'someday,' the circumstances that might arrive in the future, we miss the opportunity to live, to enjoy the beauty of the moment, and to appreciate the happiness that we can experience in the here and now.

Author and physician Dr. Ian Smith believes mindfulness to be an important aspect of happiness. It's a good idea to check in with yourself from time to time, to think about and focus on the things that make you feel good. It can help to take a periodic 'happiness inventory' and ask yourself, "How happy am I in this moment? Why do I feel this way? What do I appreciate in the here-and-now? And what can I do or change in order to bring more happiness into my life?"

When we know what our happiness triggers are, we are more likely to incorporate them intentionally into our life and to mentally retrieve and relive them when we need a happiness boost.

Simply by doing this exercise, it's likely that our happiness level will increase. When University of Pennsylvania professor Martin Seligman worked with a group of severely depressed people, he merely asked them to take a moment each evening to write down three good things that had happened during the day. These were not life-changing events, but simple things: a phone call from a friend, a sunny afternoon, a delicious cup of tea. Within fifteen days, the depression rate among the patients had fallen from severely depressed to mildly or moderately depressed in a massive ninety-four percent of the group's members.

If such a simple habit can bring about dramatic results among even the severely depressed, it stands to reason that there are other things that we can do to build and expand our own experience of happiness.

Choices

As a child, a good friend of mine, Jonathon, suffered from severe scoliosis. His spine was curved and seriously misaligned, and he required numerous surgical operations in order to correct this. "There were so many operations," he told me. "And I had to spend a lot of time in hospital after each one." In the beginning, Jonathon found himself resenting each operation. The pain the operations caused seemed much worse than the condition they were trying to correct, and lying in a hospital bed week after week was the last thing a young boy wanted to do.

"Then another boy was brought into my ward," he said. "He was about a year older than me but he seemed different. He laughed more and talked more, and I couldn't understand how he kept so upbeat. The kid had lost both legs; both had been amputated, and he was in pain a lot, as well."

"We got to talking, and we got pretty close. It seemed he had a philosophy. Just a kid, but with a philosophy. He said he just focused on what was there, and not what wasn't there. He said: "I figured out I gotta choose. I can either choose to see the shit or choose to see the sunshine. But I'm the one who chooses."

The boy's words had a powerful impact on Jonathon, and ever since he had done his best to choose to see the 'sunshine' on even the cloudiest of days.

Happiness and joy are like that. They are something we can choose in our lives. Sometimes joy will spring up automatically, almost taking us by surprise, but more often it is we who must choose it. In choosing it, we ourselves create it. Once we've chosen our attitude, we can lay out a roadmap toward greater happiness.

Although some of the barriers to happiness may be different for us as LGBTIQ persons, the solutions may not vary much from one sexual orientation to another. We are, after all, human. We all feel joy and pain, and we all make choices on how to live our lives. The human experience of happiness is accessible to each one of us if we, like Jonathan's friend, *choose* to see the sunshine.

Changing the Brain

Like all living things, we have survival instincts. Innately, it seems, our brain wants to hold onto negative experiences. In order to survive, we need to learn from those things that have had a negative impact and attempt not to repeat them. This might be good for the survival of the species, yet as individuals we must not only learn, but also find a way to mentally let go of the negatives, or we won't be able to move into a happier, more positive future.

The flip side of this is that good experiences tend to pass through our memories far too quickly — unless we are mindful of them.

Taking a moment to appreciate good things will help to cement them in our minds.

Let's again revisit the question: "What makes you happy?" For now, let's focus on the 'small' things that bring you happiness. We want to create a stockpile of these and the good feelings they produce, and hold them in reserve. They'll be important as we continue our exploration of happiness. Perhaps your happy moments include a sunny day, a great book, or a private joke with a friend or family member.

Try to remember some happy things from your past, but also be mindful of joy-filled moments as they occur now. Notice the beauty and the joyful things that are always around, and take a moment to appreciate that beauty and joy and to hold them in your memory. When you're confronted with things that are less beautiful, you'll be able to draw on these happy experiences to get you through.

University of California, Berkley neuropsychologist Dr. Rick Hanson advocates the idea of replacing negative thoughts with positive thoughts so that we refocus and retrain our brains. Hanson stresses the importance of being mindful of both positive *and* negative experiences, as both can be instructive.

His technique for changing the brain requires acknowledging — not denying or suppressing — the negative feeling, and taking time to experience the loss, the frustration, the pain. Once the negative is fully realized and understood, which could take only a moment for small stressors or much longer for deep grief (although good therapy can accelerate this process), the next step is to find a way to minimize or let go of the negative.

Relax a little, take a deep breath, use your imagination to draw a mental circle around any harmful thoughts, as if placing them in a balloon, and then release them, letting them float off and leave. Perhaps cry a little. Tears can have a wonderful, healing, therapeutic effect, and they can be shed by the emotion of happiness as well as sadness. After you're able to let go of the negative, it's time to shift your focus to something positive. Perhaps it's a happy memory of someone you're grieving, or remembering a frustrating project from the past that you've finally completed successfully.

Glen is a transgender client of mine who employed this technique effectively at work. He had been working on a big project for weeks, but his boss was unsatisfied with the result and sent it back for yet another revision. Glen's frustration made it difficult for him to make the necessary changes, and he felt himself stalling. "Then I remembered our conversation, and began to assess why I was so upset. It occurred to me that I was taking the rejection personally, as if my boss was rejecting me as a person."

Glen interrupted this negative train of thought and, after a little reflection, he could see that perhaps the way he was feeling had a lot to do with the way he had been treated in the past, when he had been rejected by his family for becoming the person he felt he truly was. Perhaps it was his self-doubt, and not his boss, that was making him feel so bad.

It took him a few moments to remember that, up until now, his boss and he had a good relationship, and his work had often been affirmed. He reminded himself that his boss wanted him to be just as successful with this project. By reasserting these things, Glen was able to get past the negative feelings that were blocking him, and so improve the project — in his boss's eyes and in his own.

By taking just a little step back, learning to interrupt the negative and shift the mind to something more positive, we can retrain our brains to access more happiness. Genetics and innate impulses can be tempered with a little training and some thoughtful effort. By regularly using our mind and our brain to access more positive states, we can create fresh neural pathways and so alter the way we function and feel. To use the language of neuroscience, 'neurons that fire together wire together.'

Our brain has an amazing capacity for learning, and it's up to us to teach our own brain the pathways to happiness.

The Limits of Success

As you build your happier life as a gay person, remember that 'success,' however it is defined, is not the key to real joy or contentment. The perfect job, the right relationship, healthy bank accounts might be worthy objectives, but experience and research concur: they alone will *not* make you a happier person. Research has confirmed over and over again the truth inherent in that oldest of sayings: money just cannot buy happiness. Though it might seem to go against logic and so many of society's beliefs, it is a fact.

A hallmark study conducted by economist Richard Easterlin clearly demonstrated this truth. Easterlin's seminal research, conducted in the 1970s, established that people are happier when they make enough to cover life's basics, but as long as the bills are paid, there is no further correlation between income and happiness.

More recent research by Adam Davidson, published in the *New York Times,* indicates that "most rich countries have reported increases in happiness as they become richer," – but the exception is the United States. Although the US on the whole is richer now than it was when Easterlin conducted his research, on average Americans are no happier now than they were then. (This could be influenced by a number of factors, including high unemployment and the vast disparity of wealth in the US.)

According to the American Psychological Association, as consumption has increased in recent decades, there is nothing to indicate that Americans' wellbeing has increased. "Compared with their grandparents, today's young adults have grown up with much more affluence, slightly less happiness and much greater risk of depression and assorted social pathology," says psychologist David Myers, author of *The American Paradox: Spiritual Hunger in an Age of Plenty*. "Our becoming much better off over the last four decades has not been accompanied by one iota of increased subjective well-being."

Happiness Habits

While material circumstances have only a small impact on the amount of happiness we experience, the mental work of happiness — retraining our brain and being mindful of our happiness — is an important step toward a happier life.

There are also several practices that have been found to increase happiness and life satisfaction, and we will be looking at some of these shortly. Simply practicing these things, regardless of your motivation, seems to increase life satisfaction. Some of these are mental shifts — allowing and training yourself to see things a little differently — while others are activities that you can use straight away. By adding a few happiness habits and healthy practices, your life as a happy LGBTIQ person really does have the potential to flourish.

Practice Gratitude

"It's not happy people who are thankful — it's thankful people who are happy."

This old adage is actually backed up by years of scientific research. In a 2005 study, Drs. Seligman, Steen, and Peterson conducted an experiment in which subjects participated in a gratitude visit. Each subject wrote and delivered a letter to someone who had been especially good to them but who had never been thanked. Amazingly, those who participated in the exercise reported increased happiness levels that lasted for one month after the letter.

In 2003, Drs. Emmons and McCullough studied the impact of keeping gratitude journals on a weekly basis. Those who recorded things for which they were grateful felt better both physically and emotionally and had a more positive outlook on life. In addition to a twenty-five percent increase in happiness levels, journal keepers also accomplished more and exercised more. By doing something as simple as counting our blessings, and being grateful for them, it *is* possible to increase our experience of happiness significantly.

When we remind ourselves that even in the darkest of times, beautiful things, large and small, happen each day, then we restore and maintain our mental and emotional balance. In recognizing the many positive things there are in life, we cultivate an authentic gratitude for all that is right with existence.

> *"Gratitude opens your eyes to the limitless potential of the universe, while dissatisfaction closes your eyes to it."*
> **~ Stephen Richards**

A gratitude journal in which you list positive experiences or aspects of your life can be helpful in remembering the best parts of your day, and when you do this, your happiness quota increases. If you have food to eat and a place to live, celebrate these things. When you manage to catch an earlier bus, train or flight, when you discover a great book, see a really good movie or see a rainbow, when the bakery has your favorite pastry, record these happy things with a word of thanks for the positive aspects. These things really are gifts; make sure you take the time — and have the awareness — to appreciate them.

Why not go further with this exercise by exploring your past and identifying key people in your development? Perhaps it was the friend who first listened to you as you were questioning or trying to come to terms with your sexuality. Maybe it was a teacher who inspired you, or who took the time to help you. Or maybe it was a family member or someone else who stood up for you at a critical time. Remember these people and incidents with gratitude for the ways they have helped and shaped you.

You might even want to write thank you notes to some of these people. Whether you send them is up to you. Expressing gratitude in writing can help you to understand their roles in your life and to appreciate all those people and events that have brought you to the place you are. You may recognize a turning point you hadn't seen before, or better understand what was going on in a relationship. Be grateful even for the difficult lessons. Everything and everyone from your past has had an influence on who you are now. And remember that, like everyone else, you are a work in progress.

When we accept these gifts with a grateful heart, we learn to appreciate all that we have been given and are reminded of how good life really is. These are important keys that fit neatly into the locks and open the doors to happiness.

Moving forward, do your best to say thank you to the people who are currently in your life — your family and friends. Be gracious to the person at the check-out counter of your local supermarket and to the person who bags your groceries. Acknowledge your waiter and remember to say a kind word or two to lighten their day. Express appreciation for the work being done on your behalf. Thank friends when they are supportive and when they are honest. Thank your boss for being a mentor. Thank your partner for all the small, routine, insignificant things that he or she does for you and with you. Develop a habit of saying thank you — and make sure it's sincere.

And here is a very important point: Remember to express gratitude for the person that *you* are. Be thankful for your gifts and skills — the unique blend of talents that you bring to the world. Be grateful for your body, in all of its marvelous complexity. Be grateful for your sexuality. All of these things make you the unique individual that you are. Embrace them, and be grateful for the ways they have shaped your life.

All we have is this moment. Breathe deep and be grateful in all things. It will improve your happiness level, guaranteed.

Gratitude turns what we have into enough, which helps to teach us another important lesson — contentment. A happy life is not about our stuff, our status or, despite our longings, even about our relationships. Contentment brings a level of happiness that grasping and straining never can. What you have and who you are — they are enough for now. As you learn more, you may be able to do more, so continue to strive to better yourself and to work on developing as a complete person, as well as a LGBTIQ person. Continue to press on, but be mindfully grateful for what was and what is as you move forward.

> *"In ordinary life we hardly realize that we receive a great deal more than we give, and that it is only with gratitude that life becomes rich."*
> **~ Dietrich Bonhoeffer**

Practice Kindness

In addition to gratitude, research has also shown that simple kindness can be a major contributor to the levels of happiness any of us experience.

One study, conducted by a University of California research team over a two and a half month period, looked at people who performed various acts of kindness. As was the case with gratitude, they found that even a month after the study concluded, participants were reporting significantly higher levels of happiness.

Another recent study, conducted by the Department of Psychology of Tohoku Gakuin University in Japan, looked into the relationship between kindness and happiness. The results indicate that happiness was increased simply by counting kindnesses performed over the course of a week, an exercise that also increased both kindness and gratitude in the participants.

If you've ever done a good deed (and of course you have!), you already know that it is an instant mood booster. The equation is really quite simple: Those who feel good do good. But doing good also makes us feel good, emotionally and physically. Those who practice acts of kindness have been shown to have fewer illnesses, to rebound from illnesses more quickly, to have a higher pain threshold, and to suffer fewer stress-related illnesses.

The impact on psychological health is even more remarkable. Those who consistently perform acts of kindness have reduced stress, decreased incidence of depression, lower feelings of hostility, increased sense of self-worth, and more joy, optimism, and emotional resilience. In other words, they have more happiness!

"There's so much strength in kindness"

~ Labi Siffre '(Something Inside) So Strong'

Acts of kindness help us to focus beyond the self, allowing us perhaps to be that person who restores someone else's faith in humanity. Even small acts have the capacity to change lives, and they can even change the world. None of this means that we have to fall into some 'good boy' or 'good girl' snare; being kind, like being gay, may in fact be our nature — and it certainly appears to be in both our interest and the interest of others.

With research to back it up, it seems clear that doing good for others will also do good for us. It's a habit that can be developed anywhere, at any time, at little or no cost. Actively work on this, make it a habit, and your happiness quota will automatically sky rocket.

Volunteering and advocacy are other expressions of kindness that pay happiness dividends. LGBTIQ groups, organizations that advocate for political, legal, and social change, HIV and sexual health charities, all depend on volunteers to help the wheels go around.

You might enjoy working one-on-one with a struggling teen, starting an older persons' LGBTIQ group, or you might prefer something less personal, like volunteer admin work. Regardless of the way you choose, you'll be helping others, and these acts will make a difference in their lives and in your own.

> *"The simplest acts of kindness are far more powerful than a thousand heads bowing in prayer."*
> ~ **Mahatma Gandhi**

Beyond acts of kindness, the next and larger step is to *think kind thoughts*. Again, remember neural pathways and 'neurons that fire together wire together.' As we've already seen, the mind is a powerful tool in our ability to create happiness. Eastern religions in particular have long understood this philosophy — the heart-mind connection to our thoughts and actions.

"There is no need for temples; no need for complicated philosophy," said the Dalai Lama, spiritual head of Tibetan Buddhism. "Our own brain, our own heart is our temple; the philosophy is kindness." Practice a philosophy of kindness and you will retrain your brain and alter your mind, making for a better relationship with yourself as well as with others. This is sure to bring greater happiness and joy into your life.

Being kind doesn't always involve doing things for others or offering a handout. Sometimes the best thing we can do for people is not to bail them out, but rather to suggest another way. There may even be times when we need to say "no" to a request that we think is ill advised. There are ways of doing this with grace, dignity, and kindness. Remember that being kind doesn't mean being gullible.

Above all, be kind to yourself! See yourself as a person of worth, doing the best you can with what you have. You are gay, and you are human. Like every other person, you also have your emotional baggage, and you're working to unpack it. What we can handle varies from day to day. Acknowledge that you're continuing to grow into the person you're becoming, and that the person you are also deserves the benefit of the doubt. Remember that you, too, deserve your own generosity, compassion and kindness.

> *"When words are both true and kind, they can change our world."*
> **~ Gautama Buddha**

Kindness is one of the most important habits we can develop on our journey to real and sustainable happiness. It is an essential key to a life lived creatively, one in which we remain healthy physically, mentally, and emotionally. Kindness costs little but pays huge dividends in our own lives and in the lives of those we touch. It's a habit that paves the way to a happy life.

Practice Forgiveness

Now we come to a practice that many gay people may find hard: forgiveness. As LGBTIQ people we may well have experienced bigotry and prejudice, unfairness and injustice. Some of us might even have been the victims of violence or of deliberate cruelty. "Don't talk to me of forgiveness!" they might say. "I hate the bastards!"

And who can blame them? The problem is that in keeping this anger alive, we block the road to any real and lasting happiness.

When Nelson Mandela died in December 2013, he was remembered not only for his powerful leadership, but also for his great capacity to forgive. Mandela had been imprisoned for twenty-seven years because he refused to accept the injustice of discrimination based on race — apartheid. After his release, Mandela said, "As I walked out the door toward the gate that would lead to my freedom, I knew if I didn't leave my bitterness and hatred behind, I'd still be in prison." Mandela used his subsequent tenure as South Africa's president to foster racial reconciliation, work that never could have been accomplished had he not chosen to forgive.

We have all been wronged. Some hurts are so deep that they leave wounds on our lives, painful memories that shape us in powerful ways. Without forgiveness, those injuries continue to fester and never fully heal. They continue to draw energy from our lives, serving as massive obstacles on our journey into the happiness that we desire and deserve.

In my experience, so many people have the wrong idea about forgiveness. Forgiveness is not about forgetting what happened, and it's certainly not about allowing someone to continue hurting us. It does not mean that we have to love or like the person who has hurt us. Forgiveness doesn't deny the wrong done to us, nor does it mean that we condone that wrong. But by forgiving — by letting go of resentment, bitterness, and thoughts of revenge — the wrongs lose their power over our life. Forgiveness is not something done for the benefit of others; it's something we do for our self. It allows the wound to heal over. Yes, there may be a scar, but it's possible to live a full and happy life with a scar. A festering wound is a painful distraction on the path to a happy life.

While some do not believe it necessary or even possible to forgive offenses such as rape or other violence, I do not believe this to be true. Personal experience, and the work I have done with so many people over the years have served to deepen this belief.

Victims in these situations may feel temporarily empowered by harboring feelings of rage and revenge, but in my experience this simply keeps them in chains to their past. I regularly work with people, both female and male, who have experienced such terrible trauma. What needs to be understood — and this can take time — is that forgiveness is not for the person who has hurt us (they so often do not merit it), but that it is a means of freeing *ourselves* from the pain and shackles of the past. It is not even necessary that the offender realize they have been forgiven. There is a healing in forgiveness that far exceeds the benefits of holding on to bitterness and maintaining any kind of victim status.

While I believe forgiveness to be important to our psychological health and emotional wellbeing, this doesn't mean that accomplishing forgiveness is easy. It is a process that may well take time, and perhaps even the help of a professional therapist or skilled counselor, to bring about.

> *"Forgiveness is the answer to the child's dream of a miracle, by which what is broken is made whole again, what is soiled is made clean again."*
>
> **~ Dag Hammarskjöld**

Not everyone can consult with a therapist, however. Here is one possible process in the journey of forgiveness that you can do yourself, without professional help. It may need to be adapted, depending on the wrong and where you are on your journey. It's fine to omit steps, or to repeat steps when necessary, in order to come to the point where you feel able to let go and move on into a happiness that may previously have escaped you.

The first step is to WANT to forgive. If you're not ready, then acknowledge this, and try to determine why. If the wound is too fresh, it's perfectly acceptable to give it more time. If there are things yet unresolved, it may be necessary to resolve them if possible. Determine what it is that makes you reticent to forgive. Once you understand this, you may be willing and able to take the next steps toward forgiveness and release.

Spend some time reflecting on the situation. You may well have done this already, but this time do your best to reflect from a more objective perspective. What was said, what happened, and how do you understand these things now? Try to put yourself, if only for a brief time, in the shoes of the person who has hurt you. Can you feel any degree of compassion toward the person or persons who wronged you? Try to tell the story from the other person's perspective (which is not the same as taking his or her side). This may help you to identify those actions that are your biggest barriers to letting go.

Do your best to identify a way that the incident has helped you to grow. Even the most uncomfortable and unpleasant experiences contain some form of learning within them. Perhaps you gained new perspectives on yourself, or met new people, moved to another location, or changed your career direction. Finding an upside in the negative and moving on in a positive way — in other words, good living — is often the best 'revenge.' If you've already successfully moved past the incident or experience, forgiveness may be close at hand, and with it can come the most wonderful relief.

When you're ready, make the conscious and heartfelt choice to let go of your anger and resentment. Some people will write a letter to the person and then burn it as a tangible symbol of letting go and putting the past behind them. As you let go, remind yourself that you are a strong and capable person and that you still have much life ahead of you. Move forward into your future unencumbered by the weight of resentment and anger, and you will find the most wonderful joy and peace in this new attitude.

In addition to forgiving others, an important key to happiness is learning to forgive ourselves. Whatever mistakes we have made in the past, now is the time to set things right. Reflect on the situation and your role in it. If necessary and possible, and if to do so will not hurt another, make amends with those you may have wronged. You are a different person now, and you have learned from your mistakes. Consider what you've learned, and then let go. Stop rehashing the story in your head, and stop beating yourself up. Even in the face of tragic mistakes, there are ways to create something positive. But dwelling on the past won't change things. So forgive yourself, draw a line under the past, determine to do better in the future, and move on into your happier life.

Cultivate Optimism

We all face setbacks from time to time, and some of them may feel overwhelming. Optimism is *learning* to focus on the bright side: to expect, and to be prepared to work for, a desirable future, no matter what circumstances we encounter. It is an attitude that can be developed — one that we *can* cultivate.

Optimistic people believe that things work together for the good and that they have some control over events in their lives. Optimists have confidence that problems — past and present — can be corrected, changed, and overcome. They can imagine themselves succeeding. It may sound simplistic, but research has proven that by encouraging negative feelings, we will bring ourselves down, while imagining a more positive future will elevate and bring us up. In every situation there is a bright side. Research by Martin Seligman, among many others, has shown that adopting a positive attitude aids in stress management and improves our overall wellbeing.

When faced with a negative event — a quarrel with a friend, for example, pessimistic people tend to see events as internal (their fault), unchangeable, and pervasive: "I'm such a loser! I will never learn! I can't get along with anyone!" An optimist sees things as external, changeable, and limited: "It's not often that we have these tiffs. Perhaps there is some stress in my friend's life — or in mine. Now that we've cooled down, I should give them a call and see if we can talk."

Optimism, like happiness, exists on a continuum. Research conducted by Dr. Christopher Peterson of the University of Michigan found that optimism can be divided into three categories: 'big optimism,' 'little optimism,' and 'very small optimism'. Big optimism would include grand, invigorating ideas — such as "Homophobia will be completely wiped out in my lifetime." While little optimism is the optimism of the every day: "I can meet this deadline and produce quality work." Very small optimism is optimism at its most basic level: "I can get through this day, with all of its ups and downs, and in the end, everything will turn out all right." All three forms of optimism are important factors in improving our experience of happiness.

Initially the goal might be to cultivate our very small optimism, depending on our circumstances. It's fine to start where we are — and very difficult to start from anywhere else — and to ease ourselves into the *habit* of deeper optimism.

Some people have found that keeping a 'best possible self' diary can be really helpful in developing a happiness habit. Experiments by Dr. Laura King at the University of Missouri-Columbia pioneered this technique. During the experiment, subjects wrote for twenty minutes over four consecutive days about their 'best possible future selves.' This mental exercise was shown to increase optimism almost immediately, and to continue that feeling several weeks later.

If you'd like to try this, spend a set amount of time each day envisioning and writing about how you would like your life to be in a year, in five years, in ten years. What will you be doing, and whom will you be doing it with? Journaling of this nature can help you tap into your deepest desires and also help you to envision yourself as happy and successful down the road, thus creating optimism and positive thoughts and feelings in the present, as well as the future.

In therapy, we call this 'future pacing,' a really valuable strategy. The subconscious mind does not really distinguish between a real or imagined event, and by vividly envisioning ourselves in a positive future, we can reap some of the same benefits that would come if it were already the actuality — and increase our chances of bringing this about.

This is also a good time to put Hanson's brain training to use. When you discover yourself having a pessimistic thought, reflect on it briefly, work to put it aside, and then replace it with a positive thought. Replace thoughts such as "Mike broke up with me! I'm such a loser! I will be alone forever!" with "No, I am a good person ... I have many good qualities. I'm sorry it didn't work out this time, but we just weren't right for each other. I will find a great relationship someday."

There's no reason to be unrealistic or inappropriately upbeat if a given situation doesn't warrant it. Sometimes bad things really do happen, and it's all but impossible to find the bright side. In such cases it's best to adopt a stoical attitude, accepting what cannot be changed and moving on when possible. If you can find even a sliver of a silver lining, your happy side will win out eventually.

Optimism gives us resilience, as well as faith in the future and in all the good things that are yet to be. When we look forward with hope, we can be happier in the now.

Practice Time Control

Few things are more frustrating than wasted time. Getting stuck in traffic, or in endless meetings that seem to go nowhere, can push us over the edge and leave us feeling anything but happy. While it's not within our power to control every minute of our time in the ways we might like, we do have some influence. Choosing how we invest our time can pave the way to a happier future.

When asserting control over the clock, remember there are things you can change and those that you cannot. Lines at the post office and waiting at the doctor's office are part of life, and while there may be ways of planning that will help you avoid these time-wasters, from time to time we all get stuck. Breathe deep, and try not to let it get to you. Use the time to indulge in a little reading or send a few emails.

Other time wasters are within our power to address. We often say we "don't have time" to pursue hobbies, to exercise, or to gather with friends, but if these things are truly important to us and we really do want them to be priorities, our happiness will increase if we make the time for them.

> *"Your time is way too valuable to be wasting on people that can't accept who you are."*
> **~ Torcois Ominek**

Here's a simple exercise that you might like to try. Sit down and document how you actually spend your time, in half-hour increments, for the period of a week. What are some things that you're doing that are not really necessary, things that are not bringing happiness into your world? If you're spending five hours a day watching television, it might be time to cut back or to add something, like walking on the treadmill, to your TV time. If your commute into work or school is consuming more time than you'd like, it may be time to plan a new route or, if possible, move closer to your job. If that isn't possible, perhaps you can find a way to make the most of things, possibly by taking public transport and using the time to read, study, or meditate.

If you're spending a lot of time managing things, keeping your home clean and organized, for example, consider offloading some of your possessions or downsizing your home. Voluntary simplicity can pay real dividends in the happiness stakes.

Sometimes our biggest time-wasters are people. It takes only one high-maintenance friend in crisis mode to sabotage our best time-management efforts. While it's important to invest time in relationships, it may be time to set boundaries. If one of these friends gets you on the phone, or if you're meeting in person, set limits up front: "I'm really looking forward to our lunch, and I will have to be on my way by 2 for another appointment. So let's enjoy ourselves now." Then follow through, even if it means the only appointment you have is with yourself.

In our hyper-connected world, it's tempting to imagine that we must constantly be checking emails and must always answer the phone when it rings. Research indicates that multitasking doesn't really work. A study by Robert Rogers and Stephen Monsell, for example, determined that participants were slower when they switched tasks than when they repeated the same task. And research conducted by Drs. Joshua Rubinstein, Jeffrey Evans, and David Meyer in 2001 also demonstrated that people lost more time as tasks became more complex. By trying to do too much at once, stress increases, and the result is that very little is done well.

"Find the love you seek, by first finding the love within yourself. Learn to rest in that place within you that is your true home."

~ Ravi Shankar

Set parameters on when you'll respond to personal emails and phone calls. Allow yourself the luxury of time unfettered by electronics so that you can focus on one person or project at a time. The quality of your work and your relationships will improve, and you'll feel less stressed if you're not constantly reminded of every other person and project.

Simplify, simplify, simplify. Change what you can. If relationships or objects no longer bring you joy, it could be time to change them. It might not be necessary to completely remove them from your life, but it could be time to re-evaluate and establish different choices and priorities. Time management, like people management, is about setting priorities. Once your priorities are understood, make sure that the path to pursue them is clear. Jettisoning those things that weigh us down and spending more time doing the things we enjoy or that benefit us will put us on the road to a far happier life.

Practice Self-Care

The care and keeping of our physical needs is important to our overall happiness. Taking the time to care for yourself in these ways is a way to honor your whole self. Finding the right ways to boost your physical health will also increase your happiness potential.

Another client of mine, Jake, had encountered a number of personal and professional setbacks that had left him seriously considering suicide. Not wanting to hurt his family by ending his life, he developed a novel plan: suicide by exercise. Knowing that his heart was weak, he took up running each night, imagining that the strain would cause a heart attack. Each evening Jake donned his running shoes and took off for the park, exercising vigorously in an attempt to trigger his own death. But as he continued the practice night after night, Jake found not only that his health improved, but that his mood improved to the point where he got past his suicidal thoughts. Later, he was able to work on the psychological aspects that had brought him to such a low.

Exercise is good for so many of the things that ail us, and so it's no surprise that there is a link between happiness and exercise. Those who exercise regularly are happier than those who don't thanks to the release of endorphins and 'feel good' neurotransmitters such as serotonin and dopamine. Studies suggest that intense exercise is no more likely to produce feelings of happiness than a consistent schedule of moderate exercise. A brisk walk increases oxygen flow to the brain and throughout the body, and automatically reduces stress. This stress reducing quality is due not only to the body's chemical response, but also to diverting attention away from the stressor.

There is an abundance of research on the positive bio-chemical responses produced by exercise in people dealing with those enemies of happiness — anxiety and depression. For some, the social aspects of exercise are also a part of mood enhancement. A healthy body image and good health elevate feelings of self-esteem, and are also benefits of exercise. They are likewise hallmarks of happy people.

Whatever the reasons, the results are irrefutable: exercise increases our feelings of happiness. If you're not already active, consider a plan to get off the couch and get moving. Of course, please don't take the risk that Jake did. If you haven't exercised for some time, then ease yourself into it little by little. If you are really unfit, it's probably wise to consult your doctor before beginning an exercise program.

Another healthy habit that has an impact on happiness is getting adequate sleep. While a good night's sleep has a positive impact on happiness, consistently happy people are shown to sleep better. In our busy, 24/7 world, it isn't always possible to get adequate rest, but it is something to strive for. Be wary, however, if you're sleeping a lot without feeling rested. This might be a sign of a medical problem, so be sure to discuss this with your doctor.

Proper diet is another key to feeling good about our self. A balanced diet that limits processed, fatty, and high-sugar foods is a proven mood stabilizer. Be sure to eat plenty of fresh vegetables, fruit, and whole grains, and stay away from processed food as much as possible. This doesn't mean you can't indulge in the occasional treat; just try not to make it the mainstay of your diet. Eat out on occasion, but fresh, whole foods prepared at home — where you have complete control over what goes into the dishes — are usually the best nutritional choice.

Food is a sensory experience that should be enjoyed; so whatever you're eating, try to savor each bite with gratitude, mindful of the way it fuels your body — and your mind.

Some people have undiagnosed food allergies or sensitivities that can affect mood. Depression and irritability may be connected to diet. If you suspect that certain foods might be mood triggers for you, begin to monitor your eating and see if you can determine a pattern. This is an area of science that is still in relative infancy, so you may need to do your own research. Be careful whom you consult, not every medical professional or website is equally reliable, and some are attempting to sell you products that you may not need or tests that are not accurate.

And while the occasional cup of coffee or glass of wine isn't necessarily a bad thing, avoid overindulging in alcohol, which is a depressant, and caffeine, which can make you jittery. Sadly, gay bars are often places where people lose themselves in alcohol and end up doing some really unwise things. Do your best not to fall into this trap. As always, moderation is key. Too much of anything can be problematic. A happy life is a balanced life.

Practice Ethics

In our competitive society, with its emphasis on success and material accomplishment, it's easy to cut corners and to adopt a 'win at any cost' mind set. Such an attitude can tempt us into sometimes sacrificing ethical principles in order to gain or accomplish a goal or target. But this just might be a big mistake.

Recent research indicates that there is a link between ethical behavior and happiness. Dr. Harvey James of the University of Minnesota discovered a relationship between low tolerance for unethical behavior and life satisfaction. This may be related to the kindness-happiness correlation that we mentioned previously. Ethics are in a sense society's attempt at fairness, a means of doing what is best for the many — a way of encouraging us all to exercise consideration and practice kindness.

While the current data doesn't track whether ethical actions in themselves create happiness in an individual, it's not unreasonable to suppose that living an ethical life will bring us happiness in the long run. An ethical life requires honesty, compassion, and a certain degree of unselfishness — a respect and a regard for the well-being of others. Although our business climate might suggest that ethics are passé and unimportant in the quest for success (when success is seen as primarily the acquisition of money and material things), business and personal ethics are important in the quest for personal happiness.

Practice ethical behavior in the same way that you practice kindness: quietly, consistently, and deliberately. Be honest with the people close to you and those with whom you work. If you're working for a company that skirts the ethical edges, it might be time to find a new employer or to take a stand on your company's business practices. Your future happiness could depend on it.

Determine Meaning

The quest to understand the meaning of life is one of the most ancient pursuits there is. It is this that spawned the birth of religion. People seek a definitive answer, but there are no simple answers, especially when things go suddenly, horribly, or inexplicably wrong. There is no simple formula to explain why people suffer.

Psychiatrist Victor Frankl, who survived for three years in the horrors of Auschwitz concentration camp during the Second World War, observed this during his time of incarceration. He noticed that those who survived the camp were able to find meaning in even the most horrendous circumstances. "Everything can be taken from a man but one thing," Frankl wrote in *Man's Search for Meaning*, "the last of the human freedoms — is to choose one's attitude in any given set of circumstances, to choose one's own way."

Frankl's influential book emphasizes the importance of finding meaning and purpose in life, pointing to our personal responsibility to something greater than ourselves, tenets that seem at times to be so much at odds with the current culture. As a European, Frankl was perplexed by the American quest for happiness. He said, "It is the very *pursuit* of happiness that thwarts happiness."

A recent study by Roy Baumeister, Kathleen Vohs, and colleagues, sought to track the differences between a meaningful life and a happy life. When asked if their lives were happy and/or had meaning, people's responses indicated that 'happiness' tends to focus inward: our needs are met and things are going well for us. A 'meaningful' life tends to be outwardly focused, often expressed by helping people in need.

People who believe that life has meaning — even if not everything makes sense — tend to have less depression, more resiliency, and a better sense of wellbeing. In short, they are happier (by our definition of happiness). When we believe we are part of something larger than ourselves and we exist for a reason, we are able to cope, survive, and even thrive. Bigots may dislike us for who and what we are, false friends may turn their backs on us, and the rough winds may blow, but meaning will act as our compass and rudder, something that will guide us safely home to ourselves.

It's up to you to determine what has meaning in your life; no one can decide this for you. But it is important to figure this out. Relationships, intellectual achievement, creating a product or process, building a business, helping or inspiring others: the list of things that provide meaning is both infinite and personal. If you can identify what has meaning to you, and can invest in that meaning, you will feel happier and more optimistic; you'll find a place for yourself in the world and know happiness in that place.

There is no single, one-size-fits-all meaning to life. Perhaps there are as many different meanings as there are people. Your meaning does not need to be static; it can and probably will change as you change and grow. And this is as it should be.

Connected to this, it is also important to identify your own skills, gifts, and abilities, and to find ways to put them into practice. Discover and focus on what you're good at, and find ways to cultivate those talents that are not used at work or in study. Happy people spend time doing things that they are naturally good at. If you wish to experience greater happiness, then you will do so, too.

Fake It Till You Make It

What we are striving for is genuine happiness, not a fake veneer of false cheerfulness that cloaks a deeper sadness. We want our happiness to be true, honest, and authentic.

Which makes this next bit of advice seem counter-intuitive. But research begun in the 1970s and 1980s that continues today confirms consistently that acting happy, even when you're not, can bring about greater internal happiness.

In 1989, Dr Robert Zajonc conducted experiments that suggest even voicing vowel sounds that approximate a smile (the long e specifically) can be a mood lifter, and in 2009, psychologists at the University of Cardiff in Wales discovered that Botox injections that pull up the corners of the mouth improve overall mood. While we know that smiling makes a positive impression on others, it also has a positive effect on the one doing the smiling.

It seems amazing, but simple things like forcing yourself to smile can actually create feelings of happiness in you. Most of us can easily recognize a fake smile, so this may feel strained and uncomfortable initially. But with practice and persistence, smiling can become a habit that will influence your mood. In addition to smiling, articulate happy thoughts and have a positive attitude as much as possible. Listen to upbeat music and dance, whistle, or sing;

research indicates that singing for 10 minutes a day not only decreases stress but also clears the sinuses and may even promote longevity.

From time to time, say out loud, or in your head, "I am happy" or "This is a good day." All of these temporary mood lifters can actually help to build long-term, genuine happiness. Assume that good things are going to happen, and remember that you deserve to have good things happen.

By habitually creating positive experiences, neural pathways in your brain will be created and reinforced. You're actually 'rewiring' your brain so that it naturally *feels* happiness. Being mindful of your happiness and working to choose and create it will help your brain to form and deepen the neural pathways of wellbeing.

In Summary

As LGBTIQ people and as human beings, we deserve to be happy, and happiness can be cultivated. The fact is that we *can* determine our own path to happiness and contentment.

Happiness doesn't simply happen, and it isn't the result of circumstances beyond our control. When good things simply happen to us there is often a temporary increase in our happiness level, but generally this all too swiftly fades. There are exercises and habits that we can adopt and practice in order to make happiness more automatic.

Mindfulness and an awareness of our own happiness triggers are important strategies when cultivating happiness. Mindfulness is also key in many of the happiness habits: living each moment, having an awareness of the positive things that happen each day, savoring and keeping them in mind.

Even the most naturally happy people experience highs and lows. But happy people learn to deal with the downs in life and to rebound in healthy ways.

The more we explore and research the topic of happiness, the clearer it becomes that we have far more power over our own happiness than we realize. No matter your past, no matter your genetic make-up, no matter your sexuality or sexual orientation, deep, enduring happiness *is* possible.

The wonderful news is that by consistently *choosing* happiness, developing happiness habits, and cultivating joy, happiness really can be ours.

Chapter Nine

Finding Friendships

"A friend is someone with whom you dare to be yourself."
~ Frank Crane

As we accept or begin to accept our orientation as gay people, it's easy to feel a little lost. How are we to fit into this new gay world?

Our social programming and many of our experiences and friendships have revolved around heterosexuality. Now we find ourselves needing to branch out and connect with others like us as well. It's natural to want to be around people who share our interests and who understand what it is like to have feelings that are different from those of the majority. Simply put, we need gay friends as much as we need straight friends.

Perhaps even more than straight people, we LGBTIQ people need friends who are like us. Our gay friends accept us for who we are and help us to affirm who we are; they are able to empathize in ways that straight people sometimes cannot. These friends may introduce us to new concepts, new realities, and new ways of seeing things. Having friends curtails loneliness and increases our experience of happiness.

Because bisexual and transgender people represent a smaller percentage of the population, finding friends who are like you may be a little more difficult, especially if you live in more rural areas, far from the big cities. As part of your journey into happiness, however, it's important to have friends who truly understand you. Again, the Internet offers plenty of opportunity for this with its groups and associations. Make the effort to get to know others with whom you have things in common, and it will pay dividends.

Pause for a moment and ask yourself a couple of questions. Why do we have friends? What do we look for in friendship? Before reading further, please take the time to jot down a list of the things you want from friendship in the space provided below – we'll need this list a little later in the book.

No cheating now. If you really want to be happy, sometimes you have to do a little thinking. Just take a couple of minutes and write down some of the reasons you think friendship is valuable. Why do we have or want friends?

Done it? Good. This list will help you to better understand yourself and help you to clarify what you want and need from friendship. And it will be really useful when we come to the chapter about relationships — and later about sex.

Why I have friends

Cultivating Friendships

Friendships are not as spontaneous as we might imagine; they are living, breathing entities. They have to be created, nurtured, developed, and maintained by both parties.

Strong friendships that endure need to be cultivated and nourished on a regular, ongoing basis. Like so many other things associated with happiness, we have some control over this important aspect of our lives, and by taking an active role in fostering companionship with others, we can increase the level of happiness we experience.

Many friendships are born of convenience; we become close emotionally with those with whom we are close geographically. Think about your school friends. Unless you're still living in the same town or working in the same industry where you see each other frequently, it's unlikely that you've remained close.

The same thing happens with friends at work; although you and your friend have a lot in common while you have frequent contact, the relationship can all too often fade if one of you leaves the company or is moved to another division.

> *"Friendship is born at that moment when one man says to another: "What! You too? I thought that no one but myself ..."*
> **~ C.S.Lewis**

If we want gay friends, then it makes sense to go where gay people are, where we can be in close proximity. Since LGBTIQ people are everywhere, that isn't too difficult, but identifying them might be a little more challenging. As we've seen, being gay doesn't mean we walk around with labels on our foreheads.

Here are a few suggestions of where you can more easily find friends who are a lot like you.

Group Activities

These days there are various groups you can join where you can meet people who share your interests — and who have similar feelings. People are social creatures, and socializing leads to friendships. Don't be afraid to reach out and connect with others just like you.

If you're introverted or nervous about meeting new people, engage in an activity that has a built-in purpose or agenda. While you'll be expected to participate, there is less pressure to initiate one-on-one conversations until you're comfortable doing so. But don't wait too long! Keep in mind that the other person might be even more nervous or shy than you are. It's up to you to make the first move. Smile and start a conversation, and you're well on your way.

Especially if you are younger or have just recently come out, a LGBTIQ support group can offer you a safe place to process your feelings and to discover that you are not alone on your journey. A shared history and shared interests can be powerful building blocks for friendship. Find a group with members close to your age so you won't wind up hanging out with people with whom you have little in common. It's not unusual for members of support groups to do some social things as well, which will give you the opportunity to get to know others and can also serve as an introduction to LGBTIQ gathering places in your area.

In addition to support groups, check out social groups and events in your vicinity that are specifically for LGBTIQ persons. An Internet search may yield a range of LGBTIQ options, from drop-in centers and yoga classes to dinner-dances and comedy shows. Gay swimmers to gay hikers, gay reading to gay chorus groups, there can be a real diversity, but you need to look for them, and you may need to travel in order to access them.

Some churches have social groups and worship services specifically for LGBTIQ persons. Especially in urban areas, you'll find a wide variety of specialized LGBTIQ groups: LGBTIQ youth groups, LGBTIQ mature groups, LGBTIQ married people's groups, LGBTIQ parents groups. You may feel more comfortable in one than another, depending on your age, life experience, and expectations.

If you have difficulty locating a group in your area, connect with your local LGBTIQ organization (chances are, there's one nearby), or contact a LGBTIQ helpline for assistance in finding a social or support group that suits you. Gay magazines and newspapers can be useful in locating LGBTIQ groups and events in your vicinity. And, of course, you could always consider starting your own group. You can be sure that there are others, like you, who would welcome the opportunity to participate.

As we will see in the chapter on gay health, if you're struggling with addiction or substance abuse, self-help groups can help you turn your life around. LGBTIQ 12-step groups exist for drug addiction, alcoholism, even weight reduction and compulsive overeating. The support of other LGBTIQ people can be incredibly helpful in overcoming addiction and getting your life together, as well as providing a place to forge deep and lasting friendships.

"No person is your friend who demands your silence, or denies your right to grow."

~ Alice Walker

You can socialize with a purpose through volunteering. There are thousands of not-for-profit organizations that would be happy to put you to work for a few hours a week: hospitals, animal shelters, food kitchens, or charity shops to name but a few. Connect with an organization that you can support; people you meet there will automatically have something in common with you. To cultivate LGBTIQ friendships, consider working with a gay activist group campaigning for social change, or a sexual health or HIV awareness charity. Not all the volunteers and employees are LGBTIQ, of course, but many will be. Working together for a common cause can be a strong and enduring basis for friendship.

Magazines such as *The Advocate, Out,* and *Pink Mag* in the US, and *Gay Times, Pink Paper,* and *Diva* in the UK contain lists of groups that you might be interested in, so be sure to check them out. If you live in other countries, check what's available in your particular area; these days the gay press is becoming more prolific and, in some ways, even mainstream. You might be surprised at what is available.

Organizations such as Gay Pride also offer many ways to meet other LGBTIQ people. This organization is a hub for out-and-proud LGBTIQ people, and through its volunteer opportunities and public events, it's a great place to meet likeminded new friends. If you don't feel comfortable marching in the gay pride parade, you can always lend a hand behind the scenes, helping with drinks, sandwiches, costumes, or banners. And who knows, one day you might be marching proudly, too.

Bars and Pubs

If you're just a bit outgoing (and if you're not you can learn to be), gay bars can be excellent places to meet LGBTIQ friends. Even the smallest towns have places that attract LGBTIQ people, and in more urban areas there are bars that specialize in certain clientele — gay, lesbian, transgender; leather, rubber, suits and uniforms; bears, intergenerational, and so on. If you're looking to enhance your social circle with new friends, an LGBTIQ bar will present you with plenty of options.

Bring a friend or go alone, but either way, don't sit back and wait for something to happen. You're there to meet people, so take the initiative. Strike up conversations with anyone you like. Compliment an article of clothing, a haircut or style, or ask noninvasive questions, perhaps laced with humor: "I was trying to think of a clever introduction, but then I realized there's no such thing. Hi, my name's Tom, what's yours?" or "Hi. I'm taking an unofficial poll. Tell me, how do *you* keep busy on Sundays?" or even "Hi. Have you noticed how everyone seems to be after the same thing? Whatever happened to simple friendship? My name's Pat, how are you doing this evening?"

Put aside any sense of your own awkwardness and focus on making the other person feel comfortable. Remember to smile and make eye contact, but don't hold a gaze too long or it could be interpreted wrongly or make the other person feel uncomfortable. Keep in mind those things about body language that we mentioned in our chapter about self-assurance: be confident and open in your posture and with gestures. Touching is a proven flirting technique, so if you're the touching sort, make sure you're not giving off the wrong signals.

Speak clearly and at a moderate volume (appropriate to your surroundings). Keep conversation light; practice making small talk with a number of people to boost your confidence and to get a feeling for what's out there. Be selective about handing out or taking phone numbers, not every evening will produce a connection, and you may have to make quite a few visits before you find someone you'd really like to be friends with.

When you meet someone who looks like they might have the makings of a friend, do your best to establish common ground and shared interests without probing too deeply. Be sure to keep it light, especially in the beginning. Let them know when you'll be back again, and that you'd love to continue chatting and getting to know them better.

If you do come home with a phone number of someone with friend potential, be sure to follow it up with a call; don't wait for the other person to call you. If that goes well, you can easily arrange to meet up for coffee or a bite to eat. Agree in advance to 'go Dutch' and split the cost. This will allow you more time to get to know each other, and to get past the small talk to decide if a friendship is in the cards.

Social Media and the Internet

Facebook and other social media provide many additional ways to connect with people. While virtual relationships are a different animal than face-to-face friendships, there is value in connecting in this way as well. Facebook will help you to better know people you see every day and to reconnect with people you knew in your past, but with whom you may have lost touch. As you meet new people, gay or straight, you'll be able to add them as online friends. Social media can introduce you to friends of friends with whom you may discover you have a lot in common. If you feel a connection, send a friend request and see what happens.

> *"Friendship is unnecessary, like philosophy, like art... It has no survival value; rather it is one of those things which give value to survival."*
> **~ C.S. Lewis**

Online friends can fulfill many of our needs in regard to companionship, but don't spend all of your time in the virtual world. Don't be afraid to reach out to these friends, once you really get to know them, for at least occasional face-to-face connections.

The Internet also offers information on a multitude of other ways to connect with LGBTIQ people. Find a discussion group by typing your parameters into any search engine to discover what's out there. Just put 'gay' or 'LGBTIQ' in front of your interest and see what comes up. Or if you're looking for a lesbian, gay, bi, or trans social group in your area, for example, but you can't find one, the Internet offers you the opportunity to reach out to other LGBTIQ people and launch your own. Some groups meet online, but since building your circle of friends is your aim, find (or start) a local group that meets face-to-face. If you're looking for anything from an exercise class to a collectors' club, you'll likely be able to find it. Join up and discover something — or someone — new.

Sites like *Craigslist* also provide options for meeting others. There's no fee to post on Craigslist; you can write your own ad or respond to those that speak to your needs. Check out the 'strictly platonic' section, or write an ad of your own. Meeting with strangers is not without risk, so be careful with initial (and even subsequent) meetings, and only meet when you have seen a couple of photographs of your prospective friend and come to know them quite well online or on Skype.

The same goes for meeting people on Facebook, Twitter, and other social media. It is important to get to know people before giving them access to personal information. Privacy settings, in general, are also important to keep in mind since even people who are not your friends can still sometimes see your information.

Should you choose to meet someone, be sure to select a public place, with people around, and a definite timeframe for your meetings. ("Let's meet at the coffee shop at 7. I'll have to be on the road by 8:30 because I have an early meeting tomorrow.") Guard your personal information until you're a little more familiar. If things go well and you get a sense that you're both looking for the same things from this friendship, plan a second meeting to take things forward.

Roommates

For some single LGBTIQ people, sharing a house with other LGBTIQ people allows for both economical housing and built-in friend potential. Friends, or friends of friends, may be looking for someone to share a place, or you can check the Internet for this kind of housing option. Generally in these situations, each tenant has their own room, so you'll have a little space of your own, but there is also shared space, meaning you'll have the opportunity to socialize with others in the house.

Before moving in, meet all the roommates to be sure that you'll be comfortable with everyone. A mix of personalities can be wonderful, but not if your roommates' quirks make your life miserable. Also establish clear ground rules on things like privacy, finances, overnight guests, cleaning, and the use of shared spaces like the bathroom and kitchen. Living with others can be complicated, and while it may not be your first choice, it might also be a lot of fun, leading to a wider circle of friends.

Friends of Friends

As your circle of friends grows, and as your sexual orientation and gender identity become known, well-intentioned straight friends might try to introduce you to every other gay person they know. They may be hoping to spark a romance, or perhaps they understand that LGBTIQ people need each other. Whatever their intentions, accepting referrals from friends is another way to increase your circle of gay friends.

Just a note: friends and relatives who try to set you up may not understand that it's possible and healthy for you to have a platonic relationship with someone of your same sexual orientation. They may ask if the two of you are 'an item' or make assumptions about the nature of your relationship. This is society talking. For whatever reason, we like to pair people up, and this type of bias creeps into heterosexual and LGBTIQ relationships. There's no need to be defensive. You *need* gay friends! Don't be afraid to say so.

Work Friends

Remember to look for friends in the places where you already spend time. Chat with people at work and decide whether you have enough things in common to meet with one or more of them after hours. Remember that the people you meet all have friends, and may introduce you to someone you'd really get along with. Suggest 'the gang' meet for a drink after work to hash over a project or debrief after a meeting. Remember, in this initial stage the objective isn't necessarily a lifelong commitment; it's to discover where there is the basis for a friendship. Just remember to ask questions and show genuine interest in other people.

You may discover that this larger group is the perfect place for you, or you may discover one or two LGBTIQ individuals — either in the group, or friends of group members — with whom you would like to spend more one-on-one time. Pursue what feels comfortable for you.

> *"Wishing to be friends is quick work, but friendship is a slow ripening fruit."*
> **~ Aristotle**

If your workplace doesn't yield any friendship potential, consider other places where you can enjoy spending time and energy. Evening classes are filled with people who are looking to broaden their horizons by learning a new skill, so these folks are likely to be open to new friendships as well. In a few enlightened communities, particularly in metropolitan areas, there are classes geared specifically for LGBTIQ people.

There are other advantages to seeking relationships in this environment: taking a class provides you with a steady and regular commitment for a few weeks (or months), and it exposes you to new learning and experiences as well as to new people. Most classes encourage active discussion and collaboration, so it may be relatively easy to make connections with your fellow students. Class discussions can segue to events: an art class might lead to a trip to the art gallery or museum and a cooking class could lead to an impromptu trip to a specialty market. Remember that you are never too old — or too young — to learn something new. Evening classes often contain a broad spectrum of people from different backgrounds, so you're bound to find someone you get on well with.

These learning adventures could lead to long-lasting friendships, or they might be brief social contacts that last only for the duration of the class. Either way, they can be fun and absorbing. At the very least, you'll learn something interesting about the subject.

Combating Loneliness

We human beings can experience feelings of loneliness for many reasons, and it's not always due to a lack of friends. It's possible to feel lonely in a crowded room, to feel isolated even when surrounded by people we know and like. When we're not in a relationship, it's easy to imagine that we're the only ones without someone, but sometimes being in a relationship is the loneliest place to be.

As LGBTIQ people, we may face moments when we feel that no one in the world understands or cares about us. Sometimes our loneliness lasts for an evening, sometimes for a season. There are ways to get through lonely times, and there are things we can do to move past loneliness into a greater sense of happiness.

Remember that occasional loneliness happens to all of us, often visiting during times of transition: a breakup, a change of location, a change of job, a change in life circumstances, or even a change in personal goals. When loneliness strikes, remind yourself that even if you feel alone, you are not alone. There are those who care about you — always — even though they might not be near. And there are people out there, just like you, who are also feeling lonely and are looking for someone to connect with. You can't always expect others to take the first step. It is not a sign of weakness to show initiative and reach out to others first.

"Language has created the word loneliness to express the pain of being alone. And it has created the word solitude to express the glory of being alone."
~ Paul Tillich

When your life changes, it takes time to build new relationships that fit with the new you. Give yourself this time, and make the effort to create these new relationships.

In the meantime, take control of the situation. Call someone who will make you laugh or who will lend you a listening ear. Keep yourself busy. Take a walk, organize the kitchen, or read a book. Better yet, write a book, or undertake a similar ambitious goal like researching your genealogy or organizing your photos. Take advantage of this time and space to complete a big project. It will give your life focus and purpose.

Get out and do something you enjoy. Attend a lecture or a concert, or get involved in a community project or an exercise program. By all means interact with others at these places, but the point of getting out is to feel connected to something outside of yourself, not necessarily to meet people unless you're feeling social.

Distract yourself by calling someone you know who might be lonely. Research has shown that interacting with others who are feeling similarly decreases our own stress levels, and there is no doubt that it can help the other person, as well. Listen to your friend's problems, using empathy and insight. Sometimes misery enjoys company, and sharing a burden lessens it for both of you. You could be the answer to each other's loneliness. Be careful, however, not to wallow in self-pity, or to support your friend in doing this. Encourage each other and offer support in positive ways.

If your life situation allows it, get an animal companion — a pet. Having a furry friend at home to greet you can make a world of difference in combating loneliness and adding a sense of purpose. And walking the dog is bound to bring you into contact with other people — as long as your dog is friendly. Dog training sessions will introduce you to other pet owners, and this will also lessen feelings of loneliness. Lots of friendships, gay and straight, have been formed in this way. Just remember that an animal is more than an accessory. A pet is a wonderful companion, but it does bring with it a range of responsibilities and restrictions as well.

The difference between solitude and loneliness is perception. Learning to live comfortably with our self will assuage loneliness and allow us to appreciate times alone as well as times of interaction with others.

One More Thing

Just one more tip about LGBTIQ friendships: so often people put friendships on the back burner when they enter into an ongoing romantic or sexual relationship. Don't! When love is new, it's easy to dedicate all of our time to the new man or woman in our lives. Remember to make time for your friends as well, and please, when you're with a friend, talk about something in addition to Mr. or Ms. Wonderful. Focus on your friend and the things you've always enjoyed talking about. Regardless of the fate of the romance, keep in mind that sooner or later you're going to want your friends by your side.

Nurture them, and keep them close.

Chapter Ten

Gay Relationships

"There's this illusion that homosexuals have sex and heterosexuals fall in love. That's completely untrue. Everybody wants to be loved."
~ Boy George

There is little doubt about it: relationships — gay or straight — can be one of the most fulfilling aspects of life and living, but they can also be one of the most challenging.

Perhaps the most important thing when looking for a relationship, is to know what you want and why you want it. So let's start our exploration of gay relationships by asking a couple of questions. Why do we have relationships? What are *your* reasons for wanting to be in a relationship with someone? What do *you* look for in a relationship?

Take a few moments now and, in the space provided, jot down some of the reasons you want to be in a relationship. Make a list; see how many reasons you can come up with. What are you looking for? What do you want out of it? Do you want closeness? Acceptance? Validation? There's no hurry, but it really is best if you do it now. I'll be waiting for you here, on this page, so take your time; it will be worth the effort.

Reasons for a Relationship

____

____

____

____

____

____

____

____

Done? Come on — get real now! Grab a pen and make a list. This *really* is the best time to do it, so put on your thinking cap and get to it.

Did you make your list? If yes, then well done! You really are getting into things! If not, well, don't tell anyone and I won't.

Now compare your answers on why you want a relationship with the answers you gave as to why you have friendships on Page 208. What are the differences, and more especially, what are the similarities?

If you really thought it out and made lists in both chapters, you might find the number of items that are identical or similar to be quite striking. You could have listed things such as sharing, support, acceptance, caring, warmth, empathy, and validation on both lists.

So friendships and relationships usually contain many of the same ingredients — which is why friendships can turn into relationships. But it is also important to recognize that we don't necessarily need to be 'in a relationship' in order to access some of these same positive qualities. Understanding this can remove a lot of unnecessary anxiety and may even help reduce a feeling and attitude that is not at all attractive, and far from sexy — desperation.

Being in a committed relationship can be a source of great happiness, but only if we're in it for the right reasons. Relationships founded on mutual loneliness or on low self-esteem are bound for frustration and can bring untold unhappiness. If we are expecting someone to sweep us off our feet for the rest of our life, or to save us from ourselves, then we are in for real disappointment. A healthy relationship doesn't give us our self-worth, and it can't save us from our own inner turmoil. Only we can do that.

As we consider entering into a relationship, it's good to be clear about our own needs and expectations. If we bring *ourselves* into a relationship — not simply our wants and demands — and have an understanding of our reasons, our needs, and our desires, we begin from a healthier place. If we also have an understanding of the needs and desires of our *partner*, then we're ready for *partner*ship. Our relationship will be healthier, and it will be a good deal more satisfying and fulfilling.

Not every LGBTIQ person is interested in a committed relationship, of course, and it's not necessary to be in a partnership in order to be happy. But partnership can be a wonderful thing if you're with the right person: a person with whom you have much in common, as well as enough differences between you to keep things interesting.

Meeting People

The first step toward a committed relationship, of course, lies in meeting people. It's possible to meet lovers and potential partners in all the places we examined in the chapter on friendships. In fact, many of the best romantic relationships are rooted in friendship: in shared values, experiences, and goals. But if you're specifically looking for a relationship, joining a support group or volunteering at the shelter might not be the most direct route.

"I met my husband in a bar," said Andy. "For a long time I was reluctant to admit it to people, because it felt kind of cheap and cliché. But now I'm cool with it, because I realize that our story proves it's possible to find true love anywhere, including on a random night in a dimly lit neighborhood pub."

If you're looking for love, a gay bar, pub, or club is an obvious and often effective choice, provided you approach it with the right attitude. Not everyone in such places will be looking for the same thing as you, so take your time in getting to know someone. Initially, you might consider bringing along a wingman or woman, but once you're comfortable with the venue, summon the courage to go alone or at least separate from your friend once you're inside.

People go to the bar or club to socialize, and while alcohol helps to make all that socialization easier, be careful about your consumption. Keep in mind that alcohol can obscure your judgment, as well as lower your inhibitions.

There's nothing wrong with having a couple of drinks, of course, but you certainly don't need to have alcohol to be there. And if you are driving, then alcohol is a definite no-no. These days, more and more health-conscious people are ordering options such as juice or mineral water. Remember the old saying: "If you need a drink to be social, that's not social drinking."

Make the effort to talk with a few different people — not everyone has to be your 'type.' A friendly smile goes a long way. If you see someone you like, simply make brief eye contact and give a little smile. If it's reciprocated, then you know you have a chance. Do make sure that the person has seen you, though, and don't give up at first try. The other person might be a little surprised or nervous, and you might have taken them off guard, so leave it for a while, then try again and see what happens.

Perhaps you have a standard pick-up line, but most people respond best to a simple "hello" and an introduction: "Hi, I'm Jeremy.

You look like you could use some company, and I know I could, too. Mind if I join you for a little while?" Or you might just ask a question that they could answer easily and as they please, such as: "Hi, I'm Sarah and I was just wondering — what's keeping you busy these days?" But perhaps the easiest and most classic is a warm smile and: "Hi, my name's Josh. How're you doing this evening?"

If you get the brush-off, move on. Don't take it personally. Not everyone is your type and you won't be everyone's type, either. There are plenty of other interesting people to be met. But if you're invited to sit, pull up a chair, or if the other person is standing, then sidle in a little closer in order to talk.

You might begin by commenting on the surroundings, the lighting, the temperature, or the music. Then perhaps move on with a simple: "Whereabouts are you from?" Be sure to ask your new friend open-ended questions to get the conversation going. Something along the lines of: "Do you ever wonder how different things would be if you still lived there?"

> *"Each person you meet is an aspect of yourself, clamoring for love."*
>
> **~ Eric Michael Leventhal**

If things are going well, then don't be afraid to lean in. Above all, listen. Pay attention to what the other person says. Respond with follow-up questions, smiles, and nods. If you feel it's appropriate, a *little* touching — a hand on the shoulder, a pat on the hand — can be effective. Keep the focus on the person you're talking to. Whatever you do, don't complain about your terrible job or (worse) your wretched ex.

If the conversation feels like it's going nowhere, find a way to excuse yourself: "It's been great chatting with you. I hope things work out for your cat," or: "Well, better circulate, enjoy your evening!" Then move on to another area and strike up a conversation with someone else. If the conversation is going really well, stick around a little longer and see where it goes.

At the end of the evening, if it feels like you've connected, exchange phone numbers. If you really are looking for a relationship, jumping into bed on a first acquaintance may not be the wisest move; it just might send the wrong signals — fine for casual sex, but perhaps not for a relationship. By all means call the next day to find out if the spark was mutual and if there's reason to pursue the relationship. "Hi, Jack? This is Sam. Just calling to say I had a great time chatting with you last night. How's things with you today?" And remember, if this one doesn't work out, don't give up. There's a whole world of different people, and another bar or club not so very far away.

Cruising

Cruising — looking in public places for sexual encounters — is an activity that remains popular with many gay people. Gay men congregate in 'known' public places (parks, bathrooms, bars), and there are specific rituals for hooking up (we'll talk more about these in the chapter on gay sex). Lesbians also participate in cruising, although the rituals may be less stylized than men's.

In my experience, many gay people who cruise are in fact seeking not simply sex — although, of course, quite a few are — but also some form of validation or relationship, no matter how brief and tenuous. We will examine this a little more when we come to the chapter on sex and what we are looking for when we have it.

I recall working with one young boy referred to me by a social worker. He had been habitually cruising local public toilets. "It's the only time anyone ever hugs or holds me," he said. What appeared on the surface to be simple sexual activity (or as his referrer described it, 'promiscuity') was for him the closest he could come to achieving what anyone might look for in a relationship.

Long-term committed relationships *have* resulted from cruising, but in general cruising is about a short-term sexual experience. While these hook-ups can be exciting, enjoyable, and even worthwhile, on the road to greater happiness, the search for a long-term companion is probably a better choice.

Online

The Internet has revolutionized the way LGBTIQ people meet and interact, giving us access to a variety of connecting points, including chat rooms and dating sites. The largest and most popular gay dating sites can be accessed for free, with (limited) messaging and profile views also for free (paid membership gives unlimited profile views and messages). Such popular sites have free chat rooms, too. Sites such as *Gaydar.net, Gay.com, Gaydargirls.com,* and *Transpassions.com* have literally millions of members throughout the world, and these sites cater to all sorts of relationships.

Your best bet in getting what you want from a dating site is to be honest, with others and with yourself. Keep it real. Do not misrepresent yourself in your profile, and be realistic in what you're looking for. If you're on the chubby side, say that; there *are* people who are attracted to the larger, more robust figure.

If you're skinny, don't hide the fact; lots of people find the very slim figure attractive. You really don't need to be a tanned body builder with pumped pecs or a curvaceous busty bombshell in order to attract a partner. Everyone has some attractive feature, and there *are* people who are looking for someone just like you.

Having a photograph on your profile dramatically increases your chances of success. Without one, people may assume you have something to hide, and the old saying about a picture being worth a thousand words is still true.

Profiles with pics are at least twenty times more likely to be viewed — and so more likely to generate responses — than those without. A passport photo that looks like a police mug shot probably isn't the best kind of pic to attract others, but there is no need to have professional photographs taken; in fact, most people prefer more natural snapshots. Pics taken with your mobile phone, or 'selfies,' are fine for this — just make sure that any photo matches your personality; that it's a genuine reflection of who you are. A smile never goes amiss. Above all, make sure your photo is recent. This will cut down on the number of profiles that begin with "Seeking someone who actually looks like their photograph," and will eliminate disappointment on both sides.

If you don't feel ready to have a photograph on your profile, or if you really do need to be discreet, then at least have a pic or two available to attach in a private message. If you are looking for a relationship, it's probably best not to send a pic of yourself showing too much. Photos that are too explicit may be effective when looking purely for sex, but can be a major turn-off for those genuinely interested in a relationship, and again, are likely to send the wrong message.

Those with experience of gay dating sites know that there is a tendency for people to lie about their age. People can shave five, ten, or even more years off their real age in order to attract others. This is rarely helpful. Sooner or later the truth comes out and no one really likes to be deceived. So don't misrepresent your age in an attempt to attract someone younger, just specify in your profile that you prefer a younger partner, if this is the case. There are lots of younger men and women who are looking for more mature partners and honesty really is the best policy here. The same is true if you are young. Most sites have a minimum age restriction of eighteen years old. If you are younger than this and access a site, then you need to clearly state your true age in any message you send. It really is very unfair — and can have major repercussions — if you fail to do this.

There is a difference between being honest and being brutal, of course, with others as well as with yourself. It's not necessary or helpful to use your profile in order to point out your every flaw. Write about your best attributes in the most positive way: you're genuine, kind, industrious, active. You like to participate in sports or enjoy taking walks. You're an outgoing, clubbing type or you prefer quiet nights in with a movie and a cuddle. If you're uncomfortable trying to create your profile yourself, enlist the help of a friend who might more easily identify your most positive attributes and personality traits.

There's the potential to meet a lot of different people on a gay dating site, so even if you're hoping to meet 'the one,' take advantage of this experience to explore a bit. Connect with several people, and don't worry if you don't hit it off with all of them. This is the nature of relationships. We get to know many people over the course of a lifetime, and clearly not all of them will be partners for life. Use this as an opportunity to see who is out there, to practice social skills, and to refine your criteria for what you're looking for in a partner.

Chat rooms can be a good choice for initial contacts. They provide instant communication as well as anonymity, giving you both a chance to get to know each other a little before revealing more private information. Because the other person is also anonymous, at this stage you can't be sure exactly who you're dealing with, so exercise caution and don't reveal too much private information.

Preliminaries over, you may want to progress to communicating through Skype or c2c (web cam). This way you'll have some of the same benefits of the chat room plus a visual, so at least you'll know if the person you are interested in has misrepresented his or her physical appearance or age. Remember that anything you do privately on c2c can be posted on Internet sites that the whole world can see, so exercise discretion as to how intimate you're prepared to be.

Mobile phone apps such as 'WhatsApp,' 'Kik,' and Internet Messengers can be helpful in continuing to communicate and move things forward.

If the conversation seems to be heading in the right direction, it's time to meet in person. Pick something public and simple: meet for a coffee or a drink. If the chemistry is there, you can have a second drink or move on to a meal or another venue, but if the date's a dud, say your goodbyes and move on: "I've got a busy day tomorrow, so I need to be going." There's no need for a second date if the first was miserable. Should your date call you, the simplest solution is not to return his or her calls, though it is kinder to be truthful and answer the call, saying perhaps that you don't see the potential for romance, or something similar. There is no need to engage in a lengthy conversation. State your opinion, wish the other person the best of luck and be on your way.

> *"However successful you are, there is no substitute for a close relationship. We all need them."*
> **~ Francesca Annis**

Just because your profiles appear to match doesn't mean you'll click, and it doesn't mean you should give up on Internet dating. If things don't work out, go back to your computer, do another search, pull up another profile, and send some more messages. The key here, as in so many other areas of life, is patience and persistence.

"I met my wife through an Internet site," said Janice. "I dated a lot of different women before I met her, many of them casually or strictly for sex. Dating can be hard on the ego, but if you keep an open mind and an open heart, sometimes dreams really do come true."

While the Internet provides many opportunities to meet people, there are also risks to Internet dating. Not everyone is polite. Racism and ageism are as prevalent on the Internet as they are offline, and the anonymity of the Internet gives people the ability to be rude and hostile in ways they might not be in person. Be prepared for some less-than-positive encounters. Dating can involve some rejection, but that's no reason to give up. You're still a good person, and someone somewhere can't wait to meet you.

The other big risk with online introductions is fraud. People will misrepresent themselves in all sorts of ways in order to get what they are looking for. Not everyone on these sites is looking for love: some are curious, some are time-wasters or pic collectors, and some are predators. Be careful not to give personal information too soon. If you have a bad experience, you don't want the person to be able to pursue or harass you.

How can you tell if someone is being honest? As you're getting to know the other person, pay attention to any inconsistencies; if they're not truthful in one area, they might be lying in others. If they seem evasive, not answering questions directly or at all, that might be another tip-off. And trust your gut. If the person seems too good to be true, well, you know the rest of the story.

Never trust a single photograph; always ask for another or, better still, a couple more. If the person is reluctant to send you another pic, it may be because they are not the person in the photo, and so cannot produce any others. These days almost everyone has a mobile phone with a camera, and there is no excuse for not being able to take pics.

It's always best to video cam before meeting in person. This not only ensures that the person you're speaking with is the person in their profile pic, but it also provides an opportunity to read body language. If you don't feel comfortable, trust your instincts and discontinue contact. If they attempt to pressure you into doing anything on cam that you really don't want or that you feel uncomfortable doing, then you can disconnect and end communication.

If, on the other hand, things go well, then you have a green light to take things further. There's no denying that countless stable, lasting relationships began online.

Other Internet Options

Sites like Craigslist also provide options for meeting others. You can write your own ad or respond to those that speak to your needs. You'll want to set up an email account strictly for these communications in order to protect your privacy, an account that can easily be closed if you need to shut down a relationship. Once you receive a response, take the same precautions as you would when working through a matchmaking site.

When meeting someone for the first time (or the first couple of times), it's wise to choose a public place where other people will be present. Coffee shops, shopping malls, or restaurants are all good places for a first date.

Intergenerational Relationships

While many LGBTIQ people prefer partners in their own age group, in the gay world it's not uncommon to find loving, committed couples with an age difference of 20 years or more. If that is your preference, and if you're male, websites such as *Caffmos.com* or *SilverDaddies.com* are dedicated to older men and their admirers.

Lesbians can check sites such as *Gaydargirls*, which, though not exclusively dedicated to intergenerational relationships, do allow women to refine their search for the age group they are specifically interested in. Lesbian dating forums also offer possibilities in this area. If you find yourself becoming involved in an intergenerational relationship, there is plenty of evidence that it can work out well.

As with every other relationship, intergenerational relationships work best when the people see each other as equals (with the possible exception of 'master-slave' type relationships, which we'll discuss in a later chapter), when partners embrace and affirm each other's differences, and when they're able to talk about concerns. You may be apprehensive about the perceptions of others, or you may be concerned that you are being taken advantage of financially (if you're the older partner) or sexually (if you're the younger partner). If you can find a way to resolve these and other concerns, you have a great chance at a successful relationship.

> *"The meeting of two personalities is like the contact of two chemical substances; if there is any reaction, both are transformed."*
> **~ Carl Jung**

Ultimately only you can decide if the relationship is right for you. You may need to learn to ignore the occasional stare, but as long as you are both consenting adults and happy with each other, there is no reason to shy away from an intergenerational relationship if that is your interest.

Life as a Couple

Let's assume that you've met someone and, after you've been together for a while, you decide to be exclusive to each other: to enter a committed relationship. Being a couple can be wonderful, and the right relationship can be a great asset in having a happy life.

One study conducted by the UK's Open University aimed at finding out how modern couples keep their relationships on track revealed that LGBT participants are more generally positive about and happier with the quality of the relationship they have with their partner than heterosexual couples. While we can speculate on the reasons for this, at this point no one knows for sure. But the survey does tell us that, for LGBT people, relationships can certainly be happy and satisfying.

Gay relationships are as varied as straight relationships, so how you and your partner choose to move forward is a mutual decision made by the two of you. There is no right or wrong way; there is no set path. As homophobia and discrimination against LGBTIQ people decrease, more options become available, so you can decide on the level of commitment and the living arrangements that work best for you.

Separate Homes

Not all LGBTIQ couples choose to cohabitate, even when they are exclusive to each other in a monogamous relationship. There's no need to rush into living together. If you're used to having your own space and a good deal of privacy, and if you like it that way, living in separate dwellings can be a good choice. Sometimes living apart is more a matter of convenience; for example, your jobs are some distance apart and your current homes are in close proximity to work. Living separately might also be prudent if you have young children who visit or live with you; not everyone is ready for an instant family, and children deserve a little time to adjust to a new person in their lives and in their home.

"Jack and I aren't ready to move in together," said Callum. "I've moved in with partners before and never really felt at home in what had been 'their' place. And I really enjoy a bit of solitude and my own company — and keeping my own schedule. Sometimes Jack stays over, and sometimes I stay at his place, but for now, I like having my own place. It seems to work just fine for both of us."

If you're both happy living separately, there's no reason not to continue to do so.

Living Together

Many LGBTIQ couples prefer to cohabitate simply as a matter of expedience, or as a means of expressing their commitment to each other. Living together offers the opportunity to live as full partners, sharing the expenses and the chores as well as all the ups and downs, the procession of moments that make up our everyday life.

"We were committed to each other, and ready to take the next step, so when her lease ran out, Tess moved in with me," said Robin. "We'd both had our fill of the clubbing and party scene, and we were ready for a more settled life together."

Tess and Robin have separate bank accounts but share expenses. "I make more than Tess, so I tend to foot the bill when we go out for dinner or do other special things," Robin said. "We've figured out a budget and a schedule that works for us, and we love being able to spend time together and share the same bed every night."

Adapting to any new living situation may take a little time and flexibility. If possible, consider moving into a new place that you choose together in order to make a fresh start and to avoid issues of territory. Negotiations on some of the mundane details of domestic life will begin the moment you cross the threshold together: closet space, furniture choices, and thermostat settings, among others. You'll also need to work out the day-to-day details: who does what chores, when and how you'll entertain friends and family in your shared space, where to go on vacation. As you have these conversations, be assertive but flexible. Be willing to advocate strongly for the things that matter, but be willing to let go of issues that are less important to you. The objective isn't to win an argument, but rather to live in harmony as much as possible. Learning to compromise is critical to happy cohabitation.

Money matters can be a major cause of discord among couples, and LGBTIQ couples are no exception, so it's best to have these conversations early and often. Be clear about each partner's financial obligations at the outset, and be prepared to be flexible if the situation changes. Consider drawing up a legal agreement that specifies who is responsible for which expenses. If you purchase property together, a legal contract is especially important. It's not romantic, but try to see it as an investment in your future that can benefit everyone in the long run.

Regardless of how long you've lived together or the nature of your relationship, your legal rights as a partner might be fuzzy at best. You may see yourselves as full partners, but if you are not married or in a civil partnership, then legally you're not related, so in times of crisis you might not be able to function as next of kin. A lot depends on which part of the world you live in. Work with an attorney who is knowledgeable on LGBTIQ rights to be sure you are both protected, or contact an LGBTIQ organization in your country for advice. Write a will that specifies what your partner is to inherit, and execute a durable power of attorney and a medical power of attorney that names your partner as your decision maker and vice versa, if that is your wish. This will guarantee partner rights (and responsibilities) if something should happen to either of you.

Civil Partnerships and Gay Marriage

Many have fought hard, and continue to fight, for the rights of gay couples to marry. More than a piece of paper, a marriage license allows LGBTIQ couples access to the same rights as other married couples. Marriage isn't the goal of all LGBTIQ persons, but it is an option that is becoming increasingly accessible for couples that want it.

Marriage indicates a strong commitment to the relationship. Many couples have been waiting for years for the right to marry, and they are not inclined to enter into it lightly.

"We waited a long time. We've been together 35 years, never thinking we'd get a legal marriage. I'm so happy I can hardly stand it," said 85-year-old Petra at her marriage to her partner, 77-year-old Jane, in 2013.

> *"At some point in our lifetime, gay marriage won't be an issue, and everyone who stood against this civil right will look as outdated as George Wallace standing on the school steps keeping James Hood from entering the University of Alabama because he was black."*
>
> **~ George Clooney**

Civil partnerships and civil unions, legal in numerous different countries, give same-sex couples many (but not all) of the rights and responsibilities of civil marriage: property rights, inheritance tax exemption, social security and pension benefits, next of kin rights in hospitals, parental responsibility for a partner's children, and others. There is a formal process for dissolving partnerships that is similar to divorce.

Gay marriage became legal in England, Wales, and Scotland in 2014, and a process was introduced to convert civil unions to marriage. In 2015, Ireland approved a referendum on same-sex marriage, joining the ranks of other progressive countries.

And in the US, after a long and hard-fought battle, the Supreme Court ruled in June 2015 that gay marriage is finally a legal right in all states nationwide.

As of 2015, gay marriage is recognized in 21 countries — including Canada and New Zealand. Civil partnerships and civil unions are now legal in an additional 18 countries.

Marriage gives LGBTIQ couples a level playing field. A legal gay marriage entitles the couple to all the rights and responsibilities of a hetero marriage, including insurance benefits, family leave benefits, and survivor benefits. It also means that separating will require a divorce, with all that it entails.

LGBTIQ people marry for the same reasons straight people do: for love and as a public celebration of commitment. LGBTIQ people also marry to have access to the rights mentioned above. The institution of marriage does come with benefits.

LGBTIQ weddings can be private ceremonies or large affairs. Some couples host a lavish party, while others celebrate with a quiet evening alone. A wedding is a wonderful opportunity to celebrate your relationship with family and friends; how you do that is up to you.

After the wedding, or civil ceremony, be sure that both you and your partner update your insurance information, legal documents, and government records to reflect your new status. Handling the details now will save time and hassle later.

"It may be that same-sex couples will save the institution of marriage."
~ Elizabeth Gilbert

If you've lived together prior to marriage, most of the cohabitation details have probably been worked out long ago, but don't be surprised if your life together experiences subtle and not so subtle changes. Such a big step may make you feel differently about yourself and your partner, hopefully more settled and more confident in your future. Continue to nurture your relationship; with the proper care and attention, it will continue to thrive.

Children

Raising children can be a wonderful, if sometimes challenging, journey! Although for decades society denied LGBTIQ people adoption rights, arguing that same-sex households were damaging to children, all current research refutes this. LGBTIQ couples and singles can be excellent parents, and are exploring parenting options in record numbers.

If you and/or your partner have children from a prior relationship, make sure they have room in your life with your new partner. Whether your children live with you or with your ex, you and your new partner will be partners in parenting. It's good to establish expectations early on: make it clear that children are to respect your new partner as a parent when the children are in your care.

Celebrating your relationship through the addition of a child can be a tremendous bonding experience, provided your bond is solid. If you're anticipating that a child will shore up a shaky relationship, think again: it doesn't work. Make sure that you and your partner are strong together before taking on the stress of parenting. If you're adopting as a single person, be sure that you have support networks in place to help you as you make the transition into parenthood.

For LGBTIQ couples in the US, having children requires enormous effort and often a significant amount of cash. Some employers provide financial assistance for adoptions, so check with your company's human resources department to see if this is included in your benefit package. While you're there, check into your company's policy about family leave. In the US, family leave varies greatly from one employer to another.

In the UK, maternity, paternity, and adoption leaves are generous and standardized, and the National Health Service (NHS) can provide in vitro fertilization without charge for LGBTIQ couples.

While many US insurance companies cover or partially cover in vitro treatments for couples who are infertile, most won't pay for these treatments for gay couples. Lesbian couples may have coverage for office visits, testing, and insemination. Still, it doesn't hurt to check with your insurer. The law and medical insurance coverage are areas that are always in flux.

Gay couples have a number of options when considering biological children. For lesbian couples, artificial insemination would allow one partner to carry the pregnancy; the egg can be fertilized by someone known or by an anonymous donor. In vitro fertilization would allow one partner to supply an egg that is fertilized and then implanted in the other partner, who would carry the pregnancy. Another option is the use of a gestational surrogate, or 'surrogate mother,' who would carry the fertilized egg to term.

Male couples who want a biological child would require both an egg donor and a gestational surrogate. Sperm from both partners can be used to fertilize the egg.

Fertility clinics have a lot of experience working with LGBTIQ persons in their quest to have children, and will do everything they can to walk you through the process. Unfortunately, not every city has a state-of-the-art facility available, which might complicate your ability to have children in this manner. Talk to your doctor about the best medical options near you.

> *"Adoption is the most intentional process on Earth."*
>
> **~ Jody Cantrell Dyer**

Adoption is another possibility for LGBTIQ adults who want children. Thanks to the Internet, it's not always necessary to live in proximity to the agency in order for them to handle your adoption, so be sure to explore your options and choose an agency with a solid history and reputation. There are agencies that specialize in LGBTIQ adoptions that are equipped to help you through the labyrinthine process. Adopting parents are interviewed, undergo a background check, fill out dozens of forms, and provide references. For international adoptions, the paperwork is even more daunting, but the agency will assist you. Not all countries will permit LGBTI couples or individuals to adopt; your agency will be able to advise you on this.

It's also possible to adopt through the foster care system and provide a home for a child who has been removed from the care of the parent. The UK welcomes adoption and fostering by suitable gay and lesbian parents. More information on this can be found on the *British Association for Adoption and Fostering* (BAAF) website: www.baaf.org.uk.

In the US, two states – Mississippi and Florida – prohibit adoption through foster care by gay couples, but most states allow single people to adopt. Working with the foster care system is generally more economical, but can require more paperwork.

In Canada, adoption by same-sex couples is legal in every province. In Australia it depends on the state, while in New Zealand, married same-sex couples can legally adopt.

You can increase the odds of a quick placement if you're willing to take a special needs child, an older child, or a sibling group. Because most adopting parents prefer to adopt newborns, this group of children can be harder to place. These can be wonderful kids, but they may come with psychological difficulties or costly medical issues; so be sure you're prepared to deal with these complications, which can be taxing both emotionally and financially.

If you'd prefer not to work through an agency, contact an adoption attorney who can provide you with advice on private adoptions.

Raising children is a profound undertaking and not something to be entered into lightly. It's a relationship like no other. It's a long-term investment in another person's life that can yield enormous happiness, but it is not without its challenges, as well as its wonderful rewards.

Open Relationships

LGBTIQ relationships don't necessarily need to be exclusive, of course. Some people prefer a non-monogamous, 'open relationship' in which either person is free to have sexual experiences outside of the main, established relationship. Such relationships can work provided that parameters are set early on, and both partners are secure enough to deal with any feelings of jealousy that might arise. Topics that need to be discussed and agreed upon might include whether partners can talk openly about their sexual interactions, whether such trysts need to take place away from the home (where accommodation is shared) and so on. There really are no hard and fast rules on this; each couple must decide for themselves if this is what they want and how best to handle things.

It's Up to You

While being gay and happy doesn't require that you be in a relationship, life with a partner can be rewarding and fulfilling. The most important thing is to determine what you want, and then find a way to make it happen.

Chapter Eleven

Gay Sex

"Sex is emotion in motion."
~ Mae West

We talk about it, joke about it, plan for it, hope for it, fantasize about it — sex.

It's a joy, a means toward emotional intimacy, a diversion, a guilty pleasure, a game of love and sometimes of power. Few things are so pursued, so primal, and so mysterious.

Attitudes about sex are shaped by our upbringing, our past. If we were raised in a family where the subject of sex was taboo, cloaked in secrecy and embarrassment, we might be a little shy and hesitant when it comes to sexual encounters. If our family and our environment were more open toward the subject, allowing conversations about sex and treating it as natural and important, the probability is that our attitude is more open.

For people who have been sexually abused, sex can be anything but pleasurable. Add to any of this a negative attitude toward homosexuality — from society or from people we know — and it can all get more than a little bit complicated.

Regardless of your upbringing or your circumstances, remember that adult, consensual sex is natural, healthy, and pleasurable.

It is meant to be enjoyed. Learning to appreciate and cultivate sexual relationships can be an important link to a happy life.

The initial contact with gay sex can be the ultimate confirmation that we are, in fact, gay, and this can be an enormously liberating experience. Even if our first time isn't 'amazing,' it can still be a strong validation of long-held feelings and an end to all of that questioning. And it may well be pleasurable enough to encourage us to try again. With a little practice and experience, we learn what feels good to us and what we want from sexual experiences.

Great sex makes us feel good physically — releasing endorphins and those feel-good neurotransmitters, serotonin and dopamine. It also elevates norepinephrine levels, the neurotransmitter that has an essential role in mediating communication in the body's autonomic nervous system. Oxytocin — the hormone that plays such an important part in pair bonding, encouraging emotional attachment — also increases during sexual arousal and in orgasm. This is true for both men and women.

In women, estrogen, the female hormone, combines with oxytocin, producing a stronger emotional attachment. In men, with higher testosterone levels, the bonding effect is somewhat muted. Because of this, men may be slower to form emotional ties, and can be more likely to see their initial sexual contact as 'just sex.' Regardless of biology, though, men are indeed able to bond and form lasting relationships with each other.

> *"We waste time looking for the perfect lover, instead of creating the perfect love."*
> **~ Tom Robbins**

While the stereotype is that gay people, and gay men in particular, can't get enough sex, recent research indicates that promiscuity might not be as prevalent in the LGBTIQ community as previously imagined. Sexual relationships, after all, may well be about much more than just the act of sex.

The research showed that a massive 92.6 percent of gay men reported their most recent sexual event occurred with a relationship partner, someone they indicated being in love with at the time they had sex.

That said, some sexual encounters are quick and spontaneous, and there is nothing inherently wrong with this. Other times sex can be a deeply emotional bonding experience, a means of taking a relationship to an elevated level.

From the routine to the extreme, sex is normal and healthy, and there are a variety of ways to experience pleasure and to provide pleasure to your partner.

Assertiveness and Sexuality

As in other areas of our existence, our own healthy sense of self will enhance our sex life. When we feel good about who we are, this is reflected in our sex life, too. Homophobia-induced low self-esteem can be an enormous barrier to creating and maintaining intimate relationships. Without a strong sense of self, there can be a tendency to play the numbers game — to constantly seek affirmation and validation through others. Low self-esteem can turn us into something of a slave to sex, using and abusing, or being used and abused in an endless effort to be appreciated and loved, to feel in control or to feel wanted and needed.

If you're finding that you're having lots of unsatisfying sex, or if you are not as sexually active as you would like, it might be time to assess your needs and assert your own expectation for your intimate life. Not everyone's sex drive or need for sex is the same. Some may have a very powerful libido, while others not so.

So for a moment, let's ask the types of questions we've asked in the previous two chapters. You might need to think and reflect a little longer this time. Why is sex important to you? What are your reasons for pursuing sex? What are you looking for in your intimate relationships?

I'll ask you to take a few moments now to note some of your thoughts in the space provided (or on a piece of paper that you can later discard). Make a list, and then perhaps try to rank them in order of importance. Remember, this is *your* list; there is no right or wrong here. No one else need see your answers. What are *you* looking for? Pleasure? Intimacy? Commitment? Take a moment now to consider your reasons, and jot down your responses.

Reasons I Have (or Want) Sex

____

____

____

____

____

____

____

____

Done it? Excellent!

Not done it? You're reading this because you want to be gay AND happy, right? And you realize that this is going to take a bit of work? Hmm… Okay. There's still time to do it.

If you did the exercise, well done! This shows you genuinely want to be happier and are prepared to work for it. Now compare your answers on why you have or want sex with the answers you gave as to why you seek friendships on Page 212, and why you want to have relationships on Page 226. Where do you see differences and, more especially, what are the similarities? What, exactly, are the things that you can obtain *only* from sex?

You might once again notice some developing themes in your lists: perhaps companionship, commitment, emotional support, maybe acceptance, human warmth, or a host of other things. So many of the things we look for in sex can be found elsewhere, in both friendship and relationships.

While sex is a wonderful thing, it's often misused. If we use it in an attempt to validate ourselves, or to shore up our self-esteem, then we may find ourselves trapped in an endless quest, a numbers game that results only in disappointment, or else constantly searching for a reassurance that seems never to arrive, convince or endure.

Rarely does sex satisfy in these ways. By better understanding your own needs, desires and motivations, you may be able to see things clearer, to understand yourself better, avoid relationship difficulties, and resist getting involved with the wrong people for the wrong reasons. All of this can help you foster the friendships and relationships — at all levels — that make you happy.

A big part in having a healthy, pleasurable sex life lies in becoming our own advocate in sexual relationships, learning to ask for what we want, and in knowing how to say "no" to acts that make us feel uncomfortable.

Just as we have human rights, we also have certain unilateral rights when it comes to sexual activity. Understanding and asserting our rights as sexual beings is an important step to a healthy and happy sex life. Here is a list of the rights you have as a sexual partner.

Bill of Sexual Rights

- **I have the right to my sexuality and my sexual orientation.**

  There is no right or wrong way to feel attracted to people. Your orientation and sexuality are yours, and they are perfectly healthy. Having sexual urges is part of being human, and these urges are not merely about procreation.

- **I have the right to sexual wellbeing.**

  You have the right to enjoy sex, and to pursue the sexual relationships that you enjoy. And you have the right to health, safety, and wellbeing as you do this.

- **I have the right to express my sexuality in any way that does not oppress another person or interfere with their rights.**

  Sexual preferences are just that: preferences. Sex is enjoyed in many different ways, and as long as both you and your partner(s) are in accord, and are above the age of consent, your sexual expression is up to you.

- **I have the right to intimacy and to sexual pleasure.**

  Sex can be a wonderful thing, physically and emotionally. You're entitled to all of the benefits of a sexual relationship, including the intimacy and all of the pleasure and joy that come with it.

- **I have the right to express and ask for what I want.**

  Sex is a shared activity that ought to be mutually beneficial. It is within your rights to make requests of your partner in order to maximize your experience. This includes talking frankly and openly about sexual matters and preferences, initiating sexual activity, and asking for specific acts or techniques.

- **I have the right to change my mind and to say "No" to any sexual activity that I don't want at any time.**

  It's natural to want to experiment sexually. This is how we discover new things about ourselves, our likes and dislikes, our bodies, and our partners. If everyone is agreeable, these can be amazing adventures. But at any time, it is within your rights to say "no," to say "stop," or to change your mind. Sex ought not be coerced, and you should not feel pressured or forced into any sex act in which you don't want to participate. As with all sexual rights, your partner has the same rights. Remember to respect this.

- **I have the right to clear information about sex and sexual health.**

  In addition to being a marvelous experience — emotionally, mentally, and physically — sex is also a bodily function, which means there are related health and medical issues that we need to be aware of. Because sex has been a taboo subject in the past (and to a much lesser degree still is), there is an enormous amount of misinformation about it in our society, and some of this misinformation is dangerous. We have the right to a clear understanding of how our bodies work, how to protect ourselves from disease and harm, and how to seek help should we need it. We have the right to good, nonjudgmental healthcare when we desire or need it.

Knowing and asserting our sexual rights allows us to celebrate our sexual relationships and helps to maintain a healthy self-esteem. Part of asserting ourselves lies in understanding our own needs and limits — and being prepared to act upon them.

Age of Consent

And speaking of rights, the age of consent for sex is 16 in the UK and the United States (higher in some states). In Canada, the age of consent is also 16, but is set at 18 for anal sex between unmarried partners. In Australia, the age of consent depends on the jurisdiction and ranges from 15 to 18. In New Zealand it is 16. Other countries and regions have differing age of consent laws.

Before you do something that could get you or your partner arrested, be sure that both of you are legally old enough to engage in sexual activity in your area of residence.

The Act of Sex

It's something of a myth that LGBTIQ people know exactly what their partners want. Some do, and some don't. The misperception is that since LGBTI people are romancing a body type that is familiar, they should intuitively know what feels good to their partner. In life and sex, we each have our own needs, desires, and turn-ons. What is mind-blowing for one person might be annoying or painful for another. LGBTIQ people may be just as insecure and clumsy in their early experiences of sex as anyone else. In the beginning, it's not at all unusual to fumble a bit, not only in the mechanics, but in figuring out how to please a partner, as well as in discovering what feels good to us.

> *"If our sex life were determined by our first youthful experiments, most of the world would be doomed to celibacy."*
>
> **~ P.D.James**

Great sex is about more than technique; it involves trust and communication as well. The right partner can bring out your adventurous side or make the most pedestrian acts exciting. Sexual practices among LGBTIQ persons are as varied as the people who practice them. There's no right or wrong way, but there are a few common practices, and the Internet offers almost unlimited information on variations.

Masturbation

Although religious dogma and old wives' tales may have tried to convince us otherwise, masturbation is not immoral, and neither is it harmful. Most often, our early exploration of sex begins with self-stimulation through masturbation, which can provide not only sexual release, but also a deeper understanding of our own bodies and pleasure zones. Because mutual masturbation is usually a part of gay sex, this information can be useful when stimulating, or making requests of a partner. As we mature, masturbation can also be used in conjunction with fantasy or pornography to excite and expand our sexual horizons.

How much masturbation is too much? Men in particular seem to feel there is some norm or limit for masturbatory activity. Frequency of masturbation is a function of many things, including libido, age, and availability of sexual partners; so unless your body is sending signals that you're overdoing it, or if it's interfering with relationships, study, or work, there's no reason to limit your activity.

For Men

While ejaculation is the ultimate physical and sensational goal of sex for most men, it is the journey to orgasm that holds much of the real pleasure and joy. When it comes to sex, tenderness and touching are also high on the list of importance for many.

Mutual masturbation is known for being easy and fast, as well as being one of the safer sex options.

Frottage — the act of rubbing against someone, while clothed or naked, sometimes to the point of climax — can be a mutually satisfying experience. Many gay men enjoy rubbing their genitals against those of their partner.

Fellatio, also known as a 'blowjob,' 'giving head,' 'oral sex,' or 'sucking someone off' is the oral stimulation of the penis, often to climax. For many men, this is their preferred sex act, and it can be performed in a variety of positions, including 'sixty-nine,' which allows for mutual fellatio — both partners mouthing, sucking, and licking the other's penis.

'Anilingus,' or *rimming*, is the use of the tongue for oral stimulation of the anus, although it may take a little practice to get used to. Some prefer to use a dental dam or non-porous cling-film when performing anilingus.

Intercrural sex is also a popular form of nonpenetrative gay sex, which involves the man placing his penis between the legs of his partner and thrusting in order to create friction. Other options include fucking the crevice between the buns, the armpits, or the space between the clavicle and chin, Apart from masturbation, this is the safest form of sex, since no actual bodily penetration takes place.

> *"The world is filled with love-play, from animal lust to sublime compassion."*
>
> **~ Alan Watts**

Fingering of the anus is a common activity in gay sex, since the anus is an erogenous area and responds easily to stimulation. This involves the insertion of one or more fingers into the anus, often going far enough up to touch and gently massage the prostate gland, which can create feelings of intense pleasure. Be sure your nails are clipped and not ragged in order to avoid tearing or other injury.

Anal sex, anal intercourse, aka 'bum sex' or 'ass fucking,' has been most frequently associated with gay men, but it is something practiced by many heterosexual men and women, too. It is also the form of intercourse most associated with the spread of HIV, and so it is best to use a condom unless you know your partner's history well.

There is no need to douche inside the anus before having anal sex. As long as the bowel has been evacuated, and the body cleaned in the shower, bath, or *bidet* prior to sex, then all should be fine.

'Barebacking' is the common term used for unprotected anal sex. When a man intentionally orgasms inside his partner's anus without protection, this is known as 'breeding'. Those who are in a committed, trusting monogamous relationship often prefer this to wearing a condom because of increased intimacy and the heightened sensitivity it can afford. The fact is, though, that people can be less than truthful about their past, or even their present sexual activities, so unless you know your partner very well, over an extended period, and are *absolutely* sure, it is safer to use a condom. Remember that when you have sex with someone, in a manner of speaking you are also having sex with everyone who has had sex with that person before you.

The anus is lined with a thin, porous membrane, and can develop small tears or abrasions caused by scratching or friction through which an infection can enter the bloodstream. A condom creates a barrier between anus and penis, preventing fluids from entering the body. In the past, extra thick condoms were advised for anal sex, but research has shown that regular condoms are just as effective.

Before you begin having insertive anal sex, use your fingers and your preferred water-based lubricant to caress, explore, and become familiar with the anus and to practice gently relaxing the muscles. Pain during anal intercourse is due largely to lack of sufficient lubricant, inability to relax, feelings of anxiety and tension, or unease with taking the passive role. Psychological factors can play an enormous part in triggering pain; so trust and good communication are essential ingredients of pain-free, pleasurable anal intercourse.

> *"My own belief is that there is hardly anyone whose sexual life, if it were broadcast, would not fill the world at large with surprise and horror."*
>
> **~ W. Somerset Maugham**

The anus has two rings of muscles, called anal sphincters. The first ring, the external sphincter, is under our conscious control. It can be relaxed or tightened at will. But the inner sphincter is not under our conscious control and has to be manipulated and gently eased and stretched in order for the anus and rectum to be loose enough to be penetrated. It naturally returns to its normal size soon after intercourse. Experience will tell you which position you prefer — doggy, missionary, on your side, face to face with one of the partner's legs raised, or any other position. Don't be afraid to experiment, communicate with your partner, and remember that, in consensual sex between adults, nothing is taboo.

Fisting is another practice popular with some, but by no means most, gay men and women. This involves gently and gradually penetrating the anus, first with fingers and then, when the anus is sufficiently stretched, with the hand itself.

A great deal of consideration, patience, and trust is involved in this particular sexual activity, and it is not without its dangers. A copious amount of lubricant is essential. In order to prevent scratching or trauma caused by fingernails, the person doing the fisting can wear latex or non-latex surgical gloves, readily available from most pharmacies.

For Women

Sex between women ranges from tender and loving to raucous and rough. A woman's tongue, lips, and mouth are highly sensitive erogenous zones used by both partners throughout sexual activity. The oral or manual stimulation of a partner's breasts and nipples is common as a form of foreplay. As with the nipples, oral stimulation of the vulva, clitoris, or vagina, called *cunnilingus*, is a common practice between women, and can include the use of teeth, lips, and tongue — aka 'eating pussy.'

Licking or nibbling the ear lobe or exploring the ear with the tongue and working on down to the nipples, navel, and inner thighs are direct routes to the vagina.

Giving or receiving an erotic massage can also be very exciting and sensual. A warm scented oil or lube can boost the pleasurable sensations, increasing the pleasure even more.

Another fairly common practice is oral stimulation of the anus, called 'anilingus.' If you are sure that your partner is free of STIs (sexually transmitted infections), then this can be enjoyed '*au na-*

turel', but if not, then a dental dam may come in handy. Putting a drop of lube on your partner's pussy before positioning the dental dam may increase the sensation considerably.

There is no need to be meek, and there is no need to rush. Take your time. Feel, listen, and explore. Pull her hair, stroke her back, and squeeze her cheeks. Taste, tickle and touch, gently or firmly caress her waist and lightly run your fingers down the sensitive area of the inner thighs.

Let your partner's body be your guide. Be adventuresome. Sex with another consenting person is no shame, and the bedroom (or wherever you choose to have sex) is no place for taboos — or, perhaps more correctly, it is the place to break taboos — so give yourself and your partner permission and the freedom to experiment.

'Frottage,' *scissoring*, or dry humping, also known as 'tribadism,' is a nonpenetrative sexual act that many women enjoy. It doesn't work for everyone, and much depends on how your body 'fits' with that of your partner. In classic scissors, women lie down, each one rubbing their vulva against her partner's vulva, thigh, stomach, buttocks, arm, or another body part. And this may also be achieved in a number of different positions, including missionary, doggy style, scissoring, or other styles. It might be accompanied by penetration with a dildo or with fingering — the use of the fingers to explore and massage your partner's vulva, clitoris, vagina, or anus, which can further increase the enjoyment.

When using your fingers, there are three cardinal rules: feel, feel, feel. If you are a woman, notice the difference in texture, the slightly rough feeling of the front (or anterior) wall of the vagina, and the soft, smooth feeling of the rest of the vaginal walls. Some women enjoy stimulation just below the urethra, at the opening of the vagina.

For most women, climax is achieved through massage of the vulva and the clitoris, either manually or orally. Both massage and fingering — self-fingering, mutual, penetrative, or nonpenetrative

— can be executed in a variety of positions. Some couples enjoy using a hand-held dildo, a strap-on dildo, or other sex toys for deeper vaginal or anal penetration.

A 1983 study first coined the term "lesbian bed death." The study indicated that lesbian couples in committed relationships have less sex than any other couples, and that frequency of sex declines the longer a couple is together. Since that time, research has debunked this myth. Lesbian couples can and do continue to have great sex long into their relationships.

Safer sex

The safest sex is sex that does not involve a part of one person's body being inserted into another person's body, and where body fluids are not exchanged. Although a 2007 study reported that the majority of gay men had no more unprotected sexual encounters than the population as a whole, the risk of disease is higher among gay men due to the greater risk of contracting STIs through anal sex. STIs can be contracted through the urethra (the tube that allows urine to pass out of the body) or through abrasions on the penis or in the anus or rectum.

The risk for HIV-AIDS from lesbian sexual activity is low, but the risk of STI transmission does exist. Bodily fluids such as blood (including menstrual blood) and vaginal fluid can spread infections. STIs can also be transmitted through oral sex if the person has abrasions, cuts or sores in his or her mouth.

Since the early reports of HIV-AIDS in the 1980s, the term 'safe sex' has led many of us to believe that we can eliminate the risks of sexually transmitted disease through the use of protective measures. While the use of condoms and other barriers can drastically lessen the risk of disease, every sexual encounter carries with it some risk. When it comes to intercourse, especially, there is no such thing as 'safe sex;' there is only safer sex. Condoms can break and are less likely to hold up during anal sex, so even if you're practicing safer sex there are risks. If you're with a new partner, by all means use protective measures but remember that no barrier is failsafe. The safest sex is with a close and trusted partner, someone whose sexual history is known to you, or nonpenetrative sex.

> *"I can remember when the air was clean and sex was dirty."*
>
> **~ George Burns**

Purchase a box of good-quality condoms (be sure to check that the date is current) and put them in places where they might be handy, such as your bedside table and your wallet. Don't expect your partner to provide them; take responsibility for your own health and wellbeing by providing, and insisting upon, protection.

The best way to get comfortable with condoms is to practice putting them on yourself when you're alone. Once you've gained some familiarity with condoms, you might want to invent sensual rituals while slipping on the condom that can heighten anticipation and excitement and increase the eroticism for you and your partner. Inviting your partner to engage in such rituals adds to the excitement and prevents any awkward break in the flow of lovemaking.

Dental dams are thin latex squares that may be used as barriers during cunnilingus or oral/anal contact. Non-latex polyurethane dams are also available, as are nonlatex condoms, for those who may have a sensitivity to rubber or latex. Because dental dams can be difficult to find and expensive, consider making your own by cutting a condom into a rectangle. As with condoms, use the barrier only once in order to avoid cross-contamination. Another handy alternative is to use nonporous cling film.

If you're using dildos of any sort, use of a condom is also recommended, especially if using the dildo with multiple partners. (If this is the case, be sure to use a different condom with each partner.)

Any oil-based lubricant used in conjunction with a condom or other barrier will reduce the barrier's effectiveness and may cause it to split and break. (When using non-latex products this does not apply.) Otherwise use only water-based lubricants created especially for sex. In addition to classic products like KY jelly, which is readily available from any pharmacy, there are many specialty varieties widely available that can enhance your pleasure; some even have fruit flavors and harmless nonirritant scents.

And one more thing: drugs and alcohol can lessen your resolve and open the door to riskier sexual behavior. Be careful when under the influence, and don't allow it to cloud your judgment when it comes to protecting yourself.

Kinky Sex

There is very little new under the heavens, and that includes sexual practices. What might once have been considered kinky in our culture or personal experience has probably been going on for centuries.

What makes it kinky is the element of being a little out of the mainstream, maybe a little bit naughty — which, of course, is part of the fun. Maybe it's a little rough, or a little dirty, or it's a bit of role-playing that goes against societal norms.

Role-playing — father-son, teacher-student, coach-player, doctor-patient, master-slave — is considered by some to be kinky because it pushes the boundaries of propriety. Costumes, specific clothing, or 'dressing up' can add to the enjoyment. If playing these games is exciting to you and your partner, there's no reason not to enjoy your fantasies in the safety of your own relationship or sexual encounter. It can be a fun and harmless way to explore new sexual frontiers.

'Good' kinky sex is consensual and pleasurable for you and your partner. It should not be dangerous or life-threatening to either of you. Sex in a public place might be considered kinky, while it wouldn't necessarily endanger your life. It could get you arrested, however, so be discreet.

BDSM (bondage-dominance-submission or bondage-dominance-sado-masochism) activities are kinky but safe when participants follow an agreed-upon script that defines roles and behaviors. Bondage and discipline sex are about gaining or surrendering dominance and control. This may be incorporated in the idea of a master-slave relationship, usually in role-play. It can include the use of restraints, ropes, handcuffs, gags, blindfolds, etc., and may take place in the home or in a specially equipped area — a play 'dungeon,' for example. By agreeing on a 'safe word,' (which would immediately halt play) as well as setting limits ahead of time and respecting these limits, both partners can enjoy the excitement without any real danger.

Other popular BDSM practices include leather, masks and harnesses, and rubber, including tight-fitting body suits with strategically placed slits. With a trusted partner, these can be exciting — and ultimately safe — sexual encounters. Be careful of practicing with someone you don't know, however. A new partner might not respect your boundaries, or might run off with your wallet or some article of clothing while you're tied up.

Spanking, being spanked, paddled, or caned – aka 'CP' or corporal punishment – arouses some people, particularly if part of a role-play. Again, as long as it is what each person wants then there is little harm — other than a sore bottom. There are those who also engage in 'electro', which involves attaching little clamps to nipples, the penis or other body part, through which a small amount of electrical current is passed. Machines designed expressly for this activity are sold online and in some sex shops.

Some people are turned on by piss play (aka 'water sports,' 'golden shower,' or 'yellow'). The issue here is that urine is *not* sterile. Viruses, bacteria, and fungi from an infected person can also be transferred to you. Infected urine can transmit infections such as hepatitis B and other nasty diseases that have not gone away with the advent of HIV. If you do engage in water sports, make sure that there are no abrasions or cuts on the skin, and do your best to avoid contact with the eyes.

Sex parties or 'three-ways' go against societal norms, which can be part of the attraction. Some men favor 'spit-roasting'; in this, one person is anally penetrated by another man's penis, and this person is also penetrated so that he both gives and receives simultaneously.

'Bukkake' is the term used for the sexual practice of several men ejaculating on another's face.

If all partners consent, then such activities can be fun; just remember not to take health risks as the temperature rises and the passion takes over. Though many experiment and enjoy threesomes and group sex, it is not at all unusual for a person to find that these things work better in the imagination than in reality. Whatever your turn-on or choice, make sure that you keep it as safe as possible.

Sex should be fun, and if a little danger excites you, there are options that feel dangerous without actually putting you in harm's way.

Sex Toys

Online and in brick-and-mortar 'adult' establishments, toys of a variety of shapes and sizes are available to enhance your sex life. Avoid those devices or products that promise to increase your size or prolong your pleasure: most of them are fraudulent in their promises. Despite the hype, no gel, pill or device will really enhance your penis or your breast size. Props for role-playing, however, can be a fun and exciting addition to your routine. Handcuffs, whips, and other instruments of authority have moved from the world of S&M into the mainstream. If these games appeal to you and to your partner, then there is no real reason not to enjoy.

Also available are vibrators, 'love balls,' 'butt plugs,' and dildos of every sort. If you or your partner enjoy using a dildo, it's best to start smaller and to choose one made of a softer material in order to avoid injury. Be sure it has a wide base so that it doesn't accidentally slip inside, and use plenty of lube. And never, never insert an object not intended to be inserted. Many a sex partner has been damaged, even killed, by the insertion of objects such as glass bottles, turkey basters, candles, and other objects into the anus or vagina.

> *"Sex should be friendly. Otherwise stick to mechanical toys; it's more sanitary."*
>
> **~ Robert A. Heinlein**

These things can get lodged or lost inside or otherwise do internal damage. If an object does become lost or lodged, seek immediate medical help. Doctors and nurses are accustomed to helping the "slipped-in-the-shower-and-it–just-happened-to-be-there" patient. The medical establishment has seen it all before. Don't allow embarrassment to keep you from getting the treatment that you need and that could save your life.

Fetishes

A fetish can be defined as a fixation on an inanimate object (the smell, texture or look of leather or rubber, panties or sneakers, for example) or a fixation on a particular physical characteristic in a person as a means to arousal. While most of us have certain types of partners to whom we are attracted, a true fetish is a focus on a specific body part such as the feet, or some other characteristic, sometimes to the exclusion of everything else. With a fetish, arousal is triggered or enhanced by this specific aspect, which is focused on and given attention.

Nonhuman fetishes are often items of clothing: boots, trainers, underwear, Speedos, even trench coats. A fetish can include fabrics such as leather, rubber, fur or lace. Role playing can also involve items of clothing: dressing up for your lover can be a fun way to experiment and to fulfill each other's fantasies. Soldier, sailor, French maid, nun, student, schoolboy or schoolgirl are just some of the possibilities. Fetishes and role-playing can be enjoyable additions to your sex life. If both you and your partner enjoy the game, indulge in these fantasies all you like. Bear in mind that there is always a human being, a person, behind the fetish, game or play and always treat your partner as such.

If, however, the fetish becomes the only way for you to become aroused, it might be best to take a step back and figure out what's going on. If you're at the point that you'd prefer to masturbate with your fetish than have sex with another human, perhaps you should re-evaluate whether the fetish has become a barrier to having a relationship.

A solution is to connect your fetish to sex with a partner. If the sight of lace gets you hot, for example, drape a lacy scarf around your partner's neck or over the erogenous zones. Feel your partner through the lace, and encourage your partner to use the scarf in the same way on you. Use your imagination to incorporate your fetish in ways that are exciting to both of you and as a way to create or enhance emotional attachment to each other.

Intergenerational Sex

While most may be attracted to people in roughly the same age group, it's not uncommon for people to be attracted exclusively to those in another age group. Once we are past the age of consent, there's no right or wrong in terms of the ages of our partners. It's okay to be attracted to older or younger partners. While some view this as a fetish or seek some sort of deep psychological meaning, for the most part, age doesn't matter. If the attraction is mutual (and legal), there's no reason for concern.

In many societies it has been considered the norm for younger men to form sexual relationships with older men who also serve as guides and mentors. There is nothing new here. History is replete with examples of intergenerational love. This can be seen from Japan to Persia, Polynesia to Europe. In ancient Rome, the emperor Hadrian took a young Greek youth, Antinous, for his lover. When Antinous died in the River Nile, Hadrian was beside himself with grief. Later, he would dedicate an entire city in Antinous's memory, commemorating him in statues, portraits, and coins that were used throughout the Roman world.

In Renaissance Florence, young unmarried men often had sexual relations with older men; it is estimated that as many as two-thirds of all men engaged in such practices. In Japan, it was common for samurai warriors to have their own personal youths whose responsibility was to look after the master's sword — inside and outside of the bedroom.

As long as it's consensual and enjoyable, it's fine. Each can bring what the other lacks to the relationship: the younger bringing youth and its energetic enthusiasm, with the older bringing experience and wisdom.

Cruising

In some locations there are specific parks or outdoor areas where men go to meet others and have sex. In towns and cities, 'tearooms' and 'cottages' are slang terms for public toilets where gay men meet to have sex. There are specific rituals and techniques for hooking up. Two men stand side by side or at nearby urinals; one or both play with the penis while exposing it to the other's view. If no one else is around, they reach for each other, or beckon the other to enter a cubicle. Or there may be cruising from one toilet stall to another. In some cases, holes have been drilled between stalls that are used to look through to the other stall, with slightly larger holes used for masturbation, giving and receiving blowjobs, even fucking — so called 'glory holes,' the ultimate in anonymous sex.

If there are no holes, a man may begin tapping with his shoe. When another man taps back, the two begin to move their shoes closer together until they touch. At this point, they may jerk each other or suck each other beneath the partition, or they may move into a stall together. They might also leave together so that they can continue their sexual adventure in a more private place.

"The first two facts which a healthy boy or girl feels about sex are these: first that it is beautiful and then that it is dangerous."
~ G.K. Chesterton

Online cruising or mobile apps allow you to hook up in real life or in virtual reality. There are sites specifically intended for brief, anonymous trysts, and you're able to specify the type of partner you're looking for. Chat rooms also allow you to explore your options; a clever and descriptive screen name can provide instant information about you, and you can respond to those screen names that seem a good match.

Cruising brings with it a high degree of risk, physically and psychologically. If your partner's sexual history is unknown to you, *always* use a condom. And don't depend on cruising to provide you with lasting, ongoing relationships. Not that it never happens, but that's really not the point.

Sex and Disability

Not every LGBTIQ person comes in a convenient able-bodied package. Some have disabilities. This does not mean that people with disabilities do not desire sex or sexual relationships. Of course they do, and they are as much entitled to these things as are the rest of us. Yet the commercial gay scene, especially, seems ill equipped to provide for their needs.

Few LGBTIQ establishments have adequate facilities for those with disabilities, often lacking ramps and wheelchair accessible washrooms. In LGBTIQ stores, much of the merchandise is displayed out of reach for those in a wheelchair.

Nor, it seems, are all disabled people treated equally within the gay community. One-time coordinator of a Canadian Gay chat line, Stephan Lock, who has considerable experience working with gay people with disability, comments, "Of those in wheelchairs, there seems to be a higher comfort level with those with paralysis, for instance, than with those with cerebral palsy or advanced MS."

Lack of acceptance forces many LGBTIQ people with disabilities to struggle in order to find a place for themselves and break free from social isolation. Finding suitable partners can prove difficult, but certainly not impossible. In fact, there are those in the able-bodied gay community who are specifically attracted to those with disabilities, just as there are those with disabilities who are attracted to able-bodied people, or to others in a similar situation to themselves.

One gay and disabled dating site is *Whispers4u.com* (www.whispers4u.com/gay).

A smaller website dedicated to disabled gay people who wish to travel is *Gay Traveller's Network* (www.gaytravellersnetwork.com/group/disabledgays).

An excellent book that many LGBTIQ persons may find helpful when it comes to sex is *The Ultimate Guide to Sex and Disability*, by Miriam Kaufman and Cory Silverberg.

"Ableism", like homophobia, is a barrier to sexual expression and happiness. Do your part in reaching out and breaking through these barriers. If you are gay and disabled, let no one tell you that you deserve anything less than the very best from life in all its aspects.

Sex with Straights

As we have seen, there are people who do not see themselves as gay but who occasionally engage in gay sex — MSM or MESMEN, men who have sex with men, or WSW, women who have sex with women. They might be curious, they could be bi, they could be in denial, or simply wishing to please. Sometimes married, these people live a heterosexual lifestyle but indulge in gay sex on the side.

These relationships can be enjoyable and even long-term, they can be one-sided and shallow, or they might be anything in between. Some straights may be "gay for pay" and engage in homosexual acts for the easy money it can bring.

If you find this attractive, it's important to be clear about what you want out of the encounter or relationship. Be aware that great gay sex won't turn a straight person into something he or she is not, any more than homosexuality can be "cured" with the right sexual experience. A no-strings-attached sexual relationship might be just what you're looking for, but sex with straights can easily fall into the category of service provider, where you're meeting your partner's needs but you yourself are getting nothing out of the relationship. If you are looking for something that involves commitment, this is probably not the best relationship for you.

Sexual addiction

Sexologists have not reached consensus about whether sexual addiction exists or, if it does, what the parameters are. As we saw earlier, puritanical ideas of sex — that it's a necessary evil intended only for procreation, but certainly not something to be enjoyed — have skewed society's overall opinion about sex, so often turning it into something that is viewed as shameful. As these ideas have been rejected, our understanding and acceptance of the variety and range of sexual appetites has increased.

In my experience as a practicing psychotherapist, however, I am convinced that sex addiction is as real as any other addiction and bears many of the same characteristics. Simply put, a person is addicted when he or she has developed a tolerance to a substance *or* a behavior, when dependence has been established, and when they experience withdrawal symptoms while attempting to stop. When a sexual behavior is repetitively and compulsively taken to an extreme, when a person feels driven to automatically engage in it — even though it may be placing them in a precarious position — then that person is out of control and has crossed the line that separates normal behavior from addiction.

There are, of course, limits to what we can and should accept in the realm of sex; pedophilia and rape are categorized by some as sexual addiction, but these acts of violence are much more about power than about sex.

A healthy libido is nothing to be ashamed of, and what you do as a consenting adult with other consenting adults and the frequency with which you do it is a personal decision. But if your desire for sex is insatiable and all-consuming; or if your quest for sexual fulfillment is starting to interfere with other aspects of your life, relationships, family, work or study; or if it is in some way placing you in danger, you may have what might be termed a 'sexual addiction.'

"Sex is always about emotions. Good sex is about free emotions; bad sex is about blocked emotions."
~ Deepak Chopra

If this is the case, then you would be wise to consider working with a qualified therapist in order to address the destructive behaviors. It's possible that you're using sex to 'self-medicate,' to distract yourself from uncomfortable feelings within, or in an attempt to answer some deeper psychological issue. It could be that your constant search might be for something else, something more than just sex. A good, experienced therapist can help you to figure this out and guide you into finding happier, more fulfilling ways to satisfy your sexual appetite.

Twelve-step support programs, such as Sex Addicts Anonymous (see below), modeled on the original 12-steps of Alcoholics Anonymous, can also be very helpful if you believe you have a sexual addiction. Meetings are closed, you need give only your first name, and nothing you say will be repeated outside of the room. You can be sure that everyone present is or has been in a similar predicament to yourself.

Internet Porn

The Internet provides the opportunity to imaginatively live out all of your sexual fantasies in the privacy of your own home. A little porn can provide a helpful sexual outlet if you're not in a relationship or if your partner is sexually unavailable for a time. Some couples enjoy watching porn together because it excites erotic feelings or provides them with some innovative ideas for how to spice up their sex lives. Whatever you're into, whatever turns you on, whatever you're looking for, you can find the porn you seek on the Internet.

The easy access to porn has led to an increase in the number of people addicted to it. How do you recognize if you have a porn addiction? Basically in the same way you might recognize any form of addiction. When dependence has developed and it becomes indispensable. When you have tried to live without it for an extended period of time and found it difficult. When pornography begins to negatively impact other areas of life, you probably have a problem. If viewing, reading, or endlessly watching pornography is interfering with relationships or other aspects of your life, you may well have an addiction.

Once again, a trained therapist can be a real asset in overcoming an addiction. As mentioned, there are also 12-step groups for sex addiction, and these groups welcome those with a porn addiction. There are also separate groups for the partners and family of addicted persons. Groups such as the previously mentioned SAA (*Sex Addicts Anonymous)* or *Sex and Love Addicts Anonymous* (SLAA) can be very helpful, guaranteeing anonymity and providing real support for anyone affected by a pornography or sex addiction problem. If you live in more rural areas, you might have to travel to a city in order to access such groups. In some of the bigger cities, you may find one specifically for LGBTIQ people. Such groups can be really helpful in overcoming a pornography or sex addiction. A quick check on any search engine will give you the contact details of your nearest support group.

Internet Sex and Phone Sex

The telephone, at one time the ultimate safe-sex tool, has given way to the Internet as a means to sexual release. Both are still in use, and each has advantages and disadvantages.

For those who appreciate visual stimulation, Internet sex will likely be a better choice. If you are in a relationship, Skype or another chat program will allow you to enjoy each other's company while pleasuring yourselves. The addition of dirty talk or roleplaying can make up for the lack of your lover's touch in these long-distance trysts. Just remember that anything you do on camera can be distributed on the Internet at any time in the future, as certain celebrities have discovered to their own detriment, so be wise in this area. If you have a solid relationship, there shouldn't be any problem, but if not, then bear this caveat in mind.

Sometimes the right voice is the only trigger you need; phone sex can be a good alternative to actually being with someone. With the phone, no one has to know what you look like, and today's ubiquitous mobile phones mean you can enjoy phone sex virtually anywhere you can find a little privacy.

Both the Internet and the telephone offer services for pay, so if you're without a partner or are looking for some variety in your sex life, it's easy enough to find one who can fulfill your fantasies. Check online dating sites such as *Gaydar* for 'Escorts' who provide such services, or simply type your keywords into a search engine and see what comes up. Remember that professional chat lines usually charge by the minute, and so it is in their commercial interest to keep you on the phone for as long as possible. Be sure you understand the charges before talking, set a time limit, and be prepared to cut the call when you have reached your limit. Keep in mind that phone sex can become something of an addiction, so take things in moderation and maintain balance if you don't want to run up massive credit card bills.

Sexual Harassment

For many years, women and their supporters have struggled for equality in what has been a far too male-dominated society. They have fought to put laws into place to prevent sexual harassment, and these rules benefit us all in creating an environment that is comfortable and respectful. Being LGBTIQ doesn't make us immune from harassment, and it's important to recognize harassment and to squelch it when it happens at work or in any other place.

In the workplace, sexual harassment includes sexual advances, demanding sexual favors, and verbal or physical harassment that is sexual in nature. Harassing comments about a person's gender or orientation would also qualify.

Harassment can come from anyone: a co-worker (gay or straight) who confesses to fantasizing about you, the client or customer who asks questions about your sexuality, or a supervisor who makes suggestive comments. If these actions and attitudes make you uncomfortable in your work environment, they can be considered harassment.

While it is best not to overreact to something minor, in general it makes sense to nip these things in the bud. Sometimes an offhand comment offends, or a joke goes too far. Although it's tempting to let it go, if it's offensive or makes you uncomfortable, it's best to say something immediately, for your own sake, but also as a means of helping a co-worker before things escalate. So speak up, perhaps employing some of the strategies and tips you learned in the chapter on assertiveness. Nothing threatening, of course, but a simple "That's in poor taste" or "I think you crossed the line on that one" may be helpful in curtailing comments in the future.

Some of your co-workers may enjoy chatting about their sexual exploits, or perhaps that co-worker is you. This, too, could be construed as sexual harassment, so if it happens and you're uncomfortable, say something. You were given a voice, so don't be afraid to use it. And if someone asks you to keep the details of your sex life private, be sure to honor that request, lest charges be brought against you. Few people really enjoy hearing about other people's sexual exploits, unless perhaps it's in fictionalized form – a novel or a movie.

If the harassment is overt — you're being touched in a way that makes you uncomfortable, or if your boss is pressuring you to have sex in order to advance in the company — ask, clearly and firmly, for the behavior to stop. It is a good idea to begin documenting the events, including as much detail as possible: dates, times, and a summary of the conversation or what took place.

If the behavior doesn't stop immediately, it's time to approach your supervisor, line-manager, or the human resources department to report the offense. The company or organization should have systems in place to handle harassment complaints, so find out what the procedures are and when you should expect things to happen. If you're not satisfied with the process or the results, or if the promised steps are not taken, it might be time to consult a lawyer or an attorney. If you belong to a trade union, then speak to your local shop steward or union representative.

Just a note of caution about sex with co-workers: before you begin dating someone from the workplace, be sure you know your company's policy on such relationships. If it's against the rules, don't do it. And even if they're not forbidden, consensual co-worker relationships can be risky. If your relationship begins to make others uncomfortable, it could open the door to harassment charges against you. So be careful and be discreet. And if the relationship should ever wane or turn sour, just remember that you will have to see that person again and again in the future, simply because you work in the same office, department, or area.

Sometimes harassment might come from someone we used to date, or somebody who, for unknown reasons, fixates on us. If you find yourself in a situation where you believe you're being stalked or otherwise harassed, you may need to take several steps to protect yourself.

Harassment of this nature often begins with frequent calls or emails. They might be threatening or fantasy filled, but in any case they are unwelcome. Keep a record of these contacts, but if possible change your number and your email address. If the person approaches you in person, on the street or at a place your frequent, do not confront him or her, but find a way to exit the situation quickly. Let someone know what is happening; call a friend or someone you can trust. Consult the police; it is possible to get a restraining order against the individual. In the meantime, change your routine and your usual hang-outs. In extreme cases, and as a last resort, it may be necessary to change your residence.

Rape

In Cape Town, South Africa, 20-year-old Zukiswa Gaca, was out drinking with friends. A man approached her, but she declined his offer of a drink, explaining that she was a lesbian. He seemed accepting, and they continued to talk. She trusted him when he offered to take her home, but when he had her alone he told her that he hated lesbians and would "teach her not to act like a man." He raped her while his friend watched.

This type of 'corrective rape' is a show of power intended to punish and perhaps 'convert' the woman. Gay rights are protected by the constitution in South Africa, as they are in the US, and by law in the UK and some other countries, and yet this type of violation, linked to homophobia, happens to LGBTIQ people — male and female — with alarming frequency. Some rapists will pick a mark coming out of known LGBTIQ gathering places. As an aware LGBTIQ person, be careful and circumspect when coming and going, and try not to travel alone. There's no need to live in fear, but do exercise reasonable caution.

Charges of date rape, at one time met with eye rolls from authorities, are now taken seriously by law enforcement and medical professionals. Date rape can and does happen with LGBTIQ persons. Sometimes incidents of date rape are attributed to 'misunderstandings' or someone 'leading someone on.' None of that matters. When it comes to sex, anyone can say no at any time. Remember your 'Bill of Sexual Rights':

I have the right to change my mind and to say "No" to any sexual activity that I don't want at any time.

And remember, this goes for your partner(s), too.

You *are* allowed to change your mind at any time, to stop what you are doing at any point, or to refuse to participate in any act, even if you agreed to it earlier. Anytime you are forced into a sex act, regardless of your history or your relationship with the person, it is rape. Men as well as women can be raped. Though, for years, victims of male rape were not clearly recognized as such, things have now changed and continue to change in this area, too. Whether you are male or female, trans or intersex, rape is rape. Period.

If, somehow, this horrible crime happens to you, seek medical attention immediately, regardless of whether you intend to press charges. The doctor will collect evidence, assess possible physical damage, and test for STIs. You may well be offered PEP (post exposure prophylaxis) in order to prevent HIV infection (more on this in the chapter on health). The medical community will not judge you; there is no need to feel shame. This act of violence is not your fault. You can't undo it, but you can take steps to make sure that your body and your psyche can heal. Good counseling can help enormously here.

Celibacy

There are a number of reasons that LGBTIQ persons might choose to refrain from sex. Some choose celibacy as a spiritual discipline or for religious reasons. Others might refrain for health reasons, as a way of avoiding HIV or other sexually transmitted infections. For those sexually inexperienced, it might be a matter of waiting for the right partner or time before engaging in gay sex. For others, celibacy is a way of resetting oneself following a relationship breakup, or a way of creating an uncrowded space in which to think and reflect, a space where greater clarity and a deeper sense of meaning might be accessed.

Although it may seem an odd choice, a season of celibacy can be emotionally and psychologically refreshing. Without the pressure of sexual entanglements, LGBTIQ people have more time to focus on themselves as something other than sexual beings. It gives us the opportunity to cultivate our abilities and talents, and allows us time and space to breathe, and to renew ourselves spiritually. A period of celibacy can help us to better understand ourselves. Without the constant pressure of sex, we can reacquaint ourselves with, and learn to rely on, our own inner strengths. And we can also put our energies into cultivating nonsexual relationships and interests.

Particularly if you have a history of dysfunctional or unhappy sexual relationships, an intentional and perhaps temporary cessation from sex in order to analyze and break the pattern can be a helpful solution.

There's nothing harmful or 'weird' about choosing celibacy. It can lead to greater awareness, new confidence, and a self-assurance that will remain with you if and when you're ready for your period of celibacy to end.

LGBTIQ people have sexual yearnings, and you have every right to act on those attractions, provided your partner is willing. Sex is to be enjoyed and appreciated, a celebration of this essential part of our humanity. An active, balanced and healthy sex life can be a valuable step on the path to happiness.

> *"Young people are moving away from feeling guilty about sleeping with somebody to feeling guilty if they are not sleeping with someone."*
>
> ~ **Margaret Mead**

One final word: sex can be like a headstrong stallion or a mighty mare that can take us in so many different directions. It is one of the most powerful forces we can encounter. Always remember that you are the rider and the master. The horse may be your constant companion, but it is also meant to be your loyal servant.

Chapter Twelve

Gay Health

"If you have health, you probably will be happy, and if you have health and happiness, you have all the wealth you need, even if it is not all you want."
~ Elbert Hubbard

Important Note: *This chapter is intended for informational purposes only, and is not meant to replace the advice or care of a doctor or of medical or mental health professionals. Every effort has been made to provide up-to-date information, but medical science in this area is advancing rapidly. Always consult your doctor, medical advisor, or suitably qualified therapist if you have any concern about any aspect of your health or wellbeing.*

Good health is a key to a happy life. In taking care of our body, we increase our life expectancy, as well as enhance the happiness potential of each moment we live.

As LGBTIQ people, many health tips are as appropriate for us as they are for any other human being. A healthy diet and regular exercise are two principal — but often overlooked — ways to keep ourselves on track and healthy. Plenty of water and plenty of rest and sleep are other important keys to living a healthy life, as are developing an optimistic attitude and positive mind-set.

Yet LGBTIQ people also have some special considerations we need to be aware of in order to keep ourselves in the peak of condition. With a little effort and self-assertion, good health can be our ally for years to come, placing us in the very best state to maintain and continue to welcome happiness into our lives.

Choosing a Doctor

Although it's not necessary to have a doctor who is LGBTIQ, it is important to work with a physician who knows of your sexual orientation and who is absolutely comfortable with that. Regrettably, very little time is spent in medical schools teaching medical students specifically about issues of LGBTIQ health. That said, it's not essential to have a doctor who specializes in LGBTIQ health, but you do want someone who doesn't judge you and who accepts your orientation rather than blaming it for any health issues you might experience.

In short, we need to feel completely comfortable with our choice of doctor. We get much better advice and information if we feel able to have open and honest conversations about all aspects of our body with our medical advisor or health care practitioner. If you can't be truthful about issues you're encountering, including sexual issues, with your doctor, then the very best advice is to keep looking for someone with whom you can.

Remember, you have the right to change your doctor, just as your doctor has the right to accept or decline you as a patient – something that, in practice, very rarely happens. So don't be afraid to shop around for someone you can feel comfortable with. Anything you say to a doctor is confidential (provided you do not disclose serious intent to injure or harm someone), so be upfront about your sexual orientation. When it comes to your health, honesty really is the best policy.

If you have insurance, especially in the US, it's possible that your coverage limits your choices to doctors who are in the plan. There should be enough variety in their offerings for you to find a physician with whom you can connect. You're probably looking for a primary care physician or GP (general practitioner), someone you can go to for general check-ups, aches and pains, prescriptions, and other routine health concerns. He or she will refer you to specialists — cardiologists, dermatologists, urologists, surgeons, and so on — as needed.

Consult your local LGBTIQ organization, center, or clinic for information on doctors in your area. This is probably your best bet for accurate information. They often have a list of doctors and medical practitioners who are known to have experience with, or be especially helpful to, members of the gay community.

In the US, gay publications may also carry advertisements for LGBTIQ-friendly physicians, or you can consult a website such as the *GLMA* site (www.glma.org) for a directory. Then cross check these names with doctors who work with your insurance plan and see if there's a match.

> *"To keep the body in good health is a duty ... otherwise we shall not be able to keep our mind strong and clear."*
>
> ~ **Buddha**

When you meet with the doctor, check out the magazines and other literature in the waiting room. See anything gay-friendly? The really 'hip' practitioners may have a little rainbow flag or decal somewhere. That's a good sign, but not seeing such things doesn't mean that the doctor is hostile. There are quite a few LGBTIQ doctors who overlook such things. When you meet with the doctor, ask about their experience in treating LGBTIQ people. If the doctor can talk the talk convincingly, you've probably found a keeper. If, however, the doctor seems uncomfortable with the subject, you might want to try someone else.

Use your common sense and go with your gut feeling. You wouldn't rush into buying a new car, so don't rush into choosing your doctor. Your health is surely more important than any vehicle purchase — it's only wise to treat it as such. And just because your family has used the same doctor for ages, doesn't mean that you need to do so, too.

A doctor familiar with LGBTIQ issues will have an understanding of your special health concerns, but should also respect you as an individual. If you tell your doctor that you're in a long-term monogamous relationship but your physician still insists on HIV screening at each appointment, your doctor's bias is showing itself. A visit to the doctor's practice should not make you feel belittled or discriminated against in any way.

There are a couple of ways you might approach this. You could politely point this out to the doctor: "Dr. Jones, would you recommend these tests to someone in a long-term heterosexual relationship? I'm concerned that you might be requiring tests that are unnecessary." Doctors are, after all, human, and it can be helpful and instructive if you're willing and able to step up on your own behalf and on behalf of LGBTIQ people everywhere. (Remember your learnings from the chapter on assertiveness.)

The doctor may have compelling reasons for a test, but if you're not satisfied, there's no reason to comply. Option two is to say nothing, to thank the doctor for their time, and simply find a different doctor. Each option has merits.

Depression

In today's world, depression has become a serious problem, with as many as one person in ten thought to be impacted at some point in life. It appears that depression is even more pronounced among the LGBTIQ population. Given the homophobic ethos and all too often hostile environment that many have had to grow into and face, it is hardly surprising that an impact has been made on the way gay people feel about themselves and about life in general.

A national study published in the *American Journal of Public Health* in 2001 found that in grades seven through twelve, lesbian, gay, and bisexual youth were more than twice as likely to have attempted suicide as their heterosexual peers. The higher rate of depression is linked to situational events such as bullying, hostility toward LGBTIQ people, rejection, and other forms of homophobia, particularly at school.

But maturity doesn't necessarily improve things for LGBTIQ people. Research conducted by University College in London indicates that LGBT adults tend to experience more mental health problems than heterosexual people. The researchers obtained data from the Adult Psychiatric Morbidity Survey of 2007, and examined the rates of mental disorder among 7,403 adults living in the UK.

Rates for difficulties such as anxiety, depression, suicidal thoughts, self-harm, and alcohol and drug dependence were significantly higher in gay respondents. The proportion of homosexual people who described themselves as being fairly or very happy was 30 percent, compared to 40 percent for heterosexual people.

It also appears that advancing years do not necessarily improve things. Another 2011 study found that depression and loneliness are also higher in older LGBT adults. Nearly four out of ten had considered suicide at some point. The study, conducted by the University of Washington's School of Social Work, cited fear of discrimination, the lack of children to depend on as caregivers, and less social support and financial security with age, as older LGBT adults are less likely to be partnered or married.

But it's certainly not all doom and gloom. More recently, evidence is emerging that demonstrates things may be changing for the better in the LGBTIQ community. In research conducted in

2013 by the UK's Open University which involved more than 5000 people, it was found that gay couples tend to be happier than their heterosexual counterparts, and more positive about their relationships. The theory is that LGBTIQ couples tend to be more focused on and attentive to each other, making these relationships more satisfying.

Researcher Richard Wight's 2012 study of gay marriages was based on data from the 2009 California Health Interview Survey. Respondents, who ranged in age from seventeen to seventy, were asked about their sexual orientation and relationship status. Wight's study found that marriage, and to a slightly lesser extent domestic partnerships, may improve the mental health of gay and lesbian couples.

Marriage has long been associated with increased happiness in hetero couples, so it makes sense the same would apply to LGBTIQ couples, although perhaps for different reasons. Wight theorizes that the ability to publicly affirm their relationships allows LGBTIQ people to feel more accepted, thereby increasing their overall happiness.

Research by Dr. John Guttmann and Dr. Julie Schwartz Guttmann conducted over a twelve-year period, indicates that while gay and lesbian couples face the same stresses that hetero couples face, gay and lesbian couples tend to be more upbeat, and to face challenges with more humor and more affection.

LGBTIQ couples also tend to share power and are better able to soothe each other during and after a conflict; both of these tendencies are healthier for the relationship and the people in the relationship.

As acceptance for diversity grows and homophobia decreases, happiness and optimism within the LGBTIQ community continue to increase. There is hope that depression will decrease in the LGBTIQ community in the years to come.

If you are feeling depressed, very often an honest conversation with someone you trust will help diminish feelings of despair and give you hope. If your feelings of depression are severe and last for two weeks or more then it is wise to visit a doctor or suitably qualified therapist who can help. Be aware though that most GPs and family physicians are not trained in mental health or versed in how to promote emotional and psychological well-being, and so the tendency is to hand out medication in the form of antidepressant pills.

There are other, more natural ways to treat feelings of depression that do not include medication, and top amongst these is therapy with a qualified therapist or counselor experienced in this area. Be sure to discuss this option with your doctor or health advisor.

If a friend comes to you to discuss his or her depressed feelings or suicidal thoughts, be a nonjudgmental listener. Be supportive and sensitive, expressing your own feelings on the person's value to you. If you, or they, are having suicidal thoughts with consistency, seek professional help immediately.

Be sure to work with a therapist or counselor who is accepting of your sexuality. A therapist who views homosexuality itself as the origin of your depression will not be able to help you find the real cause, and is unlikely to provide any truly useful treatment. If you feel you are not getting the help you need, you may just have to find a different therapist or counselor. So trust your gut, and don't be afraid to let your feet do the walking.

For more immediate help, especially if overwhelmed with thoughts of suicide, contact a suicide prevention service. In the UK, the *Samaritans* run a 24-hour helpline on 08457 90 90 90. *CALM* operates a helpline for young men who are depressed or suicidal. Their toll-free number is 0800 58 58 58 (5:00 pm to 3:00 am daily).

In the US, call 1-800-273-TALK (8255) or go to www.suicidepreventionlifeline.org to chat online.

If you live in another country, directory enquiries will probably be able to provide the number of a similar service, or you can do a quick online check.

There's been an enormous amount of study into depression over the years, a good deal of it fueled and funded by pharmaceutical companies looking for a chemical solution — one that will increase their bottom line. There has been far less focus on the study of happiness, although research in this area has increased over the years, and the research that's been done has produced remarkably consistent data. As it turns out, one of the ways to overcome depression is to focus on happiness instead. And that is exactly what we are doing in this book.

STIs

Participating in sexual activity as an LGBTIQ person doesn't make you immune from sexually transmitted infections (STIs), also known as sexually transmitted diseases (STDs) or venereal disease (VD). Knowing your partner's history and practicing safer sex can minimize the risks, but nothing is foolproof. Should you suspect that you've contracted an infection, it is prudent to seek a doctor's advice immediately.

> *'We are all born sexual creatures, thank God, but it's a pity so many people despise and crush this natural gift.'*
>
> ~ **Marilyn Monroe**

Many — but certainly not all — STIs can be cured completely with the proper medicine. Even those infections that have no cure can be managed in ways that lessen your discomfort, extend your life, and minimize the risks of passing the infection on to other partners. Your doctor or healthcare provider can help you with treatment options or refer you to someone with expertise in the area.

There are some basic rules that apply to all STIs, and to their prevention. You drastically reduce your chance of infection if you:

- Use a condom during sexual intercourse
- Use a new condom with each partner
- Have fewer sexual partners
- Become aware of the symptoms of the various STIs
- Get tested regularly if you are sexually active and not in a sexually exclusive relationship.

HIV-AIDS

It's impossible to talk about LGBTIQ health without a discussion of **HIV-AIDS**. Labeled 'The Gay Disease' when first diagnosed in the 1980s, its association with LGBTIQ people has persisted, even as we have learned more about the virus. Although we have discovered ways to curtail the spread of HIV and now have medicines to curb its symptoms, HIV remains a serious health risk, especially for gay men.

Of course, HIV is a viral infection that can infect anybody who is sexually active, straight or gay. Drug users who share needles, syringes, rinse water, or other equipment ("works") that have been used by someone infected with HIV can also contract it. Additionally, the virus can be passed from mother to child during pregnancy, birth, or breastfeeding. Worldwide, it is estimated that men having sex with men account for only five to ten percent of all HIV infections.

In the US, UK, Canada, Australia, New Zealand, and most of Western Europe, however, more HIV infections are transmitted by men having sex with men than through any other route.

In 2007, fifty-three percent of HIV-AIDS diagnoses in the US were in men who have sex with men, although this group represents only two percent of the population. A 2010 federal study indicates that one in five men who have sex with men are HIV positive, but nearly half don't realize it.

Today, it seems that more and more men who have sex with men are engaging in the high risk practice known as 'barebacking' — unprotected anal sex. So many believe that with the advent of combination therapy, HIV is little more than an inconvenience, something that can be quite easily managed by taking a few pills. Nothing could be farther from the truth.

Such people have not had to cope with this terrible infection themselves. If they knew of its dire consequences and the awful health and social difficulties it can bring into the HIV positive person's life, they might well think twice before barebacking with partners whose sexual history is not fully known to them. Many are ignorant of the fact that not everyone responds to, or is able to tolerate, the numerous and all-too-toxic drugs required for therapy. Furthermore, HIV is still a cause of death amongst quite a few of those infected with it.

I know only too well how devastating an HIV diagnosis can be. My only brother, Bob, died because of it. It is an ugly death, and I believe that anyone who has witnessed such a tragedy would certainly think twice about having unprotected sex with someone whose sexual history they did not know well.

Those who insist on risky sex at any cost may be lucky for a while, avoiding infection through chance or blind luck, or they may not be quite so fortunate. I remember counseling a young teenager of just sixteen who had contracted HIV on his very first sexual encounter with a man. He was devastated. He now had to cope with the fact that he was HIV positive, that he would have to live the rest of his life around this infection, explaining to any potential partner that he was infected, and that he would be on strong medication — and forced to deal with its side effects — for the remainder of his existence.

Lesbian and bisexual women are not completely immune from HIV infection, but it is uncommon for HIV to be contracted in this way. Women can lessen the risks of transferring infections by using a fresh condom each time a toy is used to penetrate a new person, or using different toys for each individual; by using a protective barrier (a dental dam, a cut-open condom, or nonporous plastic wrap) during oral sex; and by using barriers to avoid contact with menstrual blood or genital lesions. Be aware, however, that there is no good evidence proving that using a dental dam reduces STI transmission risk between women who have sex with women.

One of the most important things to realize about HIV is that *you cannot tell by looking at a person whether they have it or not.* Some people who have the virus have no signs or symptoms of HIV for many years, yet may be highly infectious. Others exhibit symptoms within weeks or months.

HIV can lay dormant in the system for months or years after initial infection and may not show up in a test until three weeks to six months after infection, although thirty days is a more typical window. During this window period, it's possible to test negative (called a "false negative") even though the person is positive; it's also entirely possible for an HIV positive person to pass the infection on to other partners.

If you've had unprotected penetrative sex with an unknown partner, it's probably a good idea to rapidly seek post-exposure prophylaxis (PEP). This entails taking a course of prescribed anti-viral drugs designed to lessen the risk of HIV infection. PEP is considered to be around eighty percent effective — *if treatment is begun swiftly.* The window of opportunity to prevent viral infection is very narrow, however, and delay means that the treatment may not be made available because it is simply too late to have any effect. With PEP, time really is of the essence. This procedure is not as simple as taking a 'morning after pill.' PEP is unpleasant to take, and the combination of drugs required can have toxic effects and side effects. Your sexual health clinic will be able to advise you on this.

Antibody tests, which look for antibodies produced in response to HIV, have a ninety-five percent accuracy rate when administered two to three months after exposure and a ninety-nine percent accuracy rate twelve months after exposure. Antigen tests, which look for the virus itself, are more expensive and less accurate, and therefore used less frequently, but they can give results within two to three weeks of exposure.

Professional testing is quite easy to access through your doctor or sexual health clinic. In the UK, home testing kits are available free from *Terrence Higgins Trust* (www.tht.org.uk) to gay, bisexual, or men who have sex with men. The kit arrives discretely through the post and is then mailed back in the pre-paid envelope. This service is entirely confidential. Check online for a similar service in the US or your country of residence.

These days, 'self-tests' are available which do not need to be sent off to a lab and which give results within minutes. In the US, the Food and Drug Administration has approved *OraQuick* by *Ora-Sure*, an antibody 'self-test,' and *Home Access HIV-1.* In the UK, self-test kits are marketed online by *Bio Sure.*

Home-testing kits differ from a 'self-test.' With a home-testing kit, the finger is pricked, and a few drops of blood are placed on a card that is then mailed in for testing by a lab. With a self-test, a saliva sample or drop of blood is analyzed at home. If the test is reactive, however, you will need to take another confirmatory test at a clinic or doctor's practice.

Should your test be reactive or positive, you need to meet with your doctor immediately to discuss treatment options. While *there is no known cure for HIV*, there are medical protocols that can help keep the disease in check and allow you to continue with a reasonable quality of life — provided you can tolerate the drugs. And if you test positive, be sure to notify all of your sexual contacts and encourage them to be tested as well. It is your responsibility to do this. It's important to do everything we can to prevent the spread of this terrible infection.

If you do contract the virus, living with HIV will be psychologically and emotionally easier if you can confide in people and gather or connect with a supportive community. In many ways, coming out with HIV is much like coming out as gay. It's not something that you do once and then it's over. Choose your people carefully; not everyone needs to know, at least at first. Be prepared to answer a lot of questions or to be met with stunned silence. Don't interpret this as lack of concern or as hostility. Some people will be able to be supportive immediately, while others might need a little time to get their heads around it.

There's no need to be defensive or apologetic about your HIV status. State the facts, tell them the steps you are taking to tend to your medical needs, and offer to answer their questions. You are under no obligation to tell them anyone's name. Hopefully those who are close to you will be able to walk with you, but if they can't, walk away. You'll need all your energy for this, and people who can't or won't support you will be a drain you can't afford.

Your doctor or local LGBTIQ organization may be able to refer you to a support group for people who are HIV positive, and there are many such groups online. While these groups are not everyone's cup of java, for some they are a helpful source of emotional support and a valuable means of coping better with the infection.

What of the future? Experts believe that the most effective way of combatting HIV will be through a vaccine, but such a vaccine has yet to be developed.

Recently, a drug called Truvada – previously approved as a treatment for those who had already contracted HIV – has been shown in clinical trials to have a high success rate in *preventing* transmission of HIV in people who were HIV negative but at high risk of infection. Known as PrEP, or *pre-exposure prophylaxis,* the regimen requires daily doses of Truvada.

The problem lies in adherence to taking the drug on a daily basis and at the correct dosage. It is important to be tested regularly for HIV while on PrEP since taking Truvada as a prophylaxis while you are in fact HIV positive can cause resistance to the drug to develop, which can reduce treatment options. Moreover, it is very expensive. At the moment, Truvada is perhaps best thought of as some kind of secondary safety net for those at high risk of infection, rather than as a replacement for condoms.

Hepatitis A

Hepatitis A is a viral infection that is frequently passed to human beings through feces — a very good reason to follow your mother's advice about washing your hands after visiting the toilet. It can also be transmitted through anal-oral contact, or 'rimming.' Contaminated shellfish, such as mussels and clams, that have been exposed to sewage or polluted water can also contain the virus and pass it on to those who eat them — especially raw.

Hepatitis A is rarely fatal, though it may make you feel very unwell for quite a time. It can take around two to six weeks before symptoms begin to show, and during this time the infected person is very contagious. As a result, the virus can be transmitted through kissing, rimming, etc. The illness usually runs its course within a couple of months, during which time the liver is able to recover.

If you contract this infection, it's best to wash your dishes and eating utensils separately in order to avoid infecting others. It's also wise to abstain from kissing and intimate sexual contact, too, until the infection is cleared. It is essential that you wash your hands after visiting the bathroom. With rest and good nutrition, recovery should be relatively swift and permanent.

Hepatitis B and C

Hepatitis B (HBV) and hepatitis C are two different viruses that can be transmitted through exposure to blood, semen, or other body fluids, often through unprotected sexual contact or through sharing needles used to inject drugs. Both are a good deal more serious than hepatitis A.

These infectious illnesses of the liver can cause inflammation, vomiting, jaundice, and sometimes even death. For those with HIV, hepatitis B or C can be fatal. HBV is fifty to one hundred times more contagious than HIV, and at least thirty percent of cases cannot be associated with an identifiable risk factor. Symptoms include loss of appetite, nausea, body aches, dark urine, and eventually jaundice. The incubation period for Hep B and C averages two weeks to six months.

People with hepatitis B and/or C are often unaware that they have it. It can be asymptomatic (without noticeable symptoms), something that seems to go away on its own. Because of this, those with hepatitis can pass the virus on to others before they know they have it themselves.

Diagnosis is made through blood tests, and so requires a visit to a doctor or clinic. These tests are designed to identify either the virus or the antibodies that the body has produced in an attempt to fight off the infection. No specific drugs are available to treat acute hepatitis, but lots of rest is indicated. If infected, it is essential that you visit your doctor on a regular basis so that your liver function can be monitored. Your nutritional balance also needs to be checked. It is best to avoid alcohol and drugs (especially steroids), which tax the liver, and be sure to drink lots of fluids. Most doctors advise abstinence from sexual activity until the hepatitis is resolved.

Vaccines are now available for hepatitis B, so if you are gay and sexually active with more than one partner, or with someone whose history you are not absolutely sure of and you haven't been vaccinated yet, it would be wise to do so. Unfortunately, there is no vaccine for hepatitis C.

By taking precautions, hepatitis — like the other STIs — is an illness that can be avoided.

Syphilis

Syphilis is a sexually transmitted infection that did not simply disappear with the advent of headline-grabbing HIV. It is a STI that is still very much with us, one that continues to affect gay people in quite alarming numbers. This means, of course, that many LGBTIQ people are engaging in unsafe sexual practices. Left untreated, it will lead to blindness, insanity, and death.

> *"Life is a sexually transmitted disease and the mortality rate is one hundred percent."*
> **~ R. D. Laing**

This is the disease responsible for Beethoven's deafness and demise, as well as mobster Al Capone's insanity and death. ("I will hear in heaven," said the deaf Beethoven. We do not know what Capone thought of 'heaven.') It is transmitted through direct sexual contact with mucous membranes: with syphilis sores that occur on the external genitals — on the penis, in the vagina, anus, or rectum — or in the mouth. It is killed by soap and water, but this cannot happen once the infection has entered the body.

Symptoms can vary greatly, and syphilis is difficult to diagnose in its early stages. Most commonly, the first sign is a firm, painless, non-itchy skin ulceration — or chancre — that appears at the point of contact within three weeks of initial infection. Such chancres may be seen close to the head, or glans, of the penis, on the shaft, or further down, on the scrotum, of an infected man in the earlier stages of the disease. Though more visual on the penis, such chancers are invisible in the anus and may go unnoticed in the vagina. They are extremely contagious. The sore or sores will change in appearance and become tender, painful ulcers. Sometimes they can be so small as to be missed by the infected person or by his or her sexual partner.

Secondary syphilis develops within four to seven weeks of contact; symptoms may include a rash, sore throat, fever, joint pains, and headache — all of which can be mistaken for symptoms of other problems, such as colds and flu, and so overlooked.

Infections caught in the earlier stages can be treated with penicillin, while more advanced cases will require intravenous antibiotics. If the disease is allowed to progress untreated, it can develop into what is known as the 'tertiary stage' — as happened with Beethoven and Capone. The tertiary stage is reached by around forty percent of untreated people within ten to twenty years. This is the most awful stage. Deafness, blindness, insanity, and death are all consequences of the tertiary stage of syphilis infection. And all of this can so easily be avoided. A simple test can determine infection, allowing the infected person to begin treatment and avert disaster.

If you contract syphilis, it is important that all sexual partners be notified and checked for the infection. Regardless of how embarrassing this may be, if you have been diagnosed with syphilis, it is your absolute duty to do this.

If HIV were not enough reason to take active precautions with your sex life, add syphilis and you would have to be very foolish indeed not to protect yourself from ill health and the pain that comes with it.

Gonorrhea

Gonorrhea is a sexually transmitted infection considered to be the most common of all the STIs. In the US, it is the most frequently diagnosed communicable disease. Gonorrhea can affect the genitals, anus, eyes, mouth, or throat. Many people have no obvious symptoms, but symptoms in men include a yellowish-grey or slightly greenish looking discharge from the penis, discomfort when urinating, or inflamed testicles. In women, symptoms include a burning sensation during urination, vaginal discharge, or bleeding between periods.

The bacteria that cause this infection are almost always transmitted during sex. Fingers, toilet seats, and sauna baths are safe, while shared dildos and unprotected anal intercourse are not. Kissing is considered to be quite low risk, but direct contact — through fellatio, or blow-jobs, rimming, or cunnilingus — is not.

Antibiotic treatment is available for gonorrhea, although drug-resistant strains have begun to develop. Left untreated, gonorrhea can create serious health problems, spreading throughout the body, focusing in on and seriously affecting the joints, heart, skin, and even the brain.

As with all STIs, if you have been diagnosed with gonorrhea, it is your responsibility to inform any partners, past and present, so that they can be tested and, if infected, receive the appropriate treatment.

Chlamydia

Chlamydia, like many STIs, is often undetected for several weeks because symptoms are subtle or nonexistent. In fact, most people infected with chlamydia notice no symptoms, and so are unaware they have it. Current research suggests that fifty percent of men and up to eighty percent of women infected with chlamydia experience no symptoms. Of those that do, in men, symptoms can include discharge from the penis, painful urination, and pain and swelling around the testicles. Women who do have symptoms might notice vaginal discharge, painful periods, bleeding between periods, painful intercourse, and abdominal pain with fever. If you have a history of unprotected sex, it makes sense to get yourself checked for all STIs, including chlamydia, at a sexual health clinic or in your doctor's office.

Once detected, chlamydia can be treated with antibiotics.

NGU — Non-Gonococcal Urethritis

NGU is also known as *nonspecific urethritis,* or NSU. Though both sexes can contract NSU, this is a diagnosis more commonly made in men than women, which is due primarily to anatomical differences. It is a condition commonly diagnosed in men who have been practicing unprotected sex.

Basically, NGU is an infection of the urethra, the urinary pipe that runs from the bladder to the opening at the tip of the penis. This causes inflammation and symptoms similar to gonorrhea — a yellowish-green discharge from the penis and pain when urinating. The term 'nonspecific' is used in order to indicate that the inflammation is not caused by gonorrhea. (It is often caused by chlamydia.) A lab test is needed in order to determine this. It is best to abstain from sex until NGU is cleared, and to notify partners so that they can take steps to be checked.

This particular STI is usually cleared quite quickly using antibiotics.

Genital human papillomavirus (HPV)

HPV is common, so common that most sexually active people will contract it at some time, even if they have only one partner. There are more than forty types of HPV that can be passed on through genital contact, including homosexual contact.

The infection can impact the genital area or the mouth and throat. Although it often goes away by itself, HPV can result in serious diseases, including some types of cancer. This is the infection that actor-producer Michael Douglas famously blamed for his throat cancer. There is no test for the virus, no way of knowing if HPV will cause serious problems, and there is no course of treatment for HPV, although there are treatment options for the problems caused by the virus. Your doctor or clinic can advise you on these.

LGV

This is another bacterial infection that is transmitted through sexual contact, in particular unprotected receptive anal intercourse. **LGV** (lymphogranuloma venereum) is a STI that appears to be on the increase amongst gay men. It is a type of chlamydia that attacks the lymph nodes.

Symptoms of LGV are similar to urethritis (inflammation of the urethra), and usually occur in three days to three months following exposure. In men, a painless papule or shallow ulcer/erosion may appear, and there may be groups of lesions resembling herpes infection. Left untreated, other symptoms such as vomiting, fever, and headaches may occur.

Again, treatment is with antibiotics, but this can only commence once the infection is diagnosed. Visit your doctor, health advisor, or clinic for proper diagnosis and treatment.

Herpes

Herpes simplex includes types 1 and 2. Type 1 causes sores in and around the mouth, while type 2 generally results in sores in the genital area. **Type 1** can be spread through oral contact or through sharing objects such as lip balm or toothbrushes, while **Type 2** is generally contracted through sexual contact. The infection can go dormant for periods of time, and can be spread even when sores are not present.

There is no known cure for herpes, although there are treatments available that may relieve the symptoms.

Trichomoniasis

Yet another STI, trichomoniasis, is caused by a small organism called *trichomonas vaginalis* and most often impacts women, although men can also contract the infection. Symptoms include discharge, pain when urinating, and, for women, discomfort during intercourse. Once diagnosed, this common STI is easily treated with antibiotics.

> *'A fit, healthy body—that is the best fashion statement.'*
>
> **~ Jess C. Scott**

Pubic Lice and Scabies

Pubic lice (crabs) and scabies are miniature parasites that transfer from one person to another during sexual contact. The most common symptom is itching in the genital area. Pubic lice, or 'crabs', can be effectively treated at home with lotions that are widely available. Your pharmacist can advise you on this, as can a doctor or clinic specializing in sexual health.

Shigella Dysentery

Like hepatitis A, shigella dysentery is a bacterial infection that is transmitted through oral-fecal contact. It is spread through sexual activities such as rimming or through unwashed hands. It takes only minute amounts of the bacteria in order to become infected. Shigella affects the gut, and is often linked with foreign travel. Symptoms most often develop within one to three days after infection and include severe, chronic diarrhea, stomach cramps, and vomiting. It can cause serious health problems in those whose immune system is compromised.

Gay, bisexual, men who have sex with men, or women who have sex with women, who experience any of the above symptoms are advised to visit their doctor of health advisor without delay and request a stool sample test for shigella. This is an infection that can be effectively treated with a course of antibiotics.

Hygiene

If we want to be happy and healthy in body and mind, then a certain degree of personal hygiene is essential.

Flossing and regularly brushing our teeth will keep them healthy and allow us to smile with confidence. If your teeth aren't to your liking, don't be afraid to discuss things with a dentist. These days so much can be done to enhance the appearance, as well as the clinical health of the teeth. With advanced dentistry and its painless techniques, there is no reason why anyone cannot have a healthy set of teeth and a great smile.

No need to let a fear of the dentist keep you away. If you have any kind of dental phobia, a good hypnotherapist can rapidly help you overcome your fear so that you will easily relax when visiting the dentist. Tranquilizing drugs are also available from your dentist.

Be sure to keep the body clean with regular showers or baths. Few people like a body that smells of stale sweat and unpleasant odors. Colognes and perfumes are fine, when used with discretion, but though their original use was to disguise unpleasant smells from the unwashed bodies of people who did not have easy access to baths, such strategies really do not work well today. No amount of cologne will disguise the smell of a body in real need of washing. Use mild, preferably non-scented soaps in order to avoid sensitivities, and be sure not to go overboard. It is possible to take too many baths and showers, and so remove the skin's protective oils and other helpful elements that are a natural part of skin health. If your skin feels dry, you might like to try a non-perfumed emollient body lotion or cream after washing.

Anal Sex Hygiene

Most people who enjoy anal sex are quite fastidious about keeping this area clean, but be careful not to overdo it. A simple cleansing wash with a mild soap and water is all that is necessary. There is no need to use an internal douche or enema prior to anal sex; in fact it is advised that this not be done. Long-term enema use or overuse can cause chronic constipation, and it is possible to become so dependent on them that it becomes impossible to have a bowel movement without them.

If you feel that you absolutely must clean internally before anal sex, then you may like to try syringing with a small ear syringe, available from most pharmacies. Just fill the syringe with warm water, use a little lubrication if necessary, and insert into the anus, gently squeezing the syringe. This will allow you to expel any residual fecal matter, together with the small amount of water injected. Pat the area dry — too vigorous rubbing can cause micro tears or abrasions that invite infection. As long as you exercise general hygiene, know how to relax, and use protection with partners whose history you do not know, there should be no problem.

Drugs and Alcohol

Within the LGBTIQ community, alcohol and drug use, and sometimes abuse, is all too common. Bars, pubs, and clubs are popular gathering places for people who are LGBTIQ, and when alcohol is readily available, people will drink. Alcohol lowers inhibitions, and once these are lowered, it's easier to open up to the possibility of more risky behavior, including consumption of stronger drugs.

If we have felt ashamed or rejected for our sexual orientation, or have struggled to accept it, we may use alcohol to self-medicate, that is, to compensate for or cover up feelings of low self-esteem. The easy availability of alcohol — a depressant — means that it can become the drug of choice for those wishing to numb the pain of the past or assuage the anxiety and uneasy feelings of the present.

"I made a commitment to completely cut out drinking and anything that might hamper me from getting my mind and body together. And the floodgates of goodness have opened upon me — spiritually and financially."
~ Denzel Washington

It's remarkably easy to slip into a habit that becomes an addiction. If alcohol is becoming central to your existence, if you're drinking too much or too often, if you're regularly drinking on your own, if you can't remember events from the night before, or if you need a drink to get you through life, then you are heading for — or already have — an enormous problem.

As a therapist, I believe that alcoholism is a disease, and it's one for which there is no cure. The only solution is to arrest the disease through stopping to drink completely. Though there are other models, such as 'controlled drinking,' I personally believe that if you are alcoholic, total abstinence is the only way to recover.

If you have a problem with alcohol — or if alcohol has a problem with you — then it may be time to look into a 12-step group or another approach that might work better for you. An addicted, diseased life is not a happy life; in fact it's almost certainly a sign that something isn't right internally. Intense therapy, outpatient treatment, or hospitalization might be necessary in order to dry out and stay sober.

If your drinking is causing problems, be sure to talk with a doctor, counselor, or therapist. Alcoholism has been called 'the disease of denial.' It is the only disease that tells you you don't have it. If drink has become or is becoming a problem in your life, think seriously about ending the denial and doing something about it. It really is possible to have a wonderful life, filled with feelings of joy and happiness, without dependence on alcohol.

Sadly, LGBTIQ people also appear to have a higher rate of drug addiction than the general population. Some of this is likely related to alcohol use, which lowers inhibitions. After a few drinks, doing a little cocaine might not seem like such a bad idea. Drugs give us jolts of false energy and can temporarily elevate confidence levels, offering us an artificial way of getting along, putting aside inhibitions, and suppressing emotional discomfort and pain.

The list of party or 'recreational' drugs is constantly expanding. Methamphetamine ('crystal meth'), ketamine, GBL, and mephedrone have joined drugs such as cocaine, ecstasy, and OxyContin in the lineup of chemical offerings, with new drugs appearing on a regular basis. All of these drugs distort reality and lower inhibition. Lack of inhibition can lead to other risky behaviors: more drugs, picking fights with the wrong people, driving while under the influence, engaging in unprotected sex. And after the high is over, there's usually a serious crash — the piper just has to be paid, and sometimes he can even come in the guise of the Grim Reaper.

There's no way of knowing what you're getting when taking illegal drugs. They could be cut with all sorts of substances or so pure that a single dose could kill. Drugs all have side effects. Some are temporary, others are long-term, and some are fatal.

It's not a question of morality but of health. If you're already a heavy user or an addict, maybe it's time to think about getting out. Seek treatment with the help of your doctor or healthcare provider.

If you are dependent on drugs or on alcohol, then sooner or later you will be forced to face the truth: an addicted life is not a happy life.

Sexual Difficulties

Most men experience sexual difficulties from time to time. When we are overly tired, have been drinking alcohol or taking drugs – prescribed or illegal – or when we are simply not in the mood or not really turned on by our partner, then problems can arise. If you have the occasional misfire (or not) it's probably nothing serious. If erection difficulties become the norm, however, there's no need to panic. It may take a little time to figure out what's going on, but in general this is not a permanent condition.

If you experience problems, the first thing to do is to check out the basics.

First and foremost, determine that you are really sexually attracted to your partner. Obvious though this may seem, some people attempt to have sex with someone who is not their 'type', someone whom they do not find sexually attractive, which can result in real difficulty in becoming or remaining sexually aroused.

If this is not the case, then visit your doctor for a check-up. Underlying physical conditions such as narrowing of the arteries or type 2 diabetes can cause difficulties such as erectile dysfunction, as can age-related issues, so it's only wise to eliminate any physical cause before looking further into treatment. If your doctor thinks it necessary, he may recommend medication such as Viagra (sildenafil) or the longer lasting Cialis (tadalafil), to be taken on an 'as needed' basis.

Sexual difficulties in women are more difficult to diagnose, primarily because women are constantly compared to men but are quite different from men, physically and psychologically. A man's inability to have an erection is measurable and diagnosable, while a woman's physical response (or lack thereof) is not. Often, emotional health and relationship status tend to be more important to a woman's sexual satisfaction than orgasm.

If you're unsatisfied with your sex life, there are several steps you can take to restore your sexual relationships. First, consider how things are with your partner. If there is tension in your lives or in your relationship, this can have an adverse effect on your sex life. Spend time together reconnecting, emotionally and physically, without the pressure of sex. Conversation, cuddling, and massage can be powerful reminders of why you're attracted to your partner.

Take it slow and don't rush into intercourse until you're quite sure you're ready. It may take a few sessions, but if you can find a relaxed, comfortable state, desire can reignite.

Premature ejaculation in men can often be remedied through the squeeze technique developed by sex experts Masters and Johnson. While masturbating, or working with a partner, once an erection is achieved, squeeze the head of the penis just below the corona (the cap or 'bell-end') for three seconds. This will stop ejaculation and reduce the erection. Repeat the process four or five times: arousal, erection, apply pressure. After a half hour or so, allow ejaculation. After a few sessions of this technique, the time between stimulation and ejaculation should increase, eventually allowing for full control.

If sexual difficulties persist, by all means have a conversation with your doctor. Pharmaceuticals such as Viagra have been a boon to men's sexual health in particular, but your physician may offer other suggestions as well, including literature that helps you to understand your reproductive system. Don't be embarrassed to have this conversation.

Sexual dysfunction and premature ejaculation are problems far more common than most people realize. They are difficulties I have been called upon to treat countless times in my career as a therapist. Hypnotherapy has proved helpful to many, especially those whose difficulty springs from psychological reasons, which it so often does. Above all, it's wise not to view sex as a performance. 'Performance anxiety' can disturb even the healthiest libido, distracting the mind and the emotions, leaving the body floundering.

A healthy sex life is important to your overall wellbeing, so treat it with respect and if something is out of sync, don't be afraid to seek help.

Domestic Violence

Domestic violence exists in the LGBTIQ world at about the same level as in the population generally. About one in four relationships between gay men have experienced domestic violence, a statistic that mirrors the numbers for heterosexual women in relationships. Violence rates within lesbian couples are estimated to be at fifty percent. This shockingly high number is disturbing, but it is compounded by the lack of help or services offered to same-sex couples.

> *"Many survivors insist they're not courageous: 'If I were courageous I would have stopped the abuse. If I were courageous, I wouldn't be scared' ... Most of us have it mixed up. You don't start with courage and then face fear. You become courageous because you face your fear."*
>
> **~ Laura Davis**

Domestic violence occurs at the same rate in all economic, racial, and educational groups. Many smart and otherwise reasonable people get caught in the cycle of violence. While from the outside it seems completely illogical, those trapped in abusive relationships can have a difficult time escaping them, for a number of reasons.

Domestic violence in LGBTIQ couples is similar in nature to the straight world in that the violence can include physical, sexual, and psychological abuse, with psychological abuse generally the most prevalent. The abusers, often past victims of abuse themselves, may blackmail or shame their victims into silence. Domestic violence is notoriously underreported, no matter the genders of the people involved.

Unfortunately, within LGBTIQ relationships, thepsychological abuse can be even more pronounced. Isolation is a hallmark of abusers; they work to pry victims from support systems and gradually control everything in their lives. If the victim is already estranged from family or otherwise lacking in support, the abuser is in a powerful position to leverage the isolation in order to exert control over the victim. If the victim isn't yet out at work or with his or her family, the abuser may threaten to reveal the victim's orientation. Closeted victims may also be hesitant to contact law enforcement for fear that their orientation will become public.

Even those who are out may hesitate out of concern that their complaints will not be taken seriously or in the mistaken belief that it will give the LGBTIQ community a 'bad name.' Abusers might threaten to infect their victim with HIV-AIDS or to tell others that the victim is infected. If there are children present in the home, they, too, become leverage: the abuser may threaten to hurt them or take them away.

When abused LGBTIQ people do call the police, they may not get the support they need. Because victims in same-sex relationships are more prone to fight back than their heterosexual counterparts, disputes are more often seen as mutual fights or domestic disputes rather than abuse, especially if the police are not aware of the nature of the relationship. A quarrel between roommates is not seen in the same way as violence at the hand of a partner. If you and your partner are passing as roommates, the police will be more likely to try to smooth things over.

Lingering homophobia can also impact the level of service provided. In spite of their training, there are those who still believe that LGBTIQ people are 'emotional' or somehow 'deserve' to be abused, just as over the centuries women have been blamed for violence done to them. Such bias says that your sexual orientation means you were 'asking for it,' that you 'must have done something' to provoke your partner. Do not believe this, and don't allow the people who are supposed to be protecting and serving you to get away with discrimination of this sort.

If you are a victim of domestic violence, report it immediately and do everything you can to extract yourself from the situation and the relationship. You'll need help and support in order to do this, and regrettably, at this time there aren't many specifically LGBTIQ services available. Men in abusive situations face the toughest road. Resources for women are more readily available, but that doesn't mean it's easy to make the break.

Law enforcement offices offer victims' support services, or your doctor should be able to help. Churches and not-for-profit organizations may also be able to connect you with a help center, and organizations such as the *GLBT National Help Center* (www.glbtnationalhelpcenter.org) can be of real assistance. Also, the *Rainbow Domestic Violence* website gives much useful information, together with links to some helpful resources (www.rainbowdomesticviolence.itgo.com).

In the UK, the LGBTIQ domestic violence charity *Broken Rainbow* offers help and a hotline for those experiencing violence (www.brokenrainbow.org.uk), while *Men's Advice Line* offers support and advice for male victims of violence in same sex relationships; 0808 801 0327 is their number.

If you live in another country, check online for services near you. At the very least you can find online organizations, groups, and other resources that may well be of help.

If you're in a violent relationship, remember that it is not your fault. No matter what you wear, do, say, or think, your partner has no right to hurt you, control you, or threaten you. Don't excuse your partner's behavior by blaming it on drinking, drugs, or stress at work. And don't think your partner will change. If you are experiencing domestic violence, the best way to look at it is that your partner is sick, and *you cannot cure him or her*. **Get out!** Your life might depend on it.

Stress Isn't Healthy

As LGBTIQ people, we have more than our share of stressors, and stress impacts both health and happiness negatively. Remember that stress, like happiness, comes much more from within than from without. It is the way we respond to life's experiences, much more than the actual experiences themselves, that determines our inner balance.

There are things we can do to manage our stress level. Many of them are discussed in more detail in the chapter on happiness, but here are a few additional tips.

Recent research indicates that living in a community that is LGBTIQ friendly actually significantly increases longevity in LGBTIQ people, likely due to reduced stress. It's not necessary to move to an LBGTIQ commune, but if you can live and work in a community that is accepting and where you can be open without fear of repercussions, stress will obviously be greatly reduced.

> *"The way you think, the way you behave, the way you eat, can influence your life by thirty to fifty years."*
> **~ Deepak Chopra**

Another way to reduce stress is to keep a stress journal. Track your triggers and figure out the source of your stress. By recording your stress moments, patterns will begin to emerge, and once you have a sense of what's tying you up in knots, you can develop a plan to cope with or eliminate the things that are stressing you.

Working with a therapist or counselor who can teach you how to better handle life's stresses and stressors can be very helpful.

No matter how busy you are, or how hectic your lifestyle, be sure to take time to relax and unwind. Fresh air is a wonderful, health-enhancing tonic, so get out into the open as often as you can and breathe deeply. Yoga, tai chi, qigong, meditation, and self-hypnosis are all excellent ways of remaining healthy within, so don't neglect this important part of your inner health.

With a little common sense, and self-respect, you can live the healthy, happy life you deserve. Let nothing hold you back. This is your life — be sure you claim it.

Conclusion

Bringing It All Back Home

"My destination is no longer a place,
rather a new way of seeing."
~ Marcel Proust

For each one of us, the road to a joyful, happy life is open and available.

Traveling this road may well require a bit more from us because we were born gay, lesbian, bisexual, trans, intersex, queer or questioning, and so we are not in the majority, but this certainly doesn't prevent us from enjoying life to the fullest.

Just like the stars, the trees, and the birds that sing from those trees, we have a right to be here, and to know joy and happiness while we are here. We have a right to be at home in this world.

In *How To Be Gay AND Happy*, we have seen that some of the most essential ingredients of the happiness pie are robust self-esteem, frequent and consistent expressions of gratitude and kindness, and the cultivation of meaningful relationships. In this final chapter, there are reminders of these important elements that go into making us gay people happy.

Throughout this book, I have referred to the 'LGBTIQ community.' Perhaps now is the time to ask if there really is such a thing.

The simple answer is yes and no. LGBTIQ people are part of every community; we are not necessarily sequestered or segregated into specific colonies or ghettoes. But we do have much in common, and these commonalities can build community and create links among other LGBTIQ people. These common bonds allow for stronger advocacy positions, as well as support for personal and professional problems.

Not all LGBTIQ people hold the same opinions or have the same needs — no community has complete accord. But there has always been strength in numbers when it comes to creating change, and it is among other LGBTIQ people that you are likely to find your strongest supporters and the people who will understand you the best.

> *"Happiness is not something ready made. It comes from your own actions."*
>
> **~ Dalai Lama**

Regardless of your age or where you are on your journey, it is good to understand and appreciate the needs of those who are not like you. As gay people, we have a right to expect this of others, and so others have a right to expect it of us, too. If we demand to be respected for who we are, and for our own difference, then we have a responsibility to be kind and understanding toward those who have different sexual identities and preferences to our own, towards those who are older, and towards those who are younger than ourselves.

Kindness really is one of the keys that unlock the door to authentic happiness. Again, research bears this out. A study in the *Journal of Psychology* discovered that not only does kindness make us happier, but happiness makes us kinder.

If we are wise then we will remember the advice of Scottish author and theologian Ian Maclaren: "Be kind, for everyone you meet is fighting a hard battle." Do what you can to be empathetic and helpful, and you will be rewarded with good feelings about yourself.

When you have good feelings of this kind, it's hard not to feel happy.

Our Shared LGBTIQ History

As gay people, we benefit so much from those courageous advocates who have gone before us, tearing down barriers — often at great personal risk — bringing about the changes that we now enjoy. Though we have much further to go, we have already come so very far. I encourage you to understand, with gratitude, the history of the LGBTIQ rights movement and to appreciate the work of all of those who have contributed to the freedoms we now enjoy. These brave social reformers, advocates, scientists, and ordinary people deserve our utmost respect for standing up for the rights of all of us.

Each one of us has a part to play in the furthering of LGBTIQ rights. We owe this to ourselves and to those who will follow in our footsteps. In understanding our own history and being aware of the struggles and triumphs of the past, we are in a much better position to contribute to a more accepting and just society in the future.

"If I have seen farther, it is by standing on the shoulders of giants," wrote Isaac Newton, and if we can now see farther and clearer, it is because we ourselves stand on the shoulders of so many men and women who stood tall.

In school, you will have been taught little or nothing about gay people in history, of Alexander the Great and his love for the handsome Hephaestion; of Socrates and Plato and their love for young men; of Leonardo da Vinci and his liking of youths; of Florence Nightingale and her love of women; of Alan Turing, the father of the computer, and the persecution he suffered for daring to love men; or of the many LGBTIQ people who contributed so much to science, the arts, and to the history and evolution of civilization.

For most of us, it was as if gay people had been airbrushed right out of the history books, their sexuality banned from the curriculum. Little wonder, then, that so many of us grew up thinking that heterosexual was the only viable way to be, that LGBTIQ people had played no significant role in the evolution of society and the process of human accomplishment.

With no LGBTIQ role models, and no one to look up to, we were left floundering. For so many of us, being gay meant that we would accomplish nothing, achieve nothing, and quite possibly, come to nothing.

In history classes, we may have learned of the battle for women's emancipation and of the fight for black civil rights and racial equality, but we heard little or nothing about the struggle for LGBTIQ freedom, of the lengthy, steadfast fight to end the awful persecution and prejudice based simply on sexual orientation and identity. We were not told about our own pioneers, those who fought for fairness and justice, attempting to drive things forward and make a difference. And so it is up to us to excavate and delve into the past and to remember and learn from those whose courage has shown us the way.

It is up to us to learn of people such as the clear-sighted social reformer Jeremy Bentham, a heterosexual who as early as 1785, when death by hanging was the penalty for being gay and having anal sex, advocated for an end to criminalization and the persecution of gay people. Of the pioneering German Karl Heinrich Ulrichs, considered by many to be the founder of the modern gay rights movement, who in the 1860s time and again risked everything by courageously speaking out in defense of homosexuality, urging the repeal of unjust anti-homosexual laws.

We can honor the memory of the Hungarian physician Karoly Maria Benkert — the man who gave the world the word *homosexual* — who protested the penalization of homosexuals as early as 1869. And we can respect the important work of Magnus Hirschfeld, which in 1897 (two years after the imprisonment of Oscar Wilde for homosexuality) led to the founding of the *Scientific Humanitarian Committee,* the organization that has justly been called the first advocacy group for homosexual and transgender rights in the world.

Also in 1897, the enlightened doctor Havelock-Ellis published his influential book *Sexual Inversion,* the first to suggest that homosexuality might be inborn rather than a choice.

The First Congress of the *World League for Sexual Reform,* held in Berlin in 1921, brought together gay rights leaders from around the globe. That movement, as well as the work of the liberated German thinkers, scientists, and reformers, was swept away by the Third Reich during World War II, when books were burned and homosexuals were among those imprisoned, tortured, and murdered in Hitler's extermination camps.

Inspired by Magnus Hirschfeld's work, American Henry Gerber established in Chicago in 1924 the *Society for Human Rights,* the first gay rights organization in the USA. This organization produced the first American homosexual publication, *Friendship and Freedom.* Within a few months, the society closed due to the unjust arrest of several members. Although short-lived, the society is considered a launching point for the gay liberation movement in North America.

Since the Second World War, the sexual climate has changed dramatically in the Western world, and this naturally includes LGBTIQ people. The first Kinsey report on male sexual behavior was released in 1948, documenting the surprising extent of homosexual activity in the population. Gay groups began to meet, and the publication *ONE,* produced for a homosexual audience, began in 1950. When the post office declared the magazine to be obscene and refused to deliver it, the Supreme Court decided in favor of the magazine.

The *Mattachine Society*, founded by Harry Hay in 1950, was formed in an attempt to protect and improve the rights of homosexuals. The first meeting, held in Los Angeles, included five men, and the group grew slowly over the years until 1952, when one of the original members, Dale Jennings, was arrested for 'lewd behavior.' While most men might have tried to sweep the incident under the rug, Jennings and the Mattachine Society courageously chose instead to publicize the case and expose the practice of police entrapment so prevalent at the time — and for years after. The high profile case brought sympathy and support for the organization, including financial backing. When the case went to trial, the jury deadlocked, which the Mattachine Society saw as a victory.

Five years after the founding of the Mattachine Society, in 1955, the first lesbian civil and political rights organization in the US was formed in San Francisco: The *Daughters of Bilitis*. Beginning as an alternative to lesbian bars, which were regularly being raided and harassed by police, this organization lasted for fourteen years, becoming an educational resource for lesbians, gay men and mental health workers.

In other countries, progress was also being made. In 1957, the *Wolfenden Report* was released. Commissioned by the British government, the report obtained its information through interviews of police and probation officers, psychiatrists, religious leaders, and gay men. While the report advocated for decriminalization of homosexuality, it was a decade before this became a reality in the UK, legalization taking place in 1967.

In Russia, homosexuality was decriminalized in 1917, but this was reversed under the tyrannical dictator Joseph Stalin — an oppressive and unjust legacy that the present leadership seems intent on maintaining. Despite massive pressure, criminal violence, and state sanctioned bullying, gay people in Russia continue to courageously fight for their rights today.

The 1960s saw the Baby Boomers coming of age in the US, and their impact on culture was beginning to be felt. The times were turbulent, and protests against any number of injustices were plentiful. Social change was in the air, a *zeitgeist* flowing through the fabric of society, issuing in a different way of thinking and a greater awareness of social inequality. Where once the music of the young concerned itself only with love and longing, it now spoke of broader matters, of social injustice and changing values; from musicals such as *Hair* to the songs of Bob Dylan, the times they were changing.

And then, on June 28, 1969, something would happen that altered everything for gay people in the West — an event that would prove to be a gigantic turning point in gay liberation and LGBTIQ rights.

At this time, New York had fiercely enforced laws against homosexuality. Gay gathering places were routinely raided and shut down, the patrons rounded up, herded into police wagons, and taken into custody — a harassment technique that had been used by police and law enforcement agencies for years. Once arrested, they were given the permanent label 'Sex Offender' simply for being in a gay bar.

On that balmy night in June, however, the customers in Christopher Street's Stonewall Inn, a gathering place for gay and trans people, were in no mood to walk sheepishly into the waiting Black Marias. Judy Garland, the symbol of survival in the face of adversity that so many gay and trans people had idolized, had died and emotions were running high.

What began as a routine police raid on just another gay bar was met with fury and massive opposition from those inside. For the first time, gay and trans people fought back. Shouts of 'gay power!'

rang out as queens smashed handbags over the heads of the arresting officers, and bar stools became weapons in a battle against simple injustice. The confused and frightened police retreated. Desperately calling for reinforcements, they finally prevailed — but only for that night.

Soon word had spread and the following evening saw a crowd of more than a thousand people standing firm and pushing back. Riots ensued, as police tried to reassert their authority.

Protests continued to percolate throughout the city over the next few days as gay and trans people and their supporters stood up for their rights en masse. The Gay Rights Movement had finally begun in earnest. An identity had been forged, one that cried out: "We *do* matter. We *do* have a right to be who we are. We *are* gay — and that's okay."

Four years after the Stonewall riots, the American Psychiatric Association removed homosexuality from its list of mental disorders.

Two organizations grew out of the protests: the *Gay Liberation Front*, which lasted only briefly, and the *Gay Activists Alliance*, which was most active in the early 1970s, disbanding in the 80s. Their usually peaceful but often disruptive activities inspired similar groups nationwide.

> *"Conformity is the jailer of freedom and the enemy of growth."*
> **~ John F. Kennedy**

How To Be Gay AND Happy is not a book on gay history. What I have outlined are simply a few of the important figures and milestones along the road to LGBTIQ rights. I hope it has inspired you to do your own research and discover more of the rich history of our struggle for equality. We really do stand on the shoulders of giants.

Almost fifty years after Stonewall, the work of advocacy and the push for equality continues. Perhaps you yourself, through your own actions, will add even more to our proud history. In so many Western countries we no longer need to protest for the right to gather, but ignorance, homophobia, and anti-LGBTIQ bias lingers steadfastly on, and in some areas police harassment — or neglect — remains all too commonplace. Even in the Western world, discrimination and abuse continue, and LGBTIQ people still do not have equal human rights.

For most in the LGBTIQ community, the goal of the advocacy is simple: equal treatment for LGBTIQ persons. This includes the right to live in a secure environment without fear of violence or harassment and where law enforcement is unbiased; the right to secure employment; the right to love, marry, and raise a family; as well as the right to live safely, without judgment.

By owning our history, we ourselves contribute to it. We are far from powerless. We can continue to push forward into the future, to secure rights for ourselves and for the LGBTIQ people who will inherit this legacy from us. We, and they, deserve nothing less.

Wherever you are on your personal path, remember that there are many who have gone before — people who have used their courage and inner strength to help change things and build a better world for us. Remember, too, that no matter our age, our race, our heritage, or our sexuality, we are all on this journey together.

If you are older, be sure to treat younger people — those still uncertain and perhaps trying so hard to fit in and to find their balance — with patience and the understanding you yourself would have wished for when you were younger.

If you are young, reflect on this when you meet someone considerably older than yourself, someone perhaps less 'hip' appearing and a bit behind the times. The gay world so often revolves around youth, and there is no doubt that it can appear dismissive and, at times, even hostile toward older people. Though it may seem to you to be a very long way off, remember that you, too, will one day be old. Consider that older people have had to wrestle with a different world, a world even less accepting than the one into which you were born. It could be that they have helped to move things forward, that in their own way the price they have paid has made things easier for you.

As a gay person, a member of the vast worldwide LGBTIQ community, you will have your choices, just as you will have your battles. Always hold tight to the fact that you are not alone. You are an integral and valuable part of the process called 'humanity.' So many have gone before you, and after you will come so many more.

Some Notes on Body Image

A positive body image is an important component of self-esteem, and this is especially the case among gay men. Always remember, though, that you are a worthwhile, valuable person, regardless of your size or shape. Be sure to appreciate your body for what it can do for you, not purely for its looks. As we have seen, self-acceptance is an important key to happiness.

In focusing too much on our body, we run the risk of developing all sorts of difficulties, not least amongst these being the psychological condition known as 'body dysmorphia.' Anorexia and bulimia are two such issues that have come to the fore in recent years, and young women have borne the brunt of the pressure, imagining that they must meet some specific standards of beauty that include dangerously low body weights. But it is something that is affecting more and more men, too. Also, men who are overly obsessed with maintaining a 'gym-perfect' muscular physique — particularly those taking steroids or growth enhancing drugs — may experience a sort of 'reverse anorexia,' in which the slightest reduction in muscle size produces feelings of anxiety.

Living as muscular 'macho men' or flamboyantly effeminate 'queens' are just two of the many ways gay men express their personalities and their sexuality. There are as many different kinds of gay men as there are straight men; they are simply men who happen to like men. And as we have seen, not all lesbians are butch, wearing lumberjack shirts and no make-up. Some are actually ultra-feminine, a stereotype sometimes referred to as a 'lipstick lesbian.' Again, there as many different kinds of gay women as there are straight women. Remember that while it may occasionally be comfortable and even comforting to slip into a persona, LGBTIQ people do not have to fit into any specific mold or body type.

Effeminacy — the tendency of men to display characteristics and behaviors more often associated with women — isn't limited to gay men. Neither is a woman who has traits traditionally associated with men a sure-fire indicator of lesbianism. These tendencies may be biologically determined, or they may be learned or chosen; they may occur more frequently in LGBTI people, but are certainly not limited to LGBTI people.

Regardless of their origin, there is nothing wrong with having traits customarily assigned to either gender. If this is what feels natural to you then it is absolutely fine. The sad thing is that these traits and behaviors often lead to teasing, bullying, and discrimination, even among adults. As a LGBTIQ person, you may choose to change your walk or alter the way you talk in order to 'fit in,' or you may choose not to. Either way, be assured that these and other tendencies are not flaws to be corrected, but simply a part of the person you are. There is nothing wrong with you, and there never was.

Statistically, gay men are following the same patterns as straight women, placing an increasingly high priority on physical fitness and physical attractiveness that can border on the unhealthy and the obsessive. Eating disorders are common, but often overlooked, among gay men.

Research conducted by Beth Brunner of Vanderbilt University, indicates that straight men are most likely to like their bodies, followed by gay women, then straight women, and finally gay men.

As a group, gay men have the least satisfaction with their bodies, spending more time in the gym than any other demographic group. They are still the most likely to criticize their own physical appearance.

"I want to have sex with a man, not someone who looks and acts like a woman," said Jaimie. "I'm attracted to the same attributes in men that straight women are. I appreciate a man who takes care of himself, and by taking care of myself, that's the kind of man I attract."

Such preferences are to be respected, but not when they ridicule or disparage those who do not conform to their idea of what a man or a woman should or should not be.

Says blogger Louis Peitzman, "There are, of course, gay men who don't obsess over their weight or the weight of potential sexual partners. There are also those for whom going to the gym is not an activity to build one's days around. But the stereotype of the gay obsession with body image and a six-pack is not unfounded. There is a widely held understanding that being gay means maintaining a certain standard of physical beauty, with very little room for deviation from the norm."

The desire among gay men to have a buff, hard body, or bulging muscles — so-called 'Muscle Marys' — may be a means of countering the stereotypical image of gay men being skinny, limp-wristed, and effeminate. Ironically, hyper-masculinity, also known as being 'macho' or a 'gay clone,' has in many ways become its own stereotype.

Said Robbie, "The club scene is very much a meat market, with men taking their shirts off as if advertising the goods. I take care of myself, but I'm more private about my body. I thought I'd find acceptance on the gay scene, but the trouble is, I'm judged mainly on my looks ..."

Among gay men who are overweight, the bias is worse. Peitzman, who considers himself overweight, says, "The truth is, the gay community isn't interested in embracing overweight people because we're a blemish on the image of perfection. And much in the same way, progressives as a whole can get away with ignoring anti-fat bigotry; gay men never bother examining the way they treat their overweight brothers. Ignore us or relegate us to the butt of hackneyed jokes: We just don't matter. It doesn't get better for us."

Such body fascism is, unfortunately, all too common on the commercial gay scene.

Just as it's not right for society to put us in a closet, it's not right for society to paint a one-dimensional picture of body image, male or female, gay or straight. Remember what your body is for: it provides you with life, mobility, and pleasure. It's more than bait for sex. Treat it with respect. It houses all that you are; it is not the total of what you are.

Another body concern among men, but particularly among gay men, is penis size. So many men are concerned that they are 'inadequate,' and there are those who will judge a partner by the size of his penis. In gay parlance, such people are known as 'size queens.' The average size of the fully erect penis is about 5.8 inches (14.9 centimeters) long. So if a man has six inches or more, then he has a larger than average penis. If you are young, then you may be interested to learn that the penis does not stop growing until around the age of twenty-one.

If size is a concern, remember that great sex and great relationships do not depend on the size of your equipment. Don't waste your time and money on products, lotions, pills and 'treatments' that claim to enlarge the penis; none of them really work. Instead, learn to accept, and work with what you have. An honest partner can give you valuable feedback, and you may be surprised to find that he is perfectly happy with your cock just the way it is.

Among women, breast size can be a similar concern. Again, much of this is about personal preference; there is no single body type that is sexy to everyone. Be proud of your body and treat it well. Body confidence is very sexy and very becoming!

Most of us are drawn to certain types. We might gravitate toward someone taller or shorter, younger or older, slimmer or stouter, smoother or more hairy. The person that attracts you, however, may not be attracted to your 'type'. Because someone is not interested in you sexually, does not mean that they are actually rejecting you; they may very well be attracted to a different type. Keep in mind that you will never be all things to all people — nor should you try to be, and remember this:

The only person who can really reject you is yourself.

Learn to be true to yourself and to who you are, and don't be shy to express who you are. Focus on cultivating relationships that respect and honor the needs and desires of both parties.

Just as you are not simply your sexuality, so you are more than your body. Learn to appreciate all the great things about yourself, including your unique physical abilities and attributes (beautiful hair, great feet, fabulous eye-hand coordination and so on) that aren't connected to weight or muscle tone or size. It's good to be fit and active, but be careful not to become obsessed with your looks or with the looks of potential partners and friends.

Find new role models who have healthy self-concepts and different body types. Remind yourself that you can like and admire people even if they aren't 'the ideal,' and they probably feel the same way about you.

Of course, exercise is important if we are to remain healthy and feel good about ourselves. If you really hate the gym and detest vigorous workouts, try switching up your exercise routine with walking instead of running or stretching exercises like yoga instead of weight lifting. Experiment and appreciate the new ways you can achieve fitness while nurturing your body.

Travel

Travel can be an amazing way to broaden your worldview and to gain understanding of your global neighbors. It's an opportunity to be free of the day-to-day and to let go of the to-do list. For many, it's a time to relax and refocus; for others it's an opportunity to learn about history and culture; and for others still, it is an opportunity to meet new friends and perhaps engage in new sexual adventures.

> *"We travel, some of us forever, to seek other states, other lives, other souls."*
> **~ Anaïs Nin**

Whatever our reason for journeying, travel expands our horizons and introduces us to new people, places, and things. It can also help us to appreciate what we already have; those things and people we often take for granted, back home.

One thing that most travelers learn quickly is that customs differ with culture. In some countries, holding hands is common amongst men. This does not mean that they are gay, and it might be an enormous error to assume that it does. Before traveling, check out the laws and customs of the countries you will be visiting. Above all, respect the culture and the people. One of the wonderful rewards of travel is that it really can expand the mind — provided you approach it with the right attitude. But don't forget that many of the people you will encounter may never have traveled, and so are very much the product of the beliefs and opinions that they have been exposed to.

If you're new to the world of travel or are nervous about experiencing a new culture, you might consider booking your trip with an experienced agency. These days it's easy to find tours that cater specifically to LGBTIQ people. There are a variety of agencies out there, so the one you choose will depend a good deal on what you are looking for. You can book a romantic cruise on a LGBTIQ-only ship or register as a single as part of a group excursion to Turkey or Thailand, for example. Some tours welcome the inclusion of friends or family that are not LGBTIQ. If you're looking for that, or if you're opposed to that, be sure to ask about the parameters.

In the US, Canada, and the UK, traveling as a gay couple is rarely a problem. In larger cities same-sex couples are nothing unusual and are accepted virtually everywhere. In addition to gay clubs and nightlife, many larger cities offer LGBTIQ pride gatherings and other annual events, often in the summer. The Internet provides a great deal of help locating interesting, gay-friendly destinations and activities. *Spartacus* is the classic travel guide for gay men, giving information on laws, hotels, cruising etc. For women, *Damron Women's Traveler* guide provides comprehensive international information for and by lesbians who travel. *Damron* produce a number of different guides, including a guide for men.

In more conservative areas, there may be some sideways glances; there have even been cases of bed-and-breakfast or '*pension*' owners refusing to rent rooms to gay couples. (A practice that is illegal in some countries, including the UK.) These incidents are mercifully rare, but if you think it might be an issue, ask when making your booking. There are plenty of establishments that will be more than happy to do business with you.

Most countries in Europe — especially in Western Europe — are open and have active LGBTIQ communities and activities, including nightlife. Not every destination worldwide is equally gay-friendly, however. As we have seen, homosexuality is illegal in a few countries, such as Russia, and in most African countries. While many countries in Asia have established and open gay communities, homosexual activity is criminalized in others, including Afghanistan, Bangladesh, Bhutan, Brunei, Malaysia, Myanmar, Pakistan, and Sri Lanka. In the Middle East, Iran, Iraq, Kuwait,

Lebanon, Oman, Qatar, Saudi Arabia, Syria, United Arab Emirates, and Yemen all have restrictions against homosexuality.

You don't have to like the laws of these countries, but if you choose to travel there, you are obligated to adhere to them. What you do in the privacy of your hotel room is up to you, but remember that if your partner is a local, he or she will have to remain there after you have left. So do nothing that might make their life more difficult once you are gone. In public, it will be in everyone's best interest to be discreet.

That said, even in conservative countries, there is often more leniency in larger cities; there may even be an open and active gay community. Again, be aware that there can be risks in partying with this crowd, so be smart and circumspect when making new friends.

The *International Lesbian, Gay, Bisexual, Trans and Intersex Association* (ILGA) produces maps of LGBTIQ rights around the world, and also a homophobia report that can be downloaded from their website: www.ilga.org.

The Gay Press

The gay press, once an underground movement, is now big business. These publications can be an enormously helpful tool in providing news, and keeping updated on information relevant to LGBTIQ issues, nationally and internationally. They can also help in connecting us with people, products, and services within the LGBTIQ community.

While the Internet has forced many hard copy publications out of business, others have maintained a print presence as well as an active online publication. Other publications are exclusively online. Although electronic translation programs are imperfect, reading the publications of other countries can give you a sense of gay rights and issues on a global scale.

Each publication will have its own value, its own stated purpose, and its own biases, so remember to read multiple sources for a fuller understanding of the issues and to find the information you're looking for.

In the UK, publications such as *Gay Times* and *Attitude* and online *Pink News* are popular amongst gay men, *Diva* amongst lesbians. *Trans Living* is a popular online magazine devoted to the trans community.

In the US, there is a much wider variety to choose from. Among the most popular: *OUT, The Advocate, Instinct Magazine, Metrosource, The San Francisco Bay Times, Pink Magazine,* and *Password*.

For publications in other countries, check online. Wikipedia has a comprehensive list of LGBTIQ publications sorted by country, including those publications that are free.

Putting It All Together

Is it possible to be happy as a LGBTIQ person? I hope that, after reading this book, you know that the answer is unequivocally: yes! Happiness is within the grasp of every gay, lesbian, bisexual, trans, intersex, queer, and questioning person. And it is we ourselves who determine the degree of happiness we experience.

Think back to the questions we've asked and answered over the course of this book. By now you should have a better understanding of what you are looking for when you say you want to be happy, and I hope you've actually begun to employ some of the recommended exercises and adopt some of the strategies so that you can increase your own personal happiness. You've begun to retrain your brain and establish those pathways that will help you create your own more happy life.

While it may be true that LGBTIQ people have more hurdles to overcome when mapping out their own happiest life, if greater happiness is your goal, none of these hurdles is insurmountable. Even if everyone does not accept our orientation, even if we feel rejected, there are those who understand and who are willing to walk the path with us. And when we can find within ourselves the self-esteem to accept and affirm who we are, we've taken the most important step towards a real and authentic happiness.

If there is one, single message to take away with you from this book, it is that happiness is something that is cultivated, rather than something that accidentally happens to us. It is up to each of us to take responsibility for our own happiness — not by pursuing it, but by *choosing* it.

Happy people cultivate close relationships and choose their own purpose and meaning in life. Happiness comes when we live generously and gratefully, kindly and compassionately. Happy people learn to forgive, to let go of the pains and burdens of the past, to live in the now, and to focus, with optimism, on the future.

You *can* be happy. It is your birthright. Let nothing and no one convince you otherwise. See your life as the marvelous gift that it truly is and choose to live it to the fullest.

Ahead of you lies a wonderful adventure. Wherever your life takes you, hold your head up high, let your light shine, and you really will be healthy, happy, *and* gay.

I wish you courage and love in abundance as you move forward on your unique journey.

Rainbow Champions
Celebrating LGBTIQ Diversity

Is your organization demonstrating real commitment to its LGBTIQ employees?

Being inclusive means much more than just obeying the law. Employers of excellence value and invest in their lesbian, gay, bisexual, trans, intersex, and queer staff, making it clear that they are respected and appreciated. The very best workplace is one in which diversity is encouraged and difference celebrated.

Peter Field is the founder and director of Rainbow Champions, an organization that provides assertive life-skills training for gay men and women, bisexual, trans, intersex, and queer persons in companies and corporations across the UK.

Rainbow Champions offers private and corporate training both in-house and at locations throughout the UK designed to support LGBTIQ team members and staff. Training is interactive and conducted in small groups to ensure individual coaching and personal attention.

For information about LGBTIQ assertive life-skills training with Peter and his team of expert facilitators, please visit:

www.RainbowChampions.com

Printed in Poland
by Amazon Fulfillment
Poland Sp. z o.o., Wrocław